COURTING FAME

KAREN STABINER

COURTING FAME

The Perilous Road to Women's Tennis Stardom

1817

HARPER & ROW, PUBLISHERS
New York

Cambridge, Philadelphia, San Francisco, London
Mexico City, São Paulo, Singapore, Sydney

COURTING FAME. Copyright © 1986 by Karen Stabiner.
All rights reserved. Printed in the United States of
America. No part of this book may be used or repro-
duced in any manner whatsoever without written permission except in the case of brief quotations embodied
in critical articles and reviews. For information address
Harper & Row, Publishers, Inc., 10 East 53rd Street,
New York, N.Y. 10022. Published simultaneously in Can-
ada by Fitzhenry & Whiteside Limited, Toronto.

FIRST EDITION

Designed by Ruth Bornschlegel

Library of Congress Cataloging-in-Publication Data

Stabiner, Karen.
  Courting fame.

  1. Tennis—Tournaments—United States. 2. Women
tennis players. 3. Tennis—Tournaments. I. Title.
GV999.S73 1986   796.342'0973   85–45236
ISBN 0–06–015527–2

86 87 88 89 90 HC 10 9 8 7 6 5 4 3 2 1

TO LARRY
AND MY PARENTS

Contents

*A section of photographs
follows page 117.*

Acknowledgments

It seems to me a very difficult thing to let a stranger into your life, to open yourself to public scrutiny, so I want, first, to thank the families who agreed to talk to me. I'm particularly grateful to Tom and Francine Spence, and Debbie, who talked to me at times when, I'm sure, they would have preferred to be alone. I admire their nerve. I also appreciate the willingness of the other families—the Gurneys, Foltzes, Werdels, Benjamins—to share their experiences.

Dozens of people agreed to talk about the big business of women's tennis, and how it affects a talented girl. Of those, Chuck Bennett of International Management Group was exceptionally helpful. He provided valuable contacts as well as an informed ongoing analysis of the girls' careers. United States Tennis Association official Ruth Lay was equally helpful explaining the pro-college point of view and suggesting names of other people I should interview. Coach Robert Lansdorp was kind enough to let me have access at the West End Tennis and Racquet Club.

Billie Jean King, Tracy Austin, and Andrea Jaeger shared their thoughts, and personal feelings, about the plight of the young tennis player. I also appreciate the contributions made by Parkes Brittain, Sara Kleppinger Fornaciari, Nancy Arnaout, Seena Hamilton, Betty Sue Hagerman, Glen Herb, Gayle Godwin, and Andy Davidson.

Sue Clamage and Dee Gregory of Sue's Secretarial turned the resulting tapes into coherent transcripts with speed and accuracy. Marcie Rothman, possessed of a tenacity that rivals the tennis players', went back over the material to check its accuracy and collect additional bits of information. I owe her double thanks: in addition to doing a great job, she was a devoted friend. She kept my spirits up.

Other friends, who, to my knowledge, never spent a minute thinking about women's tennis before I began this book, developed a sudden interest in the subject. For their generous curiosity, and their failed but entertaining attempts to come up with a title, I want to thank Rochelle Reed, Susan and Patrick Melly, John Seeley, Digby and Kay Diehl, Harry Shearer, Jack Nessel and Ginger Curwen, Carolyn See, Eric Mankin, and Abbe Don. Thanks to Steve Smith for his help with the players' photographs, and to Joel Siegel for the free lodgings during the 1983 U.S. Open.

I've looked forward to the chance to thank Elaine Markson in print since the day I started this book. I depend on her for her enthusiastic devotion to the good idea and her unerring, affectionate advice. I'm also indebted to Geri Thoma, who is merely the soul of calm.

My editor at Harper & Row, Aaron Asher, understood what I wanted to do, and offered encouragement, from the start. His assistant, Carol Chen, deserves thanks for putting an end to a long title search. Linda Rawson, of the Harper & Row legal department, provided essential advice and aid.

A few other sage advisers shared their expertise, and I value every suggestion that Kathy Robbins, Stuart Applebaum, and Tom Pollock made.

I had help at home, too. Greta yelled at me to get back to work, Adlai offered comfort and gentlemanly affection, and Katy provided comic relief.

Special thanks to Marika, that most steadfast companion, for not complaining about being left out of the book jacket photo, and for our long walks on the beach. She has always understood what's really important.

As has my husband, Larry Dietz. For that, for his belief in me, his warmth and support, I am very grateful.

Santa Monica, California
September 1985

". . . when I walked into the jungle, I was seventeen. When I walked out I was twenty-one. And,
by God, I was rich."

—ARTHUR MILLER, *Death of a Salesman*

COURTING
FAME

Introduction

This is the story of some extremely talented young girls—top amateur tennis players on the brink of a pro career—whose ability carries with it the promise of fame and fortune, or the threat of early heartbreak. Given the current obsessive reverence for youth and fitness, for the illusion of eternal life, a girl who succeeds in professional tennis is nothing short of a pint-sized goddess. In today's currency, she is as valued as a movie starlet once was, and for many of the same reasons. The notion of a sweet, innocent child whose outsized talent propels her into worldwide celebrity has always been a favorite, whatever the realm.

Life at the top of women's tennis has its allure. A girl can hope to make from a quarter- to a half-million dollars annually in prize money, and more than that in product-endorsement fees. She can expect to be famous—not only among tennis buffs, who appreciate the fine points of her game, but also among nonplayers, who come to appreciate her as a media darling. The fifteen-year-old with the killer backhand and the ruffled underpants is just the sort of charming contradiction who wins popular acceptance. More than any other woman athlete, a young tennis star can be sold.

It is a potent notion, for parents who would like to give their girls a wildly promising future, and for girls who like the idea of being someone special; a rather blindingly rich opportunity, the first of this magnitude for women in sports. Every year, the willing and the hopeful sign up. The ranks of the United States Tennis Association's junior program, the stairway to stardom, have doubled in the last ten years.

Making a commitment to "the life," as one young player calls it, also represents a terrifying risk. Women's tennis is so fast-paced, so cutthroat, that any girl who takes a few weeks' rest is assumed to be suffering from mental or physical burn-out. Like any entertainment, women's tennis promotes its successes and tries to cover its failures, but the sport's short history—the women's pro tour started in 1970—is littered with casualties.

There are teenagers whose nerves are so frayed or bodies so overworked that they can no longer play, girls who are has-beens at eighteen. Even well-known players are not immune. Tracy Austin and Andrea Jaeger, once among the best players in the world, are struggling to recover from injuries that interrupted their careers before they were twenty.

An essential part of any American dream is denial, so players and their parents tend to assume that the sad stories will always belong to somebody else. But even Martina Navratilova, one of the best woman players in the world, the recipient of all the rewards women's tennis has to offer, is aware of the toll. At the 1985 French Open she was asked to comment on fifteen-year-old Gabriela Sabatini, whose recent performance —and great beauty—had confirmed her status as a coming star. Navratilova ruefully allowed that Sabatini would be very good for women's tennis; she did not know if women's tennis would turn out to be good for Sabatini.

The girls in this book—Debbie Spence, the top-ranked junior girl in the United States, ready to turn pro when I started to follow her career; Melissa Gurney; Shawn Foltz; and Marianne Werdel—were all eager to take the chance. They were raised to be ambitious, and, since tennis was part of the family vocabulary, they learned to channel that ambition into their sport.

But the pro circuit did not even exist when they were born, so they, and their parents, faced the unexpected challenge of stardom. Women's tennis grew up along with these girls. By the time they were at the top of the junior heap, the pro circuit had gone Hollywood.

Since tennis is an entertainment industry, with agents and corporate investors, publicists and image problems, the story of a young girl turning pro is also the story of how excellence is bent by profit considerations. A girl like Debbie Spence plays more than tennis when she steps onto a court. She plays by the rules of another game, the game of the marketplace. She learns that it is not enough to be talented, as she is subjected to corporate scrutiny and advised on ways to increase her commercial potential. A promising player quickly becomes a member of an extended family of business relations. Private family debates about how hard, and fast, to push a child, about what constitutes a happy future, are suddenly made public. And they are made with one eye on the clock, since a girl's age is a crucial consideration in evaluating her chance for stardom.

If a girl is good—if she moves successfully from local, to regional, to national competition, and if she is attractive—she is a commodity on the fantasy futures market by the time she is ten. Her life strains the boundaries of normal childhood and changes the way everyone in her family lives.

It is a dizzying, often overwhelming experience. The girls, with the headstrong faith of teenagers, roll full-tilt at what they assume will be a glorious life. Tennis serves their needs well. It offers a lot of satisfaction, at a time when their peers are thrashing through adolescence, perpetually dissatisfied with, and confused by, their lives. Tennis is reassuring proof that a girl is unique—and the better she gets, the more people there are willing to tell her so.

In the midst of the hustle, there is little time to debate the idea itself. The best most parents have been able to do is ask themselves *how* to help their daughters survive the process. As the girls get hooked on success, there is a subtle shift in power. Parents no longer have to encourage their child; instead, they find themselves subservient to her and her future. Talent, especially profitable talent, is demanding: a family has to restructure itself in deference to it. Everyone goes to work for tennis.

Superficial sacrifices—of after-school time, weekends, even vacations—are not enough. Tennis families face a wholesale upheaval. The most mundane activities, like a family dinner or vacation, become luxurious exceptions, squeezed in between practice sessions, lessons, and travel.

What might be considered healthy interests in another child come to be regarded as distractions for the gifted, ambitious player. Girls often give up attending school because it gets in the way of practice—at fifteen, their education consists of completing an assignment and stuffing it into a mailbox, to be sent to a correspondence school. They curtail their social life to fit around their sports schedule, or find it has been curtailed for them, as their old friends, lacking shared experiences, give up and close ranks.

Outsiders—who have never been tempted on the level of magnitude a tennis family experiences—tend to regard junior tennis with contempt. They make jokes about child abuse; they assume that all tennis parents are updated versions of the old stage-mother cliché, fueled by ravenous ambition and thwarted, selfish desire, and that all tennis players are brainwashed automatons. They pridefully assert that their own children are growing up at a normal pace, with only a healthy amount of pressure.

But the difference between encouragement and obsession is merely one of degree, often only a matter of opportunity and interpretation. Women's tennis elicits strong emotions from people, inside and outside the sport, because it is alarmingly familiar.

We worship personal success. Our mythic ideal is the person who has made something of himself; we depend on our achievements to define us, to identify us in the crowd. On some level, teenage girls who become professional tennis players are simply doing what we have all been brought up to do, striving to separate and distinguish themselves. They are taught—as so many children are taught—to value achievement above curiosity, to compete rather than to explore. But they are taught so young, and their education is so public, that their example is a startling one. We instinctively try to disown it.

People who aren't quite prepared for the severity of the example—because the girls are so young, and because they are girls, in a society which is still not quite accustomed to female aggression in the name of achievement—tend to blame tennis families as if they were the perpetrators of a social crime.

In fact, they are dreamers of a very common dream. There are stage mothers and fathers, certainly, but for the most part tennis families are ambitious people laboring under the pressures of fleeting commercial appeal. Women's tennis is a renegade sport, lacking in guidelines, ripe for exploitation, located at the intersection of a parent's unfinished emotional business, a child's fantasies, and a society's infatuation with celebrities, especially the pretty, young, female variety. It is one place where a parent's initially benign desire to want a child to have a better life takes such a dramatic toll.

What happens to Debbie Spence and her friends is not an isolated phenomenon—and this is not simply a book about women's tennis. Before there were tennis stars, there were little girls whose parents urged them to achieve, parents who subscribed to the notion that, given the opportunity, their children surely would exel. A promising tennis player is a distant cousin to any child who ever showed early promise, and what happens to her and her family along the way happens, to some degree, to every family with a talented child.

1
U.S. Open—September 1983

Debbie Spence wanted to quit. This was tennis in a carnival fun-house mirror: she moved like a tiny speck in cement shoes, lumbering around an enormous, distorted court. If she lunged for the ball, it jumped six inches away. If she managed to get the ball across the net, it veered out of bounds. She worked as hard as she could and still missed even the easy shots, while her opponent simply reached out and hit the ball to wherever Debbie wasn't.

She plucked at her striped shirt, which was soaked through with sweat. Her white tennis skirt sat on her hips like a sigh. This week's panic regimen—green salads and granola bars, washed down with rivers of diet drinks—had only succeeded in making her feel weak. Debbie was still ten pounds heavier than she had been at the beginning of the summer, having preceded her seven days of starvation with three months of junk food on the run. She stared unhappily at Claudia Hernandez, her temporary nemesis, who was tall and slim and did not seem to perspire. Claudia wore a stylish, robin's-egg blue tennis skirt made out of a synthetic that looked, and rippled, like satin.

Debbie tugged at her ruffled underpants. This was beginning to feel like a disaster in the making. She looked bad, her game looked bad, and she had timed her near-collapse to coincide with the most visible tournament of the junior tennis season. The Junior U.S. Open took place during the second week of the U.S. Open, once there were vacancies on some of the twenty-five working courts (two were covered by bleachers to accommodate over 350,000 fans) at the United States Tennis Association National Tennis Center at Flushing Meadow, New York. Thirty-two girls and thirty-two boys, the elite of the world's young amateur players—including only

6

five girls from the United States, here by special invitation—competed in the shadow of the Louis Armstrong Stadium for junior titles and the dreams that accompanied them.

They were dreams of stardom. Someday, one of these youngsters could be the main attraction, playing a televised match to standing-room-only crowds on the stadium court or the adjacent grandstand court. A girl like Debbie could imagine herself holding a silver trophy aloft to the applause of adoring fans, posing for photos, holding noisy press conferences.

It was easy for a young player to be stagestruck. For two concentrated weeks, the universe was made up almost entirely of people devoted to the adulation, or involved in the promotion, of top tennis players. The promise of fortune and fame was everywhere. Chris Evert Lloyd, the number two women's player in the world and role model to young girls all over the United States, had earned $4.7 million in prize money alone in her eleven-year career, and her product endorsements had made her a media star. When she walked to a practice session, she was followed by dozens of fans, including a phalanx of aggressive little girls wielding pens and autograph books. Agents prowled the grounds, along with big-name coaches and representatives of sporting-goods firms, all ready to help an amateur player become a professional and, they hoped, a celebrity.

Debbie had earned the right to believe that it all might happen to her. Although formal junior rankings for 1983 would not be released until early in 1984, all the talented amateur players and their parents had the statistics in their heads: Debbie Spence, who had turned sixteen only a few weeks ago, would be ranked number one in the United States in the 18-and-under girls category, which was the oldest amateur age group.

A year ago she had been ranked eleventh in the 16-and-under age group, a respectable, if anonymous position, but this year her game had taken off. She won all six southern California sectional tournaments in 1983, as well as the National Junior Hardcourt Championships, and at one point in the summer had racked up sixty-eight match wins and only two losses. She pounded her way through the Junior Wightman Cup camp, a competition camp for top American players, and won a coveted spot on the Junior Wightman Cup team. She received a special invitation to the Junior French Open and got all the way to the finals before she lost. It was only her first year in this age group, but she was on her way to being the best.

For most of the summer, exhilaration had kept her mounting exhaustion at bay. She had survived two month-long trips, alone, dragging four tennis racquets and her luggage through airline terminals and motel lobbies on two continents.

But in the last few weeks, her energy had begun to lag. She had never been away from home for so long, and the mundane details of life on the road, from doing her laundry to setting up practice sessions, were wearing her out. Her last stop before the Open had been the USTA Junior Grass Court International Championships, where she lost to another highly ranked player. Now she was at the U.S. Open for the first time in her life—aware that USTA officials and East Coast agents might be curious about her, might drop by to watch the match—and she was playing tired, staring at a potentially embarrassing defeat. This was only a second-round match. With Debbie's record, people would expect her to steamroll right into the finals.

She glanced up into the bleachers. Claudia Hernandez's friends and family were bunched into an impromptu cheering section in the front rows. Debbie knew what they were thinking. They figured Claudia had a chance to score an upset. It would be quite a coup, and they cheered her every move with surprised, high-decibel delight. Debbie used to be able to ignore the spectators if she felt they were rooting for her opponent. Sometimes she even played better because she got angry. But today she felt her strength sapped by their enthusiasm. She flirted with self-pity: Why weren't people pulling for her?

Debbie was ahead five games to four, serving for the first set —but what was more important to her, what preyed on her mind, was that she had been ahead 3–love, lost her concentration, and with it, a comfortable lead. The middle of a match was not the time to think about how badly she felt. She had only made more work for herself.

If she did not pull herself together and take this set, she would have to win the two sets that followed, in ninety-degree heat and high humidity—or face the humiliation of letting what should have been an easy win go down the drain. Under better circumstances, she was known for her ability to come from behind, but today she didn't think she could do it. And she had so wanted to make a good impression here. The pressure was almost more than her frayed, undernourished nerves could bear—because partly, secretly, she wanted Claudia to beat her so that she could relax and have an excuse to rest.

She turned to the ball boy, but he was not watching her. He had his eye on two girls in the bleachers who were meticulously applying fresh coats of mascara, blusher, and lipstick, pausing only to giggle and check their handiwork in their wraparound reflector sunglasses. They managed the particular teenage trick of simultaneously noticing someone and acting as if they hadn't, which only made the ball boy more determined to evoke a response. He combed his hair with his fingers. He shot smiles in their general direction. He straightened his official 1983 U.S. Open polo shirt. He did not notice that Debbie stood at the baseline waiting, her ponytail and bangs hanging in sodden rivulets, her face blotchy from too much sun, her patience about to give out.

She tapped her foot and cleared her throat loudly; the ball boy turned, shrugged, and tossed her a ball. As Debbie prepared to serve, she imagined what her father was going to say when she called home tonight. If she somehow managed to win the match, he would probably still grouse about how poorly she had played. If she lost, he would yell at her for losing in only the second round to a girl she should have beaten. He would complain about having to pay $56 per day for her hotel room while she hung around for the less important doubles competition, and would not be consoled by the fact that it was a bargain player's discount rate; it was still a stretch for Tom and his wife, Francine, both of whom taught at a public junior high school. He would probably remind her of how expensive phone calls were from a Manhattan hotel room to Cerritos, California.

When he finished interrogating her about how, exactly, she had faltered, they would both hang up impatiently and, separated by 3,000 miles, fret over just how much was at stake. For, although they argued a lot, Debbie and Tom Spence were not at odds over Debbie's tennis; in fact, they had been partners since Tom gave his four-year-old daughter a racquet to drag around the court while he drilled his older daughter, Terri.

If tempers were short—if even the long-distance credit-card calls, insignificant as part of the total budget, were enough to spark an argument—it was because the past year had confirmed the family's hopes, had said, in effect, that Tom had been right to push his daughter all these years. Even though a loss to Hernandez could not damage Debbie's ranking, it would bruise the family's collective ego at a particularly vulnerable moment.

For the Spences faced an intimidating decision: now that Debbie was a USTA-sanctioned prodigy, the best 18-and-under player in the whole country at sixteen, what were they going to do with her? The family had moved forward together for nine years—Debbie played, Tom coached, Francine acted as chauffeur and emotional buffer between her husband and daughter—always setting a goal and trying to work toward it.

If Debbie had been ranked anything lower than number one, Tom would have argued that she still had to prove herself in the juniors. Life could have remained the same. Debbie would practice after school, play the southern California junior circuit on the weekends, and travel to national and international junior tournaments when the budget allowed. At least she would have had a goal; she still would have been working to become number one.

If Debbie had wanted to go to college on a tennis scholarship in two years, she would have had to continue playing as an amateur. Her sister Terri, two and a half years older than Debbie, had spared the family a decision by choosing what she saw as a normal life—college, home, and family—over life on the pro circuit. She went on to become a championship college player. But Debbie was her opposite. She wanted a career.

Starting on October 1, 1983, the formal beginning of the 1984 junior tennis ranking year, the only amateur goal left for Debbie was to tread water. The best she could hope for would be to rank number one for three years in a row, until she was too old to compete. The worst that could happen would be that an even younger girl could take the top ranking away from her. She could be a has-been at seventeen.

Or she could turn pro.

It was such a tantalizing thought, and a durable American dream. Only the trappings changed. For over sixty years it had been a Hollywood cliché: kids got off the Greyhound wanting to be movie stars, to leave their dull lives behind for a life of wealth and fame. Now, a national obsession with physical fitness had made sports the glamour industry of the eighties— the new show business—and this generation's dreamers included young girls like Debbie, who knew, with the same headlong certainty that sent would-be stars stampeding the movie-studio gates, that they were going to make it.

They had the chance for independent wealth before they were old enough to vote, and celebrity status that extended far beyond the grounds of Flushing Meadow. Top women tennis players competed for $11 million in prize money in 1983 on a year-round, worldwide circuit, while their agents competed for endorsement dollars and planned investment strategies. The right girl, right now, could make as much as $2 million a year in endorsements, on top of what she earned on-court. Given the current cult of the well-tuned body, these women were in demand, not just for sporting-goods endorsements, but for all sorts of consumer products; an attractive, aggressively fit young woman decked out in a skimpy tennis costume had tremendous popular appeal. She could become immune to the daily financial concerns which plagued mere workaday mortals, and become a national heroine in the process.

It took a tremendous gamble which might never pay off. Girls ran the risk of having a career cut short by debilitating injury or psychological burnout—or worse, of being stalled in the never-never land of mediocrity, earning the equivalent of a teacher's salary in a field where thirty-five-year-old players were senior citizens. To cash in early, a girl had to give up thoughts of college, look for the easy courses in the high-school curriculum, and try not to worry about having to enter the job market in fifteen years with no skills and little education.

All that Debbie Spence and her parents had to do was trade in her adolescence for a more structured, disciplined, and isolated life, never knowing what the end result would be. There might be wild, exciting promises in women's pro tennis, which did not even exist when Debbie Spence was born, but there were no guarantees.

That was the real reason Debbie did not want to talk to her father on the phone. She preferred the heady fantasy of the future, when she would be one of the pros who drew a crowd, who flew home to a condo and a sports car—while Tom, who functioned as Debbie's part-time coach and still could not finance his daughter's tennis without help from his father, had to worry about the present. He had to keep both his go-for-broke daughter and the endless expenses in line. Although he wanted Debbie to have her chance, he was afraid of being rushed into a premature decision. He was not going to give in to his daughter's enthusiasm—and his own desire for a little financial relief—until he was satisfied that she was ready.

The end of their conversation would be the same as the end of almost every long-distance conversation they had. Gently, but quite firmly, Tom Spence would remind his daughter of what he jokingly called the first economic rule of junior tennis.

"Come home," he would tell her, "as soon as you lose."

The thought made Debbie angry—angrier still when she realized that she had let her concentration wander again. In truth, she held her parents partly to blame for the way she felt. She might not be worried about losing if her mother or father had come with her. Tom didn't know how lonely she got hanging around the lobby of the Essex House, watching the other players check in with their parents. He didn't know how hard it was to find a practice court by yourself; resentfully she assumed that the girls who had traveling coaches or their folks with them were playing better tennis than she was. And he didn't know how hard it was to eat regular meals when going to a restaurant in Manhattan was out of the question—hadn't her doubles partner been mugged in front of the hotel last year?—and going down to the hotel dining room alone made her feel weird. What did he expect of her?

She took a deep breath, brushed her bangs off her damp forehead, and adjusted one of the enameled metal clips that kept stray short hairs out of her eyes. No matter how badly she felt, she refused to give her father the opportunity to say that she couldn't cope with pressure. She had to get back into this match. If only she'd given herself more time off. The last two tournaments—the Junior Grass Court International Championships in Philadelphia and the Junior National Championships in Memphis, Tennessee—had been particularly rough. Debbie knew she was running out of energy and had called her parents from Philadelphia to ask if she could skip a Canadian junior tournament and come home. She could rest for a week, play with her cocker spaniel, Sweetie, watch some TV, bring her scrapbooks up to date, and let her mom cook for her.

Francine had been getting nervous about how listless Debbie sounded on the phone, so she was all for the idea. But three days after Debbie got home, an official from the USTA called to invite her to compete in the three-day qualifying rounds for the main draw in the U.S. Open. It was a huge compliment. If she managed to survive three days of qualifying rounds, she would get to play the pros. It was a sure way to get noticed. If she survived the first round, people would remember her name, and if she got any further than that, she would be a certified phenomenon. Tracy Austin had guaranteed herself a place in tennis history by making it to the quarterfinals of the U.S. Open as a junior player. So much for taking it easy. Debbie was adamant. She had to go.

It meant turning right around and heading for New York ten days before the junior competition began. Debbie packed her bags, tried to forget that she'd been the one who asked for some time off, and promptly lost in the first qualifying round.

Now she was paying (as was her father, literally, for the extra nights at the hotel, food, and phone calls) for her mistake.

Debbie did not win another game in the first set. Claudia Hernandez won it 7–5. As the girls began their second set, Tom Werdel stopped by court 20 to watch. His daughter Marianne, who would be ranked number three in the 18s, was Debbie's doubles partner and frequent singles competitor. Her match on the adjacent court was just getting under way, so he had a little time to check in on Debbie. He was concerned about her. His daughter had been sleeping in Debbie's room to keep her company since the Werdels arrived in Manhattan, so Tom knew that Debbie was feeling worn out.

He could see that she was not playing her usual game, and he had nine years of evidence to back up his appraisal. Debbie and Marianne had been trading victories since they were little girls—this year Debbie was first in the 18s sectional rankings and Marianne second, according to the Southern California Tennis Association; the year before, when they were the top two players in the sectional 16s, those rankings were reversed.

Tom approached Warren Rice, who worked for Debbie's father as an assistant tennis coach at Cerritos Community College, and had come to the Open at his own expense, in the hope that he could promote his career as a coach, by working with Debbie in such high-profile surroundings.

"She can't win her match like this," said Tom Werdel. "She's got to run her ass off."

"She's not using her shots," said Warren, without taking his eyes from the court. When Debbie looked despairingly in his direction, he held up a clenched fist next to his face.

Both men watched for a few minutes more. Behind the bleachers, the man who ran the food concession booth began talking loudly about his imaginary stock portfolio, joking that he was just selling snacks until he got the good word from his Merrill Lynch financial adviser. Tom Werdel left to see how his daughter was doing. Warren Rice, who grew up playing football and basketball in Compton, a poor black neighborhood in Los Angeles, and came to tennis "too late to make it as a pro," wondered if he was about to lose his chance to be a paragraph in a sports story about Debbie Spence, winner of the Junior U.S. Open. She was a tough, tenacious player, and he had seen her prevail in a three-set match plenty of times before, but today she wasn't placing her shots well. The ones that usually skated right inside the line were bouncing just beyond it, and her trademark stamina seemed to have deserted her.

This didn't look like one of those matches where Debbie won by outlasting the other girl. Her frustration had started to show: she slapped herself on her thigh with her racquet and uttered a few select, but acceptable, epithets. She glanced over at him imploringly.

There was nothing he could do to help her. So Warren talked to himself about her shots, applauded the good ones, and made sure he had a positive expression on his face every time she turned toward the bleachers.

But the second set went even more quickly, although Debbie made Claudia Hernandez work for her 6–3 victory. If she had to lose, going to deuce five times in the match game was a dignified way to do it, a last reminder that Debbie was a player who never gave up.

Claudia rushed over to her excited, cheering friends. Debbie moved more slowly, hoping to avoid the crowd of people at the gate. She pulled on her cotton sleeveless tennis sweater, smoothed her hair, collected her racquets, and left the court. Eyes down, she accepted the condolences of a few onlookers before Warren, sensing her distress, pulled her away from the crowd and escorted her in the direction of the players' lounge.

Behind court 20 there was a small plot of burned-out grass. A short, distracted black woman ran across it, her shoulder bag bouncing against her side, her hair tousled. Claudette Benjamin was looking for change for the pay phone, so she could call her cousin on Long Island. Rather than take rooms at the Essex House, Claudette, her husband, Carl, and their seventeen-year-old daughter, Camille, were staying with their relatives to keep expenses down while Camille competed in the main draw of the U.S. Open. Last year Camille had been a junior player, and she and her parents had traveled the same circuit as the Spences and the Werdels. But when Camille came up number one in the 16-and-under category as a fifteen-year-old, the family decided to take a chance. Camille Benjamin skipped the 18-and-under age group entirely and turned pro.

According to the Women's Tennis Association, Camille was among the top fifty women players in the world—usually hovering between forty and fifty on the WTA computer. She lost here in the first round of the women's singles, having had the unfortunate luck to draw sixteenth-seeded Kathy Jordan as her opponent. She lost in women's doubles. Today was her first mixed doubles match with her partner, Gary Donnelly. Claudette was ambivalent about it. She did not want her daughter to lose, of course, but classes at Highland High School, in Bakersfield, California, started tomorrow, and it would be nice for Camille to be home for the first day of classes. The Benjamins had loaded their belongings into the car this morning, prepared to run straight to the airport if she lost. But now she and Donnelly had won the first set. Claudette had to put the relatives on notice: the Benjamins might be back for another night.

It was hardly a glamorous existence, but it was the big time, and it represented an unspoken challenge to someone like Debbie. If she was all that good, what was she waiting for?

The next morning Debbie was her buoyant, chattering self. At breakfast she told exaggerated stories about how mad she and her father had gotten on the telephone. She giggled about parents in general with Melissa Brown, a junior player from Scarsdale, New York, whose doubles partner was Claudia Hernandez. Debbie and Marianne Werdel were to play Melissa and Claudia this afternoon. It was a match Debbie particularly wanted to win, because it would buy her time to hang around and because it would be a minimal revenge for yesterday's singles loss.

Debbie seemed eager to get out to Flushing Meadow. Everything was fine until her breakfast order arrived. She had asked for a cup of hot chocolate, no food, which was her compromise between desire and discipline, but after a single sip she looked dismayed. This was not the way her mother made hot chocolate. Her mother used milk. This was runny, made with water, and lukewarm. Debbie was unable to cope with the disappointment. She had reached her tolerance level, both for being alone and for being unhappy; somebody else was going to have to handle the hot-chocolate problem for her. She began to whine.

"How am I going to drink this," she said, in such despair that Warren Rice immediately summoned a waiter, ordered a new cup for Debbie, and started talking about everybody's plans for the day. He didn't want Debbie seen moping around the courts, looking like a loser. He ushered her out of the Essex House restaurant to the rear entrance of the hotel, where the USTA had buses and cars waiting, and made sure she was on her way in a players' car before he got on the bus.

By the time she and Marianne began their doubles match on one of the outlying courts at Flushing Meadow, she had regained her composure. Marianne had dominated her singles matches so far, and her enthusiastic, self-assured attitude was contagious. Although the two girls had little in common— Debbie was an average student prone to practical jokes and hamstrung by a tight budget, while Marianne, more reserved in her behavior, brought home A's and was expected to follow in her parents' and older sister's footsteps and attend Stanford University—tennis had turned them into close friends. They had been doubles partners since they were seven, Marianne always a full head taller, with powerful shoulders and long legs, Debbie smaller and fast on her feet. They were used to playing with each other—and they were both aware that, from now on, they would have fewer chances to do so.

For the first time in their lives, they would not be making the rounds of the southern California junior circuit together. Debbie would get back home just in time to start her junior year at Cerritos High School, but Marianne was not returning to Garces Memorial High School in Bakersfield, California. She had convinced her parents, despite their initial misgivings, to enroll her in Nick Bollettieri's Tennis Academy in Bradenton, Florida, a $1,485-per-month live-in facility for about two hundred of the world's best players, both amateur and professional. She would attend classes in the mornings at the private St. Stephen's Episcopal School, one of two schools attended by academy students.

The decision seemed to enhance Marianne's game. She had dispatched yesterday's singles opponent so quickly that Tom Werdel almost missed the conclusion of his daughter's match. Parents of other players, USTA officials, and two spectators with briefcases who worked for one of the sports management firms came up to Tom and his wife, Corinne, to offer their congratulations and inquire about Marianne's plans. It was hard for Debbie not to be envious: her friend was playing the way she should have played, getting the recognition she had wanted so badly, and had the luxury of having both parents around to help her keep her spirits up.

Debbie was going to miss Marianne. There was little chance they would see each other before the USTA Junior Indoor Championships, which were to be held over Thanksgiving break, and Debbie wasn't sure how much time she wanted to devote to junior tournaments this year. So she and Marianne had personal reasons to win their doubles matches: every victory delayed their leave-taking a day. They went after Brown and Hernandez with a pleasant vengeance—not the way they did in singles competitions, where their rankings and individual reputations depended on it—but like pals, with smiles, dramatic moans, and stern on-court conferences. With just a bit of abandon.

"It's nice for the girls to play doubles," observed one spectator. "That way, they get to have some fun."

If major international tennis tournaments reflected something of the host country's personality—Wimbledon, with its stiff-upper-lip formality and love of tradition, or the French Open, where Parisian devotion to the good life extended to gourmet morsels sold at the stadium—then the U.S. Open confirmed this country's status as the world's preeminent capitalist.

National singles championships had been held at the West Side Tennis Club in Forest Hills, New York, from 1924 until 1977, but by the mid-1970s tennis had grown too large for that historic site. Flushing Meadow Park—which had been, at various points in history, a dump site, the home of the World's Fair in 1939–1940 and again in 1964–1965, and temporary home to the United Nations between 1946 and 1949—could accommodate more fans and more fanfare. It represented the chance to move away from the private-club atmosphere of the past, and make tennis into a mass entertainment for the future.

Flushing Meadow resembled an open-air shopping mall. Anyone who stood to make a dollar off of tennis was doing so. Actually, he was probably making a dollar and change, since the presence of a large, captive, and fairly affluent audience made it possible to charge inflated prices. The International Food Village was a formidable outdoor dining area where people eagerly parted with $6.25 for a pita bread filled with tuna-fish salad from Cutforth & Atkins, Purveyor of Fine Foods, or bought a $3.25 Stolichnaya vodka and tonic from Chesterfield's Bar.

It was not your standard spectator fare; certainly, it was a gustatory notch above the hot dogs, peanuts, and beer served to baseball and football fans across the subway tracks at Shea Stadium. But then, tennis had never been the standard sandlot sport. Its natural habitat was the country club, its training ground, the private lesson; as late as the 1950s, blacks and Jews were regularly excluded from tournaments. In 1969, Arthur Ashe, the first black player to rise out of a public-parks program, instituted the National Junior Tennis League in an attempt to make tennis more of a people's sport. The program might have skewed the demographics of the player roster, but the fans, for the most part, were people who could afford to slip away from the office for a weekday jaunt to Flushing Meadow. They were people with money to spend; they were predominantly white and well-off.

There were plenty of entrepreneurs eager to help them part with their cash or credit card. Around the circumference of the stadium and grandstand courts, spectators could walk up to a booth and subscribe to *World Tennis,* the monthly official magazine of the USTA, published by a division of CBS, or its competitor, *Tennis,* published by Golf Digest/Tennis, Inc., owned by the *New York Times.* For close to $100 they could emulate their favorite player with a complete tennis outfit from Fila, Ellesse, or a handful of other designer sportswear labels. Feron's, a tennis supply store, offered a complete U.S. Open souvenir line, from seat cushions to sun visors. Once suitably attired, the weary fan could cool down with a Sedutto ice-cream cone for $1.50 or a soft drink for $1.25, or bulk up with any number of fast-food snacks.

In case a wayward potential customer managed to miss the two major shopping areas, entrepreneurs with umbrella carts rolled around the grounds selling Italian ices, more plastic seat cushions, and souvenir clothes.

The equipment manufacturers staked out the walkway that led away from the two main courts, in front of the U.S. Open Club Building, where they set up shop for anyone who wanted a racquet restrung or a shoe resoled. That accomplished, said player could take two steps and sign up for a tennis vacation at the Rod Laver Tennis Resort.

The Open catered to fans' psychological needs as well: there were futures for sale here. By the second week of the tournament, with half the pros eliminated and the newest style in junior players on display, spectators had a choice between the name brands like Martina Navratilova and Chris Evert Lloyd, who promised a dependably exciting match played on one of the better courts, where there were bleachers to sit on, and the unknown juniors, who might be next year's hot property. The adventuresome shopper who was willing to stand through a match—or, having been on such a safari before, knew to bring a collapsible chair—could invest, vicariously, in a young player's future.

A heroine in the making had allure for everyone. People who had played tennis for decades loved to scrutinize the girls' games and then announce, often loudly, their choice for most promising player. Parents brought their young daughters, many of them decked out in name-brand tennis clothes from headband to socks, and paid rapt attention to their seven-year-old's analysis of a player's backhand. Teenage boys prowled the courts looking for cute players of the opposite sex. The younger junior girls watched the older ones and studied their outfits and hairdos, just as some of the older juniors studied the pros to learn the latest celebrity fashions.

There were more serious investors, too, business people who might want to have a literal stake in a girl's future. A coach who came to the U.S. Open with one of his charges was always on the lookout for other talented players who might be dissatisfied with their current coach and ripe for recruitment. Representatives of the big sporting-goods firms like Wilson, Prince, and Adidas wanted to make sure that players who used their equipment had everything they needed—including the company's insignia on their racquets, which was why some reps stocked stencils and vials of spray paint in their briefcases. If the W on Debbie Spence's Wilson racquet was getting a bit faint, Bob Shafer, Wilson Sporting Goods Co. promotion manager, Far West region, could quickly help her restore it to its original bright red color.

Juniors were not allowed, formally, to accept equipment, which would have been the same as accepting money, which would have meant they were no longer amateurs. But everyone—the USTA, the sporting-goods companies, the agents, the players themselves—wanted the girls to look good. They were living billboards for tennis in general and for the equipment they used, and manufacturers wanted to reserve space early, in case a girl grew into a talented professional whose endorsement meant increased sales.

There had to be a way to exploit a junior player without compromising her amateur status. The solution was a "loan" program. Technically, apparel and equipment companies let talented juniors borrow what they needed, pretending that someday everything would be returned. Debbie Spence had collected $7,500 worth of equipment this year—$4,000 in Fila clothing, $3,000 in Wilson racquets that retailed for $200 each, and $500 in Nike tennis shoes.

Agents from the three big sports management firms—International Management Group, based in Cleveland, Ohio, and ProServ and Advantage International, Inc., two Washington, D.C., firms—courted the juniors as well. A player could not sign a representation contract until she turned pro, but again, there was no time, on either side, to be coy. If an agent established a rapport with a family by offering advice and guidance, whether it be on a tournament schedule or the name of a decent restaurant in a strange town, then perhaps the girl would choose that agency to represent her. If a player impressed an agent, perhaps the agency would choose to recruit her, and help her make the transition into the professional ranks.

Everybody, it seemed, had something to buy or to sell, which quickened the pace of the proceedings and imbued every match with life-or-death significance. It also obscured the fact that, on some level, Debbie and Marianne were simply gifted children—prodigies who showed exceptional ability at an early age, no different from youthful musicians, dancers, or academics. Their parents were like so many other proud parents, pleased and a little awed at their offspring's accomplishments, willing to make sacrifices to accommodate the development of their daughters' athletic skills.

But there was a crucial distinction: these girls were extremely marketable for a very limited period of time, and the combination of potential money to be earned in an emphatically finite career was a volatile one. Other kinds of talent might require family sacrifice, and the devotion of a young mind and body to a single pursuit, but in tennis excellence and commercial opportunity were intertwined. This particular talent held a tantalizing promise: no one stood to win as much, as early, as a girl who turned pro.

She was simply the most bankable prodigy around. Women tennis pros had the highest popularity, and profitability, quotient of all women athletes. The best ones could make the leap from their specific sport into general acceptance; in the eighties, the sweaty blonde in a terrycloth headband replaced the bobbed blond starlet of the twenties as a contemporary icon. But they also had a brief shelf life. They peaked physically in their late teens and talked about retirement, or played for sentimental reasons, in their early thirties.

"These days, the men, if they're really good, never finish college," observed Arthur Ashe in his U.S. Open television commentary. "And the women, if they're really good, never finish high school." The cash register was ringing, the biological clock was ticking, and women's professional tennis was only thirteen years old, lacking in tradition and guidelines. In the confusion and noise it was hard for people like the Spences to know what to do. The internal pressure to excel was compounded by the external pressure to cash in before it was too late.

2
Bakersfield Ginny

The Laurel Glen Tennis Club, on Ming Boulevard in Bakersfield, California, was a brand-new facility at the edge of a neighborhood that barely had a present, let alone a past, where the fall crop of tract homes had just broken through the soil and Central Savings, sensing opportunity, had taken up residence in a spruced-up trailer next to an empty lot which would eventually be its permanent home.

MYTI-GOOD Realty was across the way, along with franchise food outlets for every taste and clusters of small shops to meet every need. There was no history here, just potential at every intersection. An enterprising individual could build a future. Driving down Ming Boulevard, it was easy to feel optimistic.

Debbie Spence was in town in late September because she had been invited to compete in the qualifying rounds of the $50,000 Ginny of Bakersfield, a middle-level tournament sponsored by Virginia Slims cigarettes, which also ran the more prestigious Virginia Slims circuit as part of its World Championship Series. Every morning she and her mother threw their bags into the back of Francine's road-weary Datsun 280Z, checked out of their room at the E-Z8 Motel, and drove to the Laurel Glen Tennis Club. If Debbie lost they would drive the 130 miles back home to Cerritos, having saved a day's motel bill. If she won they would drive back to the motel, check back in, and repeat the procedure the next day. So far she had survived two qualifying matches.

"The Ginny Circuit," explained the promotional brochure, "is where you can see up-and-coming players from around the world. Many of today's top-ranked players, like Andrea Jaeger, Tracy Austin, Pam Shriver, Bettina Bunge, Sylvia Hanika, and Barbara Potter, got their start in tournaments just like this one."

To Debbie's mind, this tournament marked the beginning of the end of her amateur athletic career, although it was really the beginning of what could be a long transition period. In the two weeks since the U.S. Open, the Spences had made a decision: Debbie had to get a Women's Tennis Association computer ranking as the first step toward turning pro.

She had to play six sanctioned professional tournaments in a year—by September 1984—to get on the computer. With luck, or with an agent's intervention, the process could take less than a year. Sometimes a girl could get a "wild card," a special invitation directly into the main draw, through an agent who believed that she had potential and lobbied on her behalf, or from a tournament promoter who thought she had drawing power. Otherwise, she had to hope for an invitation to play the qualifying rounds, and pray that she wouldn't be eliminated before she got to the matches that mattered. If she didn't get into six pro tournaments in a year, the Women's Tennis Association would ignore her first tournament and start counting time from the date of the next tournament she entered.

The rankings, which were revised every two weeks, were computed according to a complicated formula that awarded more points for a Virginia Slims victory than a Ginny win, and more points for a Ginny victory than for a match won on the USTA Satellite Circuit, the lowest rung on the women's professional tennis ladder. Anything above 50 or 60 was considered a very good ranking, high enough to get directly into the main draw of a major Slims tournament; above 120, a girl could still compete in many of the less prestigious tournaments. Anything below that made turning pro a murkier issue, because it meant traveling the circuit to play qualifying rounds, spending money without necessarily winning any, which was an expensive gamble.

But Debbie wasn't thinking about that at the moment, as she waited to play her last qualifying match. She was one victory away from the main draw, and she was eager to play, to show that she was an adult who could handle the stress of playing the pros. She assumed that she would end up with a good ranking; all she needed was her family's support and a chance to play. When she called her father at night from the E-Z8, she badgered him about which pro tournament he would let her play next.

With her mouth set tight, she went about her business: she found a practice court, warmed up, and then followed the winding path over to the court where she would play her match.

In the middle of that path, looking lost, was her mother. While most of the mothers here sported carefully cultivated tans, Francine was almost painfully white—a pale face hidden by big rosy sunglasses, platinum hair, and arms and legs that clearly did not spend a lot of leisure time outdoors. She wore a white eyelet top with thick straps, red bermuda shorts, red sandals, and an expression of forced cheerfulness. This much excitement sat precariously close to panic for her.

At thirty-seven, Francine had spent her life surrounded by, and devoted to, children, without having much of a childhood of her own. She was the eldest of seven children, and when she was fifteen her stepfather had informed her that he considered her an adult, capable of sharing the responsibility of raising her siblings. She left home at seventeen to marry Tom, her high-school sweetheart, and then followed him up and down the state of California, first north to San Jose State University, then south to Cal State, Long Beach. She grabbed her own college education along the way, between babies.

They had three daughters—Terri, now nineteen and engaged to be married, Debbie, and Rhonda, eleven. Both she and Tom became teachers, and, for the last year and a half, they both had taught at Chester A. Nimitz Junior High School in Huntington Park, near Los Angeles, where the spray-paint graffiti was in Spanish and the student monitors called themselves "commandos." Tom taught physical education. Francine taught science and eighth-grade girls' health. When she could she attended the Calvary Chapel of Downey on Sunday mornings with Rhonda, the only one in the family with the time, or the inclination, to accompany her.

Francine had watched Debbie play for years, all over southern California. She was used to spending her weekends on the freeways, pulling into one tennis club after another, the same ones year after year, seeing the same cars in the parking lots, talking to the same parents. It was an informal, casual universe, and there had been a comforting, if deceptive, familiarity to it all. When she and Tom discussed the need for one of them to travel with Debbie to pro tournaments, Francine agreed to go.

The extent of her travels, until now, had been an annual camping trip, visits to family in Oregon, and a single trip to Florida. Francine rarely traveled to the major national tournaments with her daughter, partly because of the expense, and partly because the tournaments were usually scheduled over holidays so that the girls would not have to miss school. She felt that she should be home with Tom, Terri, and Rhonda, and Tom's parents, instead of sitting in a motel with Debbie. In the past year Debbie had seen New York and Paris. Francine thought the traveling would be fun—a chance for her to see some of the world, and spend time with her daughter.

She never imagined that she and Debbie would sit in their room at the E-Z8 at night, calculating how much Debbie would have won at this tournament if she were already a pro. There had been no way to anticipate how utterly helpless she would feel, watching her daughter compete for the chance to have a future.

She managed to give Debbie a brief pep talk, but as soon as the match got under way Francine retreated to the snack bar for a Coke. When she returned, she approached the court hesitantly, watched for a few minutes, and then edged back toward a set of temporary metal bleachers that faced the opposite direction, toward the club's main court. From here she could watch the match without letting Debbie see her. The other girls had always teased Debbie about how nervous her mother got during a match, but nerves on the junior circuit were nothing compared to this. Yesterday, Francine admitted, she had come close to tears when Debbie's doubles partner, Marianne Werdel, lost her singles match.

"Mom, go order me something please." Debbie came off the court a quick victor, having guaranteed herself a berth in the main draw and taken the first step toward a computer ranking. She changed into shorts and a T-shirt with fashionably rolled-up sleeves and joined her mother in the club's coffee shop.

"Their salads look pretty good." Francine saw herself as the "advise person" in the family, and one of the things she wanted to advise Debbie against was poor eating habits.

"I'm *sick* of salad. I go places and eat five salads. I don't want a salad."

"What do you want?" said Francine.

"A cheeseburger."

Francine didn't want to argue with Debbie; she had won her match and deserved to savor the victory. So she went over to the counter to place the order while Debbie sprawled in her chair and accepted congratulations from people who passed by. One admiring twelve-year-old stopped at the table with her mother to ask Debbie if they could see the skinny gold bangle bracelets she wore on her wrist. They were exactly the kind the twelve-year-old wanted—primarily because Debbie, who was the best eighteen-year-old in the country, wore them, and if it was impossible to copy Debbie's game, an admiring youngster could at least imitate her style.

Francine returned with a cheeseburger and a cold drink for Debbie and a cold drink for herself. Debbie was in the midst of telling the twelve-year-old and her mother how she had gotten on the list for free Fila sportswear. Debbie appeared at every tournament wearing a Fila outfit. She had been on the Adidas list before, but the consensus among her friends was that Fila and Ellesse were the more prestigious sportswear lines.

"You write them a letter in September with your ranking and your record," she explained, to a rapt audience, "and they issue a list in October. They only accept the top ten or twenty kids in each age group, though they make some exceptions. Once you're on they usually won't kick you off unless you quit tennis or do something really bad. You get two shipments a year—eight skirts, sixteen shirts, four T-shirts, and socks."

While she talked, Debbie disassembled her lunch. She took the top of the bun off the cheeseburger, gazed warily at the sauce, which looked like fattening Thousand Island salad dressing, and tried to scrape it onto the paper plate with a knife. She dabbed at the meat with a paper napkin to mop up the excess grease.

"It's really not that much stuff," she said, with mild dissatisfaction. "Ellesse gives more. But the woman said if I ever needed anything just to call. So I've already gotten three shipments and I've only been on the list since January. As I did better I wrote her more often. It's just getting up the guts to tell her what you need. When I went to the Junior French she sent me a package with Fila pens, a Fila towel, a Fila bathing suit, sweaters, and two vests."

She looked down at her plate and grimaced. Her calorie-conscious efforts had turned her lunch into an unappetizing mess. The bun was broken in three pieces, and the hamburger patty was dotted with napkin lint.

"Mom, this is gross," she said. "Get me another one."

Francine dutifully went back to the counter to order Debbie another cheeseburger, which she wolfed without making any revisions. Then a snack-bar employee appeared at their table with a third cheeseburger. When he realized the mistake, he simply offered it to Francine for free. Delighted, she sat down to eat her own lunch. But Debbie was already thinking about what she'd like to do next. She started to get up from the table, and Francine asked her if she would like to clear her plates.

Debbie started laughing. "Sure, Mom. You go right ahead."

"That's another reason Debbie has to turn pro," said Francine, as she hastily wrapped her sandwich in a napkin, dumped the paper plates and cups in a garbage can, and hurried out the door after her daughter. "She wants a Porsche, a maid, all of it. She sees it everywhere."

For all the cordiality among tennis parents, who subscribed to a misery-loves-company philosophy and constantly swapped horror stories about outpost motels, questionable umpires, and other parents, there was a competitive edge to their relationships, as well as their daughters'. Family was a stronger bond than shared experience: the first thing tennis parents did when they met at a tournament was to bring each other up to date on their girls' victories.

When Carl Benjamin saw Francine Spence at the Laurel Glen Tennis Club, he politely inquired about that morning's match and offered his congratulations. Then Francine asked Carl how Camille was doing, which gave him the chance to announce that Camille had recently beaten Lisa Bonder, who was ranked thirty-sixth in the world and had had two very good wins the week before.

The Benjamins and the Spences had known each other for years, and shared a mild sense of isolation. Temperament—and financial limitations—had made them outsiders. Camille was one of only a handful of black players on the circuit, and her father and mother kept to themselves when they traveled. Carl Benjamin felt it was premature to be chatting with the agents and well-known coaches. The family had always done well on its own, and he preferred to keep things that way. The Spences had never been part of the sport's social and political inner circle because they didn't have the money to travel to the big junior tournaments, where useful friendships were struck.

Francine trusted Carl, so she blurted out the question she really wanted answered. Was Carl glad that Camille had turned pro? During a hectic year designed to accustom Camille to the rigors of the circuit—she played almost thirty tournaments—her ranking had refused to budge. Inexplicably, she had suffered a string of first-round losses in her last half-dozen tournaments. The optimistic explanation was that the transition from top sixteen-year-old to anonymous pro had taken a psychological toll, but the losses were troublesome.

Camille would earn just over $44,000 in 1983 and spend about $25,000 in expenses. No agent hounded her with a product-endorsement offer. No coach hustled her, hoping to enhance his reputation by taking credit for her game. When she was home she still took lessons from Andy Davidson, the teaching pro at the Bakersfield Racquet Club, over in the older section of town.

The money Camille brought in took some of the pressure off Carl, a Bakersfield Junior College mathematics teacher, and Claudette, a physical therapist, but Camille was hardly living the life Debbie dreamt about. In fact, there was little difference between them. Like Debbie, Camille still lived at home and attended the public high school. She took her homework with her on the tour.

Francine wanted to know: Was Carl satisfied?

"As long as she plays well enough to get into the tournaments," he said, "I'm happy."

Francine was always trying to make sense of what was happening; her brain was the active site of an ongoing debate. All she did, nine years ago, was agree to her husband's suggestion that the girls learn to play tennis in their free time. Tom was a good tennis player who was so busy juggling jobs that he hardly had a spare moment for his children. In addition to teaching school, he coached after-school athletics and taught tennis to other people's children in the public-parks program. If he brought his girls along, he would get to see them, and teach them a sport at the same time. It seemed like a logical solution.

Initially, the girls were reluctant to give up their time after school and on weekends. But Francine agreed with Tom: a structured activity was the best way to keep youngsters from wasting time.

"They didn't like having to go out and hit with their father at first," said Francine, "but we didn't offer them a choice. When your kids go to school you don't say, 'Do you feel like going to class today?' Of course you don't. It's the same thing with tennis. My husband made them do it . . . when they're young you don't give kids those decisions. Kids wouldn't choose to do all this practicing and work.

"It's generally one of the parents who pushes the kids into it," she said. "With my husband it was tennis and that was it. Terri and Debbie were out there on the tennis court seven days a week when my eldest was nine and Debbie was six and a half. It took me a year to convince him they should have a day off."

Lately, she found that she had a new adversary in the fight to maintain a balance between tennis and life beyond tennis. Debbie had a reputation as a fighter among the top junior players—"People know. She'd rather die on that court than give up," Francine often observed—and she had begun to fight off-court as well, for the right to devote herself exclusively to her game.

"Now, Tom thinks one day off every two weeks is enough," said Francine. "I say a day a week. Debbie thinks one day every two weeks—she'll *say* a day a week, but then the first day she's off, she goes to play tennis. The first day back from the Open was her day off and what does she want to go do? Go to the tennis workout. I called home from work and my older daughter said, 'Debbie's crazy. She's running up and down the stairs, she's so excited about going to play tennis.' "

Francine didn't quite comprehend this kind of obsession, nor was she sure that it was entirely healthy. She was troubled that Debbie had come home from Flushing Meadow pleading exhaustion as the excuse for a poor showing, only to head for a tennis court as soon as she got back. During the hours Francine had to herself here in Bakersfield—and she was alone most of the day, between the matches and the marathon three-hour practice sessions that often spanned the time between matches—she wandered the grounds and wondered about her middle child.

She tried hard to understand her daughter's behavior. She knew how alienated Debbie felt from the other high-school kids, and how eager she must have been to tell her friends at the tennis workout, many of whom only wished they could grow up to be like Debbie Spence, about her summer tour. And the fact was, Debbie had trouble relaxing. Rest was boring, if periodically necessary. Anything other than tennis and rest, like school, was unnecessary and a pain.

Only tennis engaged her attention; even the long practice sessions were preferable to the huge category of things that were not tennis. Ever since she had first displayed an ability, and a desire, to win, when she was seven years old, there had only been tennis and distractions from it.

Now there was the new challenge of getting on the computer. In deference to that—she did not want to upset her daughter—Francine cut down on her requests to take it easy. She made fun of herself for worrying about time off, and declared that the idea of Debbie developing a hobby or spending more time on schoolwork seemed forced at this point; an artificial purgatory. What else did teenage girls do? They discovered boys, or drugs, or both, and Francine could hardly recommend that her daughter make a concerted effort to follow suit.

The alternative was to take a hard line—to insist that Debbie invent something else she liked to do, and do it—and hope that Debbie's tennis would not suffer. Francine still believed that another interest could actually improve Debbie's game by taking a little of the pressure off. But what if she was mistaken? Did she really want to push what was essentially only a theory about raising children, when Tom had gotten such great results with his approach? Tom's credo was "Always give a hundred and ten percent, even when you're practicing," and he swore that total dedication was essential to a successful career as a tennis player. Francine did not want to jeopardize her child's future for the speculative advantage of a well-rounded adolescence: how could any mother risk robbing her daughter of fame and fortune for the sake of a hobby, or A's instead of B's?

If she had failed to make a dent after all this time, perhaps she needed to look at tennis in a more positive light. There was no point to being a shrew. The young pros here in Bakersfield were friendly, mature girls, and Francine had to admit that she would be pleased if Debbie grew up to be like one of them. She listened to her daughter, and tried to absorb her enthusiasm: at lunch Debbie announced her intention to take correspondence classes next year, instead of attending the public high school, and minutes later Francine echoed this position, as if trying it on for size.

Francine wanted to believe that a pro career, and the sacrifice it called for, was a good idea. Francine had never had an opportunity like the one her daughter now had, and she could not bring herself to stand in Debbie's way. Debbie had the chance to be someone special—not just another average student who took the predictable route through school, marriage, and children, but an exceptional individual. She was unique in the family, and Francine, despite her superficial worries, wanted Debbie to develop her talent. With envy in her voice, she spoke about how her husband, the second child in a second marriage, was raised. "My husband's parents had two sons, and they devoted their lives to giving their boys a better life," she said. "My mother had seven children; she was busy just raising us."

For all her concern, Francine was proud that she and Tom were able to give their girls more than they had had. She seemed almost giddy, in a girlish way, when she thought about the exciting life Debbie had in store.

The possibility that it wouldn't pan out—that Debbie would turn up twenty-five without fulfilling her promise, and without other interests or skills—did not really frighten Francine. She might not be sophisticated about the workings of the tennis establishment, but the woman who had helped raise a family at fifteen had a blunt understanding of survival.

"At least they're females," she said. "They might want the knowledge of a college education but they don't *need* it to live. The male, his family is going to depend on him. I mean, I think a girl should be independent—but later on in life she may not have to be."

Debbie defeated two opponents in Bakersfield before she lost in the quarterfinal round. Had she been a pro, she would have earned $1,250 for three days' work. She would have made more than Camille Benjamin, who earned $450 for her first-round loss. Debbie and Francine were thrilled.

$1,250. The thought of it made Debbie bold and impatient. A few days after she got home, she approached her father with a plan. Instead of waiting until next year, Debbie wanted to quit school right now and get her diploma through a correspondence course. She had all of her reasons lined up. If she stayed in public school the teachers would give her a hard time about all the traveling she did. Even the more understanding teachers expected her to make up classwork as soon as she got back from a tournament. And a normal high-school schedule would hinder her progress because she'd be limited to practice sessions at night and on the weekends.

She could tailor a correspondence course to fit her travel and practice needs. As long as she could find a mailbox, it wouldn't matter what city she was in or what time it was when she did her schoolwork. If she wanted to do an English assignment at eight o'clock at night, after her last workout, she could do so. She might actually do more work than she did now, because there wouldn't be a conflict between school and tennis.

To bolster her position even further, Debbie invoked the act-of-God argument. What if it rained on the weekends and she wasn't able to practice at all? What if the weekend when it did rain was the weekend before an important pro tournament? How was she supposed to take the next step, and put herself in the position to turn pro, if she couldn't work on her game?

Tom was taken aback by the suggestion. Carefully, he tried to explain his position to Debbie. School had not hurt her tennis so far; after all, she had managed to become number one in the 18s while she attended public school. He reminded her that he and Francine were her allies on the issue of excessive absence. They had interceded on her behalf last year, when the principal received a complaint about Debbie's missing thirty to forty days of school a year because she had something else she preferred to do, and made sure that the teacher who protested was apprised of the special circumstances. He didn't foresee a problem with the teachers this year, but if there were any, he was ready to step in again. As for the rain argument—it might have worked if the Spences had lived in Oregon, but it wasn't very effective in southern California.

His measured response only inflamed Debbie's temper. She had convinced herself that continuing in school was the one thing that would keep her from ever again doing as well as she had at Bakersfield. And now her father, the one who always demanded more of her, no matter how well she played, was saying that school was more important than tennis. He was talking like a parent and a teacher, not a coach.

She teetered in an awkward place, between adolescence and a premature adulthood, uncertain of how to assert herself and defensive about being ignored. Since she was unsure of herself, she tended to be rigid in her demands and suspicious of every disagreement. If Tom didn't see her point, it was because he wasn't taking her seriously; obviously, he still thought of her as a child. He had been hesitant, at first, about Bakersfield, worried that the traveling and time off from school were going to be hard on her. Even though she'd played her heart out at the Ginny, to prove that she was ready to devote herself to tennis full-time, he still wasn't behind her. She knew what he really meant. He wasn't going to let her play enough tournaments to get a ranking. He was going to let her down.

Enraged, Debbie began to yell at her father: "What have I been doing for so many years! I'm trained, and I'm ready, and now you're telling me no! You mean I can't practice as hard as I want? I worked seven years to do this, and now I'm close to being ready—and now you tell me no."

Tom was startled by the outburst—and rather impressed by her reasoning, although he didn't admit it at that moment. She was right: He had taken her this far by demanding all of her free time and concentration, and she had responded in good faith, giving the game her all. She had grown up to be a fine player, and now she assumed that she would be encouraged to progress to the next level of competition. Maybe he'd been wrong to insist on public school. Maybe he had been defensive, too, unsettled at the notion that his daughter would want to exert some control over her own life. He was used to being in charge, and he wondered if he had disagreed with her merely to remind her of who made the decisions in this house.

The matter was dropped temporarily. On October 7 Debbie received another surprise phone call, inviting her to compete in the weeklong Florida Federal Tennis Open, a $150,000 Virginia Slims World Championship tournament, starting October 10 in Tarpon Springs, Florida. The semifinalists from the Bakersfield Ginny were supposed to go, but one of the two players had dropped out. Debbie could be her replacement if she liked.

It was a step up in status from the Bakersfield Ginny and a chance to move one tournament closer to a computer ranking. The call came late Friday afternoon, and Sunday morning Debbie and Francine were on a plane.

Before they left, Tom informed Debbie that he and Francine had made a decision. Although they were not prepared to let Debbie take a correspondence course, they would allow her to drop out of high school and complete her classwork through an independent study program. She would have a weekly meeting with a teacher to review her progress, but she no longer had to attend classes.

3

Separation

Tom Spence stood in his driveway holding a bag of garbage. He had forty minutes to clean up the house before he drove to Los Angeles International Airport to pick up Francine and Debbie, who were to arrive this afternoon from Tarpon Springs. For the second time in three weeks he was in charge of the house, and Rhonda, and he wore the befuddled, vague look of someone who was not in his natural habitat. Usually, he worked with the Cerritos Junior College women's tennis team after school, and a couple of nights a week he taught at the local public courts until about eight. On the weekends he either hit with Debbie or drove her to a local junior tournament.

But that schedule was very quickly becoming part of the past. Debbie was gone more often, and when she was home she balked at practicing with Tom, complaining that he was too critical. By default, not by choice, he was suddenly spending more time at home.

He dumped the garbage, walked back inside, and stared at the living-room floor, which was covered by a sea of yellow tennis balls he was sorting, to see which ones still had enough bounce in them to be used for lessons. There were tennis racquets under and on top of the coffee table and tossed across one of the chairs.

The Spences had lived in Cerritos for twelve years. They were part of a population boom that would make Cerritos the fastest-growing city in Los Angeles County between 1970 and 1980 and erase the memory of the city's beginnings—it was incorporated in 1956 as the City of Dairy Valley, home of more than 100,000 cows and a like number of chickens, but only 3,500 people. Cerritos, with 15,000 new homes, situated snugly between three freeways that put Los Angeles only a traffic jam away, was the perfect place for a young family to settle.

First the Spences moved into a small house at the edge of the Ponderosa Homes development, on a street that backed up onto Artesia Boulevard, the four-lane main drag. One year later, driven to look for a bigger home by his expanding family and the unending traffic noise, Tom tried to find a house they could afford with a yard big enough for a tennis court. Failing that, he and Francine settled for a bigger house on an inside street in the same tract, and put in a swimming pool. The girls continued to practice at the nearby public courts.

Ponderosa Homes, built in 1970, sat adjacent to the 91 freeway, a new road that took Cerritos residents west to the beach, or east to Interstate 5, just as Artesia Boulevard did, but faster. It was an archetypal middle-class neighborhood—cul-de-sac streets, a comforting uniformity to the architecture, children yelping as they belly-flopped into backyard swimming pools, dogs barking at imaginary intruders. Older kids, looking bored, stood on the street corners for hours at a time.

When Tom first moved his family into the neighborhood, the kids hanging around on the corner bothered him. They weren't doing anything with themselves. He vowed to Francine that his little girls were not going to grow up that way.

For Tom, like Debbie, had no patience for sitting still. He preferred perpetual motion, and left the philosophizing to his wife. He had always been a fighter, a boy whose older brother was taller, better-looking, and smarter than he was. There was nothing Tom could do about being short and rather nondescript, and nothing he particularly cared to do about his grades, which were usually C's. So he turned to athletics in self-defense, as a way to get his parents to notice him. His brother hadn't conquered sports yet. On the tennis court Tom could compete and win, as he could not at home: it was a place where he could build his confidence, out of his brother's long shadow. So he offered Terri and Debbie his personal legacy— he taught them the game that had provided him with an identity.

What he did not take into account was that his second child

would be as scrappy a kid as he had been, and that her growth as a player would neatly intersect not only the growth of women's professional tennis, but her own need to assert her fledgling identity. When four-year-old Debbie Spence first took a racquet in her hand she did so not out of any love of the sport, but because her father told her to, and he told her to not out of some fantasy of success and fame, but because he wanted his girls to be active and involved.

At that point, the only pot of gold at the end of the tennis rainbow, for women, was a college scholarship. The pro circuit was barely two years old and the stakes were laughably low. "The problem wasn't which tournament to play next," recalled Billie Jean King, one of the founders of the women's tour. "The problem was how to get from your match in New York to your match in Los Angeles with three dollars in your pocket."

But women's tennis was a popular sport to watch, and it profited from the exploding interest in physical fitness, which made any athlete an instant role model. Tennis grew into one of two lucrative professional sports for women, golf being the other, and Debbie Spence found herself facing a choice that hadn't existed ten years earlier. Tennis could finance a college education, or it could be a career, right now.

She wanted the career and the adulthood it represented, and she pursued it with breakneck speed. Gone were the days when Tom had to push and prod her to practice. In the past few months, without warning, Debbie had started to change. It wasn't black-and-white—she was aware that his word was still law, and fearful that he would disagree with her about how she should progress—but, tentatively, she had begun to talk about making her own decisions about tournaments, and schedules, and the future. Too often, Tom Spence found himself involved in what was, for him, a distasteful pastime—waiting for the phone to ring and Debbie to tell him if she had won or lost.

He did not dare travel with her, although he had when she was playing southern California tournaments, when she was younger. He had always been fiercely concerned with her game, eager to dissect her matches, solve problems, and plot strategies. But he was hardly a master of linguistic diplomacy, and very often he came off sounding unintentionally harsh in his criticisms. Lately, his style had begun to grate on Debbie's nerves, and she maneuvered to keep him at a distance. These days, he said wistfully, "Debbie wants to feel like she's doing it herself, and she feels she knows what she has to do to get ready, and she can do it and doesn't need my help. It's her teenage rebellion. Me not being there takes a lot of pressure off—off me, too."

When she embarked on her first long trip alone, at the beginning of the 1983 summer tournament season, Tom had attempted to lay down the law, insisting that she call home nightly, even when she was in France with the Werdels for the Junior French Open in June. Then Debbie missed a night's transatlantic call and, coincidentally, won the next day's match. She worked up a superstition that she would continue to win as long as she continued not to call, until Tom, in desperation, called the Werdels' hotel room and asked them to instruct Debbie to get to a telephone immediately. She broke down and called the following day, and won anyhow, but since then not calling home had become a tiny emblem of independence. Even when she did call, she didn't have much to say. "She just says whether she won or lost," said Tom. "I'll try to ask her what she did or didn't do well, but it's not much of a conversation."

It was a difficult transition for a man used to being the voice of authority in his family. Any father would eventually face separation, as his children grew up and shaped their own lives, but Tom was facing it early, and on a literal, as well as psychological level. Debbie wasn't around. For that matter, neither was Francine. The success they had all so hoped for had separated him from his daughter and his wife.

It seemed to be happening so quickly. For years, Tom had paced his daughters' progress with a string of challenges. Each time they reached a goal he had set for them, he defined a new one to keep them from becoming smug. He set the carrot dangling just a bit further in front of their noses and encouraged them to chase it. At first there were informal matches against the kids who played at the public courts after school. By the time Debbie was eight, she had run out of worthy opponents. Tom entered her in a public-parks tournament, and then, when she was nine, he took her and her older sister to the West End Tennis and Racquet Club in Torrance, California, forty minutes from Cerritos, to audition for coach Robert Lansdorp, whose pupils included the then thirteen-year-old Tracy Austin. Debbie and Terri were the youngest players Lansdorp had ever accepted.

Debbie started playing USTA-sanctioned southern California sectional competitions, and Tom noticed a difference between his two daughters. Terri was good, but she was not as committed as her younger sister was. Years later, when Terri chided Debbie for picking up temperamental bad habits from the other players, Debbie would hurl the definitive insult at her older sister: clearly, Terri didn't understand because Terri was not a *competitor.*

Debbie racked up impressive rankings among southern California juniors. As a ten-year-old, she was number eight in the 12-and-under category; two years later, she was number one. She was number two twice in the 14-and-under age group, and by then she was so good that she had to begin playing "up" with the older girls, since her contemporaries had little chance of beating her. She spent only one year in the 16s, ranked number two, and now she was number one in the 18s.

When she got to the top of the junior heap, she did exactly what her father had taught her. She looked ahead for another challenge, and the only one that attracted her was turning pro. Two years earlier, in a local newspaper interview, she had talked about using her tennis to finance her college education, but now college seemed like a step to the side—or, given the way the tempo had picked up, a chancy step backward.

Besides, the young pros she knew seemed perfectly happy. Last year seventeen-year-old Lisa Bonder, a first-year pro, had invited Debbie to see the players' lounge at a Virginia Slims tournament. Debbie was impressed. Lisa told her how well the players were treated—better facilities, and more amenities, than a junior was used to—and about the money she could earn from endorsements. You could have all of this, she told Debbie. Just turn pro.

It was a frustrating irony. Tom had raised Debbie to be competitive, always eager for a new challenge. He had taught her to strive for excellence. He had been so successful that she was ready to strike out on her own before he was ready to let her go.

Tom Spence ran his fingers distractedly through his hair and checked his watch. He had on his hands one normally rebellious teenager with an abnormally narrow range of interests and a bad case of arrested development ("I've got twelve-year-olds in my class who are more boy-crazy than Debbie is," he said), because any social evening had to start late enough to accommodate afternoon practice and end early enough to ensure that Debbie would be well-rested for a morning workout. And, for the moment, he had a winner, which made all of his words of caution sound foolish, the flutterings of a nervous parent.

Debbie had fought her way to the quarterfinals again at the Virginia Slims in Tarpon Springs, before she was defeated by Zina Garrison, ranked tenth in the world. This time she would have collected $3,350 if she had been a pro. It was an honorable defeat that followed two impressive victories, over seasoned pro Betsy Nagelson and Michelle Torres, an amateur who was already on the computer, up near thirty, but had not yet turned pro.

She had also shown herself to be a marvelous good sport. Debbie's doubles partner was Shawn Foltz, a new student of Robert Lansdorp's from Indianapolis, Indiana. When the draw was announced they were in the nightmare position everyone dreaded: their first match was against Martina Navratilova and Pam Shriver, the best women's doubles players in the world. There was no chance that Debbie and Shawn would win. The question, in a situation like this, was whether they would be able to win a single game.

Rather than getting depressed, the girls decided to have a

good time. If they could not offer the spectators suspense, they could at least be entertaining. They appeared for the match with Band-Aids pasted all over their bodies, an acknowledgment that they were about to become casualties. They applied roll-on, glitter-flecked cologne to their arms and legs and wore a lot of makeup, all of which cracked up their opponents, delighted the crowd, and made the ensuing 6–0, 6–1 loss much easier to take.

Debbie was doing everything she could to prove that she deserved to graduate from the juniors. Tom believed he had a responsibility to keep up with her, despite his reservations. He was not one to ponder how Debbie got to this pass. He was not going to stay awake nights wondering if he had done the right thing, to push her the way he had. Right or wrong, he had pushed her, and he would not be undone by second-guessing. Tom competed with daily life in much the same way he taught his daughters to compete on the tennis court. You never complain about the draw: you study the opponent and devise a strategy for victory.

He had agreed to let Debbie leave public school, even though he was not pleased at the prospect, because he saw her point—she deserved a clear chance to follow through, after all these years of hard work. For a man who had devoted his working life to education, it was a particularly difficult admission to make, but he gave in. He could hardly ask Debbie to wait because he wasn't ready. He would have to adapt.

"I knew she couldn't handle school and that tournament situation at the same time," he said. "But being a teacher, mentally accepting correspondence, I wasn't ready. . . . When I was in high school I don't think it would have bothered me as much to make up the work and get C's, and accept that. But Debbie can't accept that. She's in a world where everything has to be outstanding. Number one.

"There's too much pressure on her in class, because she feels like whatever is said to her makes her feel bad. Even though you may not mean it to be. You never had to spank Debbie. Just say something harsh and it really hurt her. In school, if she gets behind, she feels like she's being intimidated, and she can't handle it. She's vulnerable."

He consoled himself with the notion that independent study had an important advantage over correspondence. "It's more intimate," he decided. "It gives the feeling of school." With that, he was reconciled, able to dismiss the issue and move on. Now he wanted to revamp Debbie's training and tournament schedule. Tom felt that his daughter would have to work even harder to develop the stamina she needed for the pro circuit, and he wanted her to continue to play junior tournaments, to stay match-tough, while she collected her six pro tournaments for the computer ranking. He was prepared for complaints about the increased workouts, and a battle over the junior tournaments, since Debbie would not want to face a possible defeat from a girl ranked lower than she was, but he was going to insist on those basic requirements.

Francine might be the parent Debbie talked to, but Tom was used to being the parent Debbie heard from, the voice of authority. He had to be ready with a plan.

Debbie's performance in Bakersfield and Tarpon Springs had convinced him that they couldn't wait as long as he might have liked. "This is a cut, this year," he admitted. "The best go on, and the others settle. Maybe they accept mediocrity. We've got to change the pace and give her some more goals."

He would continue to talk about having all the time in the world to decide, and would pay lip service to the notion that his daughter might not turn pro at all, but his comments were little more than a defense mechanism. Debbie was like an unannounced candidate for political office: she knew what her intentions were, as did everyone around her; the pretense that she might do something else was meant to diminish the pressure a bit and accentuate the moment when she made a formal announcement.

The real question was, what would qualify her to step up into the pro ranks? On that issue, Tom set higher standards than his daughter did. But then, her feeling that a ranking in the top 120 would be good enough was based on her impatient desire to turn pro. Tom's assessment—that she would have to be in the top fifty—was based on money.

"I feel the kids have given up so much, and worked so hard, that if they can't get sixty thousand dollars before expenses, thirty-five thousand dollars after, well . . ." he said. Then he hesitated. Like his daughter, he tended to be impressed by what sounded like a lot of money. When he thought about how quickly a career could end, though, even being in the top fifty seemed insufficient. Earning prize money without having endorsements might not buy the independence his daughter dreamed about. Tom Spence was beginning to understand the magnitude of the gamble Debbie was about to make.

He was doing figures in his head. "How long will this seventeen-year-old be able to make that much money? Four years? She's made a hundred and forty thousand dollars. So I wouldn't say that being in the top fifty would make me comfortable. I'd like it higher. That's where the hard part comes, a few years from now. 'Here I played junior tennis eight years, pro for four, and I'm still nowhere.' How will they look at themselves then?"

But there was no time to speculate about the future. Wrestling with the present took all of Tom's energy. He had a folder bulging with pamphlets and tournament applications and media guides from the USTA and Virginia Slims, which explained the intricacies of obtaining a ranking and had, for the moment, confounded him. Debbie could take the low road without too much difficulty and play the USTA Satellite Circuit, where she might rack up more wins but would earn fewer computer points for the victories. Or she could take the high road and go for the Virginia Slims and Ginny circuits, which awarded more points per match because of the risk of being eliminated much sooner by tougher opponents.

The second option was more attractive. If Debbie played well, she would come onto the computer high. The only problem was that Tom didn't know how to crack the circuit and get his daughter into the better tournaments. He read all the obscure rules and regulations and began to have the sinking feeling that he had temporarily lost control of Debbie's future.

He had to face the fact that he had done nothing to further his daughter's progress since the day she got back from the U.S. Open and started talking about getting experience on the pro circuit. He could not claim credit for the invitations to Bakersfield and Tarpon Springs. Stephanie Rehe, a thirteen-year-old who also worked with Lansdorp, had received a wild card into the main draw at Tarpon Springs courtesy of International Management Group, but no one had gone to bat like that for Debbie. Her participation was more of a fluke: if another girl had not fallen ill, Debbie would not have been invited. She was merely the beneficiary of another player's bad luck.

That kind of felicitous coincidence wasn't good enough. Tom wanted to have a more aggressive plan, the kind that required contacts with agents, or tournament officials, which he did not have. He wished, not for the first or the last time, that he were good at politicking and that he and Francine had more money and fewer obligations.

Publicly, they always insisted that traveling alone was good for Debbie because it taught her to be self-reliant. Privately, they were beginning to see the disadvantage: they did not know any of the people who were in a position to help them, and they had arrived at a point where that help suddenly seemed essential, where the ability to win no longer sufficed.

He had learned a sad lesson, this past summer, about exactly how disenfranchised a position his daughter was in. Each year the Wimbledon Committee invited certain girls from the United States to compete in Junior Wimbledon, working from a list of recommended players compiled by the USTA. Although Debbie had been on her way to her number one ranking, she was not invited.

Tom was sure there had been an oversight, so he wrote a letter to the USTA reviewing his daughter's record. But he was writing to strangers. The letter got him a polite call—there was nothing the USTA could do—and nothing more, and he imagined that he might have gotten a better response if he'd established a rapport with the people who ran the junior tennis program. If he and Francine had been able to travel to the big national tournaments, as the Werdels often did, he wouldn't have been just another anonymous tennis parent asking for help.

He dumped the folder on the table and headed out to the car, having failed to come up with an idea about how to proceed before he picked up his wife and daughter. He shook his head in frustration. Debbie doing so well should have been good news, but it had a depressing edge. Tom didn't know what to do next. All he knew was that you had to win the right matches to get ahead in this business. And to play those matches, you had to know the right people.

4

Anaheim Junior

At the end of October, with no pro tournaments in sight, Debbie Spence grudgingly gave in to her father's demand that she remain "tournament-tough" and agreed to compete in the Anaheim Junior tournament. It was one of the six sectional tournaments she had swept the year before, so this year she arrived at the Tennisland Racquet Club, part of the Disneyland Hotel complex, feeling bored and resentful. She had already conquered this challenge, and did not understand why she should have to do it again.

There was none of the anxious thrill she had felt in Bakersfield or Tarpon Springs. Playing in the pro tournaments was like being onstage; it was exciting and dramatic. But this was bare-bones junior tennis—not even a national tournament, just a sectional competition—and Debbie thought it beneath her dignity. The woman at the club's front desk was so unimpressed at the presence of sixty-four talented junior players that she dismissed any inquiries about the tournament with a vague wave toward the courts and continued her monologue about someone's sloppy backhand. Behind the club, the air was full of the sickly aroma of chewing gum and soda pop as the girls waited to start their matches. There were no bleachers to accommodate fans—only a few folding chairs set up on the small grassy area in front of one of the courts.

For that matter, there were few fans. The spectators were mostly parents and friends, which in Debbie's case only made her more upset. Since it was Sunday, Francine had taken Rhonda to church. Debbie had come to Anaheim with Tom, which made her jittery, Anthony, a boy she often hit with, and Shawn Foltz, her doubles partner from Tarpon Springs.

The two girls had become good friends over the past several weeks, even though they seemed very different. Shawn's raucous, unpredictable laugh and a weakness for whisper-and-giggle sessions were the only reminders that she was fifteen. She seemed older, and more worldly.

Shawn had what the magazines called a fashion sense, even when she was limited to tennis apparel. Today, her Häagen-Dazs boysenberry T-shirt was the same shade as her fingernails and the stripes in her shorts. Three tiny earrings—rarely the same ones two days in a row—nestled on her right earlobe, a style Debbie would copy before many more weeks had passed. She had a sure hand with her nail polish, mascara, and eyeshadow.

She also had a sense of humor, like Debbie. But today her presence rankled Debbie, because she was a reminder that the world was unjust. Shawn got to spend the day as a spectator, digging little rocks of lime-green gum called Nerds out of a box and chomping contentedly, while Debbie had to work. Shawn, who was in her first year in the 18-and-under category, was already on the computer around 150, which meant that she could play a pro tournament from time to time to get experience. She was enrolled in a correspondence high-school program administered by the University of Nebraska.

Debbie was so envious. Clearly, some people's parents would do anything for their children. Shawn's parents didn't even live together all the time, because they felt it was important for Shawn to have her mother with her wherever she went to work on her tennis. Last fall, when Shawn was fourteen, she had decided she wanted to attend Nick Bollettieri's Tennis Academy in Bradenton, Florida. Her mother, Pat, had rented a condominium near the academy and spent the school year there. Her father, Wally, who developed retail liquor stores, stayed behind in Indianapolis with her younger brother Brett.

But Shawn disliked the academy's rather rigid discipline—traveling back and forth to school on a bus with the other players, group trips to the mall or the movies, strenuous workouts—so this year she had come to California to see what Debbie's coach, Robert Lansdorp, had to offer. Since he had no live-in facility, he invited Shawn to live at his house while she made up her mind. When she decided that she wanted to stay, Pat began making arrangements to head west and Shawn moved in temporarily with the Spences.

As far as Debbie could tell, her new friend had the perfect life. Shawn could spend the morning socializing. Debbie was starting a match under the watchful eye of her father, who had staked out the bench just outside her court. Shawn's parents were always finding ways to help her out. Debbie's father had gotten a letter from Parkes Brittain, the director of women's tennis for Advantage International, saying he'd be glad to be of help if the Spences needed advice on scheduling pro tournaments—and here she was playing the juniors. Her father still had to figure out what to ask about, before he could take advantage of the offer.

In the meantime, Tom Spence was doing what he knew best, working to get Debbie into the best physical shape possible. Now that she was out of school, Tom had her on a new training schedule. "Debbie'll get up in the morning and do some of her independent study work," he said, watching his daughter intently as she began to play, "and by nine-thirty or ten she's down at the park hitting with a guy for about an hour. She'll come home and go to independent study, if she has to be there, to do work for an hour"—and suddenly he raised his voice so that his daughter could hear, saying, "Nice lob, Debbie. Sure took you long enough to use it.

"I keep telling her she's got a great backhand lob," he said. "Anyhow, then she'll go down to West End at one-thirty, have a half-hour lesson, and play two sets with top-flight players. That's about another hour and a half. Then there's a two-hour workout, and drills. She goes there Monday, Wednesday, and Friday. Tuesday and Thursday she'll hit one hour in the park and then play a set with Anthony here." Tom gestured at the teenage boy sitting next to him, who was silently watching Debbie. "Then she goes to another workout and plays sets. Five hours Tuesdays and Thursdays, then one hour of aerobics. Saturdays and Sundays, normally, should be tournaments."

That was the sticking point. Debbie didn't want to play local tournaments like this one because she thought it was beneath her—which is to say, she was afraid it wasn't beneath her, that she would lose and embarrass herself—but Tom insisted on what he knew was a stiff pace, and implied that her unwillingness was a sign that she couldn't keep up. "I'm concerned," he admitted. "She looks a little lethargic, not as sharp. But my logic is, 'OK, if she continues working hard she'll increase her stamina and play better in the long run.' It might hurt her today—she might not play as well right now—but two months from now I figure she'll be playing better. I'm not sure. But I hope I'm right."

He did not feel he could alter his position, now that he had taken a stand. Still, as he watched Debbie play, he wished that there were a way to give her a break without seeming to have second thoughts.

"I'm waiting to take a couple of days off," he said, "as soon as it rains."

Tom was not the only one who noticed that Debbie was a little slow. Although she won the first set, she remained at the baseline afterward to practice her serve, instead of sitting down to take a brief rest.

Midway through the second set her mother and younger sister arrived from church. Tom's father also appeared. Jack Spence was seventy-nine years old, favored oxford-cloth pinstripe shirts and worn suspenders, and had spoken with the aid of an electronic voice box for ten years, since he had been diagnosed as having cancer of the larynx. He was extravagantly proud of his granddaughter: unlike other parents and relatives, who seemed to make a conscious effort not to appear too wrapped up in their offspring's performance, he walked right up to the chain link fence around the court and clung to it for a moment, watching her.

Jack had contributed $3,000 a year to Debbie's tennis career since she was eleven years old. It was money he had made in the metal piping business and felt no need to spend on himself and his wife, Marie. They had lived in Carson, halfway between his son's house and the West End Tennis and Racquet Club, for forty years, the last three years in modest comfort in the Vista Del Loma Mobile Estates. He saw no reason to alter their way of life, just as he saw no reason to continue drawing a salary from the family business, even though he continued to work part-time. The money would go, instead, for things his sons and their families wanted. He didn't need it, and he took great pleasure in being able to help out.

He and Tom's mother also contributed time: with a working son and daughter-in-law, they often had to serve as Debbie's chauffeurs. When she was in school, they had shuttled her to the tennis club and back, and when the last-minute invitation to the U.S. Open qualifying round had come, it was Marie who got up before dawn to ferry Debbie to the airport.

Debbie won her match with a more than respectable score of 6–2, 6–1, and when she walked off the court her grandfather was the first one to congratulate her. Shawn was off talking to someone else. Tom got up from the bench slowly, already analyzing Debbie's game with Anthony, while Francine hung back, her arms around Rhonda, trying not to appear too excited. When she did approach Debbie, she leaned over awkwardly for a kiss, and said quietly, "Tough match, hm?"

Debbie stared at the ground and gave her mother a perfunctory kiss and an offhanded "I guess." Under no circumstances was she going to allow herself to appear happy at a junior tournament, not even when she was winning.

Then she stepped back and announced that she wanted to leave, right away. Despite the fact that she did not yet have a California driver's license, Debbie intended to take one of the two family cars and drive twenty-five miles to the University of Southern California, near downtown Los Angeles. It was a statement, not a request. Debbie had already arranged to meet Beth Herr, a new pro and one of Lansdorp's pupils, for an hour or two of practice at the USC courts. Francine, Tom, Rhonda, and Shawn could all go back to Cerritos in the other car. It was a modest revenge for having to play Anaheim, and a reminder that Debbie was capable of making decisions for herself.

Francine blushed and laughed. The secret was out. For a couple of weeks, ever since she'd passed the Department of Motor Vehicles written test, Debbie had been doing a little driving—mostly the half-hour trip to West End—to take the pressure off her parents and grandparents. It was almost legal, after all: Debbie just hadn't had time to go in and take the driving test.

Tom laughed too, although he was clearly irked that Debbie had made tennis plans without telling him. He was also a bit embarrassed that he did not know the best directions for getting to USC. He consulted a few people and then picked up a stick and traced the route in the dirt at the base of a tree for Debbie, who was too impatient to pay much attention.

The rest of the family departed more slowly, stopping to talk to other parents as they headed for the parking lot. Carolyn Gurney, who had two daughters working with Robert Lansdorp and a third waiting in the wings, stood in the middle of the walkway watching her eldest, fourteen-year-old Melissa. She always picked a position at some oblique angle to the court, so that Melissa or twelve-year-old Lucinda, called Cinda, could not see her. Carolyn did not suffer from visible nerves, like Francine. She stood out of sight because she did not want the girls to become dependent on her. They had to learn to be self-sufficient, no matter how difficult a match became.

The following weekend Melissa Gurney, a first-year player in the 18-and-under category, upset Debbie Spence, 7–6, 6–0, by playing a steady baseline game while Debbie's usual accuracy, and then her confidence, deserted her. The victory was so unexpected, and so lopsided, that it got attention. Advantage International, the smallest and newest of the big three sports management agencies, only six months old, was always on the lookout for an early clue to a girl's promise. In Parkes Brittain's mind, this single victory over Debbie Spence "put Melissa on the map." Jeff Austin, Tracy's brother and an acquaintance of the Gurneys, also worked for the agency, and he contacted the Gurneys to say that Brittain looked forward to meeting them at the USTA Junior Indoor Championships over Thanksgiving.

After the match Debbie broke into sobs in front of everyone.

However upset Debbie might be at losing to Melissa Gurney
—and at the attention the agents paid to younger girls like
Melissa and Stephanie Rehe, when she was the one who
needed help, now—she could not allow herself to dwell on it.
Her outburst at Anaheim had been a mistake, a sign of weakness that she regretted. Robert Lansdorp frequently admon-
ished her about her mental game, her tendency to doubt herself and let that doubt affect her performance, and told her she
had to walk onto the court confident if she was going to win.
In the weeks that followed the Anaheim tournament she
worked hard to regain her equilibrium.

She thought a lot about that humiliating loss, and finally
came to the conclusion that she simply had not played her best
against Melissa Gurney because she had been unhappy—
which protected her from the thought that Melissa might be
a better player than she was, and left open the comforting
possibility that the outcome might have been different if she
had been in a better mood. The reason for her less than ster-
ling performance, of course, was that she had played under
protest. Now she had played well in two professional tournaments and lost too soon on the junior circuit. All that meant,
as far as she was concerned, was that she was right: She didn't
belong in the juniors anymore. She needed the new challenge
of the pros.

The girls always had their reasons for losing, but the notion
that an opponent was simply a better player was rarely among
them. At this early stage, parents and coaches espoused a
sky's-the-limit philosophy, essential if a junior girl was going to
realize her full potential; however unrealistic it might sound,
they insisted that any player could be beaten, even a Martina
Navratilova or a Chris Evert Lloyd. Robert Lansdorp encouraged his pupils to believe that they could one day be one of
the best players in the world, since that belief would fuel
performance. There would be plenty of time, later, for adjusting to a player's actual level of achievement.

When a player won, she told herself it was because of superior natural ability; luck had nothing to do with it. But a loser

looked for an extenuating circumstance in self-defense, whether it be a referee who favored the other girl, bad wind, bad weather ("bad," in either case, meant that conditions favored the opponent), or temporary bad health. If all else failed, a girl could dismiss a single loss to a particular player as a fluke, and, having decided that such a thing could never happen again (unless there were those extenuating circumstances), she could go on believing in herself.

Debbie blamed her loss at Anaheim on her negative state of mind—and, by extension, on her father, who had talked her into the tournament and then, insult on top of injury, told Carolyn Gurney he was thinking of sending Debbie to the USTA Junior Indoor Championships over Thanksgiving, and could she share a motel room with the Gurneys so that Francine wouldn't have to go? To Debbie, his actions indicated a traitorous lack of faith. He had undermined her performance.

She had to get back on the only safe track—she had to ignore bad news, and bad breaks, and work to play her best. Tom always told her: As long as she competed against herself, and tried to better her own best game, she would come out on top. If she started to focus on the specific identity of her opponent, if she came out onto the court next time against Melissa thinking only of the last time they had played, she would be defeated. Not by Melissa, but by her own insecurity.

So she worked even harder in November, and spent more time at the West End Tennis and Racquet Club with Shawn Foltz, who was a useful ally because she seemed so immune to gloomy self-doubt. They had been having a wonderful time lately—Shawn's mother had found an apartment in Torrance only ten minutes from the club, and brought Shawn a new Dodge Conquest, which gave the girls amazing freedom. They could drive over to the mall to shop between workouts, or they could drive to a restaurant for lunch instead of eating at the club. Debbie had gotten her driver's license, so she no longer had to come and go on her parents' or grandparents' schedule. As a reward for being talented, they had been sprung from all the usual restraints of being a teenager.

Today the girls sacrificed lunch and ignored their homework for the chance to use Robert Lansdorp's teaching court while he took an hour off. There were over two hundred balls spattered around the court. Tufts of fluorescent yellow tennis-ball lint were wedged in the crack that ran under the net and around the perimeter of the court, and tiny yellow tumbleweeds danced in the air. Debbie was all over the court, dashing off every couple of minutes to dig a fresh stick of gum out of a brown paper bag, yelling at Shawn and goofing off. A portable radio played so loudly that the words were distorted, and only someone who had memorized the lyrics to "Jeopardy" and "Affair of the Heart," like Shawn, could sing along.

At one o'clock the gate to the court swung open and Robert Lansdorp glared at the girls. He was an imposing figure, six-foot-three and in the midst of a weight gain that would add twenty-five pounds to his big-boned frame, with a leonine shock of sun-reddened hair and ruddy, lined skin. His slurred, booming drawl was the result of a childhood spent in the Dutch East Indies, where he was born, and in Holland; the raspiness of his voice a consequence of chain-smoking and almost twenty years of barking orders across a tennis court. One of the first things he told people about himself was that he had reduced almost all of his students to tears at some point in their instruction. He liked to bait them—to say something outrageous, on purpose, to see if they would stand up to him. He preferred people who did, although it was not his style to demonstrate that affection.

He regarded Debbie disapprovingly. She was wearing a Panama Jack suntan lotion T-shirt, and, while Francine liked her daughter's oddball outfits—she believed they were an indication of Debbie's independent spirit, her healthy disrespect for the constraints of proper attire—Robert was a pragmatist. Weird T-shirts did nothing for a girl's image. Worse yet, Debbie was wearing shorts. Robert informed her that she could not have her lesson unless she changed into a skirt.

"He thinks it's more feminine," Shawn whispered, as she began to round up tennis balls. "Robert says there isn't enough femininity on the court."

Debbie rushed over to her bag, fished out a skirt, and looked

around. There wasn't enough time to go down to the clubhouse to change. If she did, Robert would probably hassle her
for being late. "I don't want to change in front of him," she
said to Shawn, who shrugged her shoulders helplessly. Debbie
ducked out the gate, ran a little way up the walkway that
separated the courts, and changed her clothes where no one
could see her.

Robert was amiable enough while he and the girls collected
the balls and loaded them into a shopping cart. But when they
were done Shawn took a seat at the edge of the court and
Robert suddenly became a bullying monster: he griped and
moaned and insulted Debbie while she served a shopping
cart's worth of balls at him. Then he caught sight of her chewing gum, which by now was a mass of rather sizable proportion.

"Goddamn wad in your mouth," he hollered. "About as
much class as my dog. It's gross."

"No it's not," said Debbie.

"Yes it is," said Robert. "Like a six-year-old. Not like a young
lady."

Meanwhile, one of the emphatically fit and eternally sun-
tanned young men who worked at the club came up the walk,
leaned on the chain link fence that surrounded the court, and
started to flirt with Shawn. It was the middle of the day on a
weekday and these girls weren't in school. He wanted to know
if Shawn and Debbie were on a school team, and Shawn coolly
informed him that she and her friend played in tournaments,
not on school teams. They weren't in school. They didn't have
to go to school, because they were both in special programs.

"I get it," he said, realizing that he was being snubbed.
"Rhodes scholars." He slunk away.

Shawn smiled and settled back to watch Debbie's lesson.
She was glad to be here, even if her new home still resembled
an oversized motel room. Pat had come out with only a few
of their possessions. The bulk of their things—the stereo com-
ponents, the video recorder, the television, Pat's fur coats—
would not be delivered until a driveaway company pulled into

the apartment complex in Pat's Chevrolet station wagon sometime around Thanksgiving. But Shawn was indifferent; she regarded her lodgings on a utilitarian level. "It's fine," she said offhandedly. "I mean, it's just a place to sleep. I won't be there much."

She spent most of her time at the club. Like Debbie, she found that people who didn't play tennis weren't very much fun because they couldn't understand what it was like to be a serious junior player. There were problems being friends with girls who were your competitors—you didn't want to let your doubts or fears show too much, lest the other girls begin to believe that they had a mental edge—but at least they understood, and sympathized with, what you were going through.

The girls usually kept the tension level down by making friends with players who were at a slightly different point in their development, which was why Debbie and Shawn got along—Debbie was getting ready to turn pro, while Shawn was just getting used to her first year in the 18-and-under competition. Or they ran in a pack, which provided companionship and allowed them to let off a lot of steam without feeling too emotionally exposed.

This past weekend they had been involved in an annual social ritual, the celebration of Robert Lansdorp's birthday. Debbie, Shawn, Melissa and Cinda Gurney, and a few other Lansdorp students plotted an elaborate practical joke that revolved around several rolls of toilet paper, two pie shells filled with shaving cream, and a fancy cake. At nightfall, at a rather hysterically nervous pitch, the group headed for Robert's house. First they snuck around the yard and house, wrapping toilet paper everywhere. Then they crept up to the doorstep, left the cake, and rang the bell. The plan was to pelt Robert with the cream pies, but the girls chickened out at the last minute. They ran away, edged back—and suddenly Robert appeared and began chasing them. Shawn and Cinda Gurney took the opportunity to turn on him with the pies, and then they all went inside and ate cake.

For all his gruffness, the girls adored and depended on Lansdorp, who had taught all of them, with the single exception of

Shawn, since they were eight or nine. "He yells and it's scary at the moment," said Shawn, "but you know it's not real, because a minute later he's saying, 'Hey baby, what's happening.' He cares."

But he also seemed to comprehend, in a way that a child or a hopeful parent might not, how exhausting a career in tennis would be. The flashes of compassion, or affection, were brief interruptions in an endlessly tough program designed to prepare the mind, as well as the body, for a life of demanding isolation. On a subtle level, Lansdorp taught his charges that they could depend on no one but themselves.

He strode to the net and beckoned Debbie over, to explain that he wanted her to change a particular movement. She needed to bend her knees more and move into the ball.

"You understand me?" he asked.

"No," she giggled.

"That's because you're stupid," he said, turning back to the shopping cart of balls.

"Airhead," Shawn yelled at her friend from the sidelines.

After another cart's worth of mostly successful effort, Lansdorp smiled a phony smile. "Thank you, ma'am," he said. "You're not as dumb as I thought you were."

Halfway through the hour lesson Lansdorp allowed a short break, and Debbie immediately ran over to Shawn to inquire about the boy who had been talking to her through the fence. At the moment, Shawn had more of a social life than Debbie did. They each wore a gold tennis ball on a thin chain around their necks—"what every junior tennis player wants," Shawn said reverently—that was given out by the USTA to winners of USTA national junior tournaments. Debbie had received her gold charm for the 1983 USTA Junior Hardcourt Championships held at the beginning of the summer, but Shawn had yet to win a national junior tournament. Her charm came from a boy who won and gave it to her. Debbie had a friend who played tennis with her, but she didn't really consider him a boyfriend.

Toward the end of the lesson, a group of boys passed by the

court, and Debbie glanced over at them and missed a shot. Lansdorp jumped on her.

"Hey. You want to look at the guys?" he yelled, loud enough for the boys to hear him.

"Yeah," said Debbie, mortified.

"You looked enough? You start looking at boys already, you're never going to make it, baby."

"You'd better worry about your Stephanie," said Shawn, jumping to Debbie's defense. Stephanie Rehe, who had just turned fourteen, looked and acted older. But it wasn't her ability to attract attention from members of the opposite sex that made the other girls jealous. Stephanie had a corporate suitor—Chuck Bennett, an account executive at International Management Group, who had been getting Stephanie wild cards into pro tournaments since last spring.

"She's not getting ready to turn pro yet," snapped Lansdorp.

It was true: Lansdorp's advice to Stephanie Rehe's family was to wait a few years before she thought about turning pro. But that only made Debbie more resentful. Another player, not as close to turning pro as Debbie was, got the wild cards she so desperately wanted.

The reference to Stephanie Rehe stuck with Debbie through the rest of the lesson, and as she walked back toward the clubhouse she ruminated on the need for a positive mental attitude. Being jealous of another girl was as damaging to her game as being intimidated by an opponent. It would sap her energy; it was a waste of time.

She tried to convince herself that she was not losing the competition for Robert Lansdorp's attention.

"He says we're all his favorites," she said, as she headed for the TV room to relax. "He tells us that. All the time."

5

West End Tennis and Racquet Club

There was no way that Robert Lansdorp could love all his girls equally, although it was a pleasant sentiment, and a useful tactic if it soothed a girl's fragile ego. It was bad business in a sport where a young girl, singled out for talent and beauty, could make a lot of people wealthy. Lansdorp seemed to be on the brink of his own professional breakthrough, and he wanted to make the smart moves, which required a sharp eye for his next potential celebrity and a willingness to play favorites.

He had an instinct for self-promotion, an appreciation of how to enhance his position in the tennis community. He had begun teaching tennis in the San Diego public-parks program in 1967, where he remained for three years, until 1970, when a position opened up at the Jack Kramer Club in Rolling Hills Estates, just down the coast from Los Angeles. He worked there for eight years, and then opened the West End Tennis and Racquet Club with five other investors. His star pupil, fifteen-year-old Tracy Austin, turned pro in 1978, and in 1979 became the youngest player ever to win the U.S. Open singles title.

Thanks in part to her reflected glory, Lansdorp was on his way. He drove a 1978 Lincoln Continental, midnight blue with camel trim, vanity license WESTND, and appeared to take great pride in being too busy to return phone calls that were usually from parents eager to turn their children into tennis stars. There were less happy aspects to the Tracy Austin story in the years that followed—Austin and Lansdorp had had rocky relations since 1980, when Lansdorp began to complain that he was not getting the credit he deserved and Tracy began working with other coaches—but the fantasy of being Lansdorp's next Tracy Austin was too potent to be diminished by such details. There were several calls daily, most of them either ignored or politely turned away. Lansdorp, at this point in his career, could afford to be extremely selective about his pupils.

He was known for being a disciplinarian: If one of his pupils managed to have fun playing tennis, that was fine, but he was not interested in taking on children whose intention was to have a good time on the court. He wanted kids who took the sport seriously, and he tested their dedication constantly. He would purposely cheat somebody like Debbie Spence, calling balls out even if they were in, to see if she got so rattled that she gave away the next ten points.

"The parents are usually a bit scared of me," he admitted, almost proudly. "I come on nasty. I had one guy who was sitting on the court and yelling at his daughter while I was giving her a lesson. So I said, 'Why the hell don't you get off my court or take your kid someplace else? I don't care if you stay here.' So he got off the court."

Few parents were willing to stand up to Lansdorp. However they felt about his methods, or his brusque manner, they knew that he turned out top players. He had established himself as the man for a tennis prodigy to see in southern California.

But there was one thing Lansdorp did not have. He did not preside over a physical fiefdom to compete with the one run by his East Coast competitor, Nick Bollettieri.

It was not for want of trying, but so far, Lansdorp had nothing to show for his efforts at corporate recognition, beyond a few personal product endorsement contracts. Still, he liked the psychological implications of being an institution—so he invented one. In September of 1983, he had announced the formation of the Robert Lansdorp Tennis Academy. The setup was the same as it had been since West End opened: Lansdorp gave private lessons for fifty dollars an hour and, with five assistants, presided over two consecutive workout sessions three days a week, running from 2:30 to 5:00 and 5:00 to 7:00 P.M. The only new element was the name. To commemorate the change, and to make sure that the academy without walls would be properly promoted, Lansdorp's forty pupils received T-shirts and sweatshirts with the words *Robert Lansdorp Ten-*

nis Academy over the breast pocket and a graphic—a circle containing a racquet, a net, a likeness of Robert himself, and the initials *RLTA*—on the back.

Lansdorp also signed a contract with International Management Group. ProServ, the Washington, D.C., firm that was IMG's chief rival, had provided a financial foundation for Bollettieri's academy by rounding up sponsors like Suburu, Prince racquets, Penn tennis balls, Ellesse, and Nike to provide goods, services, and sometimes funds. Lansdorp felt that he had arrived at the point in his career when he should be able to cash in on his reputation. He hoped that IMG would be able to enhance his public profile with more, and more profitable, endorsements—and then, someday, help him acquire a well-endowed home of his own on the West Coast.

In return, he was expected to call the IMG offices to tell Chuck Bennett, and junior recruiter Jim Curley in the Cleveland office, about the players who deserved their attention. Many of the girls showed particular promise, including Debbie, Melissa Gurney, Stephanie Rehe, and Shawn, but IMG could not promote a group; the agency depended on Lansdorp to separate out the players who could be successfully exploited. Theirs was a symbiotic relationship based on Lansdorp's ability to provide exploitable talent and IMG's ability to turn that talent to financial advantage.

To formally consolidate his position, Lansdorp issued an ultimatum to the members of his new academy: if they worked with any other coach, they would no longer be allowed to work with him. The man who wanted his pupils to wear his likeness on their backs was not going to let anyone else take credit for his current crop of prodigies.

Specifically, he insisted that his pupils stop working with Larry Easeley, who had replaced Lansdorp at the Jack Kramer Club and worked with several families who still had memberships there, including the Gurneys. Having established himself as a conduit to a major sports agency (an attractive fact to parents of players who wanted to reap the rewards of a pro career), Lansdorp was in a strong bargaining position. He might not be the only game in town, but he was the best one, so, in his own business interests, he indulged his tendency to be a tough guy. Some of the girls might have cried when they learned that they had to stop working with their other coach. A few of the parents, who lived closer to the Kramer Club than to West End and liked the convenience of an occasional lesson or workout there, complained about the longer commute. But Lansdorp stood his ground—and, one by one, the families canceled their other lessons.

Larry Easeley said he was hardly surprised by the move, and criticized the Kramer Club for failing to support a strong junior program to rival Lansdorp's. But the defections weakened the program even further, and Easeley was forced to leave the Kramer Club and take a job coaching men's tennis at Long Beach State University.

The maneuver improved Lansdorp's position, but it heightened the already existing tensions between the girls and forced him to become a diplomat as well as a coach. He needed to perpetuate the happy notion that all the girls were equal to avoid alienating, and possibly losing, a student who might be six months away from her peak. He became cautious about traveling with one girl too often. When he did travel, he was careful to work with the girls whose parents were paying his way, and to explain to his other pupils that he was not ignoring them, but only doing the work he was paid to do. When he attended a tournament where several girls were playing, he did his best to watch parts of all of their matches.

Still, the economics of the situation were inescapably unfair, and everyone knew it: Debbie Spence's parents had never been able to afford the travel expenses Lansdorp required when he traveled with a player. It might be nice to have him accompany Debbie, especially if she was going to play a big pro tournament, but it was a luxury the Spences simply could not afford.

Later in the day Lansdorp took out his wallet to show off a picture of his true favorite, "my pride and joy," his seven-year-old daughter, Stephanie. She was a budding tennis player, but Robert Lansdorp, father, had a much different attitude about the sport than did Robert Lansdorp, tennis coach. "I'd have mixed feelings about it if she wanted to become a tennis pro," he said. "I love this game, but I'd rather see her go into music. It's one of the greatest ways of expressing yourself, of lifting yourself out of a depression." Lansdorp, when he could get off the tennis court, listened endlessly to the Rolling Stones and country music.

"The road is hard," he said. "I would like her to play tennis where she could have a good time."

He was starting to have trouble giving her lessons, for exactly that reason: he did not know how to teach her to enjoy playing tennis, only how to be good at it. And the tactics he used on other people's children offended him when his own daughter was the target. "When you teach somebody else's kid you can be very tough and mean because it doesn't mean anything. They expect it, in a strange way. But if a father says things, it's a more emotional thing. I can't say to my daughter, 'You stink. Get out of here.' To be really tough is impossible."

As an interim solution, he had begun using his daughter's middle name when he wanted to distance himself from her. If he called her Stephanie, he was being her father; if he spoke to her as Stephanie Michelle, he was speaking to her as a coach.

He put Stephanie's picture away and lit another cigarette. "I've never seen a kid who's born only wanting to play tennis," he said. "It's a matter of motivation. If you want your kid to be a tennis player—or a piano player, whatever—then you motivate them. You brainwash them into thinking there's nothing else in the world."

Robert Lansdorp was simply not sure he could ask his own child to endure what his pupils went through, even though he knew how vast the potential rewards could be. "Tennis is the most egotistical, self-centered . . ." he began. "It creates a highly selfish individual. The girls always look at themselves as being very great and special. They're a bunch of bitches, that's what they are. They get along as long as they're not too close. Once they start competing for the same place, it all changes."

Along the way, too many of the girls changed: the emphasis

on competitiveness, and individual achievement, took a toll. He had thought about it during his birthday party, as he looked around the room at his girls—about how temporary their friendships were, and how they would eventually be replaced by the relationship between a girl and her future.

Impatience had been at the core of women's professional tennis since the "Women's Lob" pro tour debuted in 1970, but with the growth of the circuit and Tracy Austin's debut, the quality of the restlessness changed. A collective frustration among women possessed of a single desire—to develop a profitable professional sport for women—gave way to more individualized frenzies. Adults who sought recognition, as a group, set the stage for children, who, ten years later, would strive to be separated out from the group. The tour had expanded, but the perspective of the players had shrunk.

In the fall of 1970, two years after the introduction of open tennis, women's tennis was a political issue—Billie Jean King and Rosie Casals threatened to boycott an existing tournament to protest the fact that men stood to collect twelve times the prize money being offered to women, an alternate tournament was hastily thrown together in Houston, Texas, and the World Tennis Women's Pro Tour was born. At first it was nothing more than nine disgruntled women who signed one-dollar contracts and found themselves quickly suspended by the USTA for their radical antics.

But Philip Morris, makers of Virginia Slims cigarettes, agreed to put up one-third of the $7,500 in prize money, and slowly, the circuit grew. During the first year there was only $30,000 in prize money to go around, and the big money-winner was Ann Haydon Jones, who took home the lofty sum of $9,000. In 1973 the USTA tried again to squelch the circuit by setting up its own women's tour, but the rebels formed the Women's Tennis Association that same year, and were able to negotiate, as a group, to merge the two women's circuits.

Virginia Slims became a formal sponsor, and the WTA continued its fight for prize-money parity and media attention. Finally, when physical fitness started to become a national obsession in the late 1970s, women's tennis found popular acceptance—and profited, quite literally, from the coincidence of concerted effort and social trend. In the early 1970s, it was a milestone for Billie Jean King to approach $100,000 in career earnings. By the early 1980s, a dozen women had passed the one-million-dollar mark.

The growth of the circuit brought the recognition those nine pioneers had dreamed of—both personal and commercial rewards. But it also spelled the end of the camaraderie that had marked the sport's beginning. Suddenly women were competing not only for prize money, but for endorsement money that could quadruple a woman's earnings. There was no lid on endorsement money; it represented absolute financial independence and protected a player from worrying about what to do in that interminable *after* that came at the end of her competitive career.

The emergence of several young stars in the late 1970s and early 1980s—Tracy Austin, Andrea Jaeger, Kathy Rinaldi, Carling Bassett—increased the commercial tension and contributed to an essential, unavoidable estrangement among the players. As more youngsters got into the game, a gap developed between the present and the past. The new girls knew little of the days when the bleachers were empty and the pockets of the players, nearly so. They knew nothing of shared goals.

They grew up in an era of wild commercial success, and, for the most part, they grew up separated from their peers. They traveled with their parents or a coach, and were watched over by an agent. A promising new pro could contemplate the notion of $150,000 for clothing, racquet, and shoe endorsements, the day she signed—Parkes Brittain found that he could line up the basic endorsements for a hot young player with ease—because of her individual appeal. A girl quickly learned the importance of self-interest.

Billie Jean King was dismayed enough by the change in attitude to enlist Philip Morris's aid to develop workshops for new pros—she wanted to teach them about the history of the sport, and advise them on how to handle their responsibilities to the press, and to tournament promoters and sponsors. Tennis fifteen years ago was "totally different" than what she saw today, she said, "because there wasn't the madness," and because the desire to compete was rooted in a different kind of dream.

"I used to read about Alice Marble, Helen Jacobs, from the time I was eleven, when I first started tennis," she recalled, referring to two champions from the 1930s, women who collected multiple titles and whose achievements would inspire a young Billie Jean to excel. "To me, they were my foundation, the reason I had a place to play and the reason the styles of play were what they were. Why we wore what we wore. I thought it was all fascinating. These kids don't seem to care about that."

Billie Jean tried to engage young players in conversation at tournaments. She liked to dissect a player's game and place it in context, to discuss what a girl's backhand owed to an older player's style. But she found few willing conversationalists. As a thirty-nine-year-old player who was years past her heyday, she had credibility problems. The girls ignored her, just as they often ignored their parents. They were too full of themselves and their exclusively personal aspirations to listen. At fifteen or sixteen, momentum was all; distracting questions of motivation and intent, a waste of time.

Tracy Austin, the woman who changed the pace of professional tennis by turning pro at fifteen, whose early success haunted the West End Tennis and Racquet Club like a happy ghost, had been unable to complete a full season's tournament schedule since 1980. Injuries had kept her out of competition for five months in 1981, five months in 1982, and limited her to eight tournaments in the first six months of 1983. She dropped out of the June 1983 Wimbledon competition and had not competed since. She approached her twenty-first birthday plagued by recurring problems with her back and shoulder. Although she had become the youngest athlete to earn $1 million in prize money in August 1980, after only two years as a professional, her prize money for 1983 had dipped to just over $72,000. Twice in 1980 she had been ranked as the best woman player in the world, but in 1983 her international standing slid down to number nine.

Thanks to her startling debut, she was in a position to live off the profits from her investments for the rest of her life, if she so chose. Her endorsement contracts had brought her more than $5 million between 1978 and 1983, and showed how broad her appeal was: Tracy sold shoes and racquets, but she also sold Canon camera equipment on television, 7-Up, Avon cosmetics, and Knudsen dairy products.

That pain-wracked young body was an extremely commercial commodity. If some of the corporations who retained her services as a spokeswoman were starting to grumble a bit, to wonder, aloud, how soon she might return to competition, no one had yet suggested dumping her. Her Spalding racquet contract had expired almost a year ago, so ProServ had begun talking to Kennex about stepping in with a racquet endorsement offer.

All the people who had invested in Tracy Austin's image—Tracy herself, ProServ, the corporate clients, and, on a psychological level, the players who idolized her—were convinced that she would recover and return to dominate the sport. She would spend the last months of 1983 in Australia, with coach Tony Roche, in a three-month intensive fitness and conditioning program designed to get her back on her feet.

In the meantime, she continued to visit the West End Tennis and Racquet Club from time to time, to fulfill her business obligations and keep herself in the public eye. One day right before she left the country, Tracy Austin could be found in a cramped upstairs office at the club, suffering not so silently while an assistant poked pins and rollers into her hair and worked on her makeup.

Tracy was at the club to pose for photographs for a promotional calendar for Gunze, a Japanese firm which marketed a Tracy Austin line of signature sportswear. Between 1979 and 1981 the company had owned Japanese rights, but in 1981 it signed a five-year contract, the largest women's clothing contract in the history of the sport, to market the clothes worldwide.

Each year the company had new photos taken for a glossy, color promotional calendar, regardless of what Tracy Austin did on the tennis circuit. The fact that she was a pretty blonde who had been at the top of her sport, for however brief a time, was more important in Japan, with its love of tennis in general and blond female players in particular, than were her current troubles. She had achieved international star status: her allure, and its commercial value, transcended her athletic career.

For now, her life was comprised of such ancillary activities. She had again lent her name to a charity tournament at West End for the South Bay Children's Health Center, as she did every year, and planned to be back from Australia in time to make an appearance, which would guarantee more media exposure for the event. And her agent had just received a call from the producers of the television series "Hart to Hart," inquiring about whether Tracy would be available to portray a tennis star in an upcoming segment.

She was a rather astonishing phenomenon. After only two full seasons she had become the object of pity and sympathy, as much as admiration, and yet the public continued to believe in her. People seemed to have a vested emotional interest in her recovery. It was as if the last few years had been a halluci-nation. The real Tracy Austin was the commercial image, the smiling, successful young adult; all the pain and disappoint-ment was a fleeting illusion.

Sara Kleppinger, senior vice-president at ProServ and Tracy's agent from the beginning of her pro career, marveled at how eminently salable her client was. "I think even some-body's name is important sometimes," she reflected. " 'Tracy Austin' is a perfect name. Pretty and feminine."

Kleppinger, a lawyer who liked to joke that she had made a career "on the court, not in the court," waited for Tracy at an umbrella table on the patio at West End, wearing a yellow short-sleeved knit shirt, a white sweatband, and a white tennis skirt. An affable type with a practical short blond pageboy and a frank expression, Kleppinger had been hired in 1973 to do public relations for the sports-oriented law firm of Dell, Craighill, Fentress & Benton. She went to law school on the side, and became a lawyer in 1978, just in time to handle the affairs of Tracy Austin when she turned pro.

Their careers blossomed together. Tracy became a tennis star, and Kleppinger became a senior vice-president when the law firm was transformed into ProServ in the spring of 1983. Tracy had the talent; Kleppinger, the ability to turn that talent into profit and exposure in the media. Between them, they created a new, mythic ideal by which players would judge themselves. For the top girls, who were serious about turning pro, playing well was no longer enough. The true champion showed her ability early. An entire generation of tennis families began to worry that sending a daughter to college would consign the girl to unprofitable obsolescence.

"Given the intensity of the pro level now, you can't really go to school and play tennis on the same level as the other girls can," said Kleppinger. "And a year or so in college might be it as far as most of the girls go. So then the kids start thinking, Should I go to college at all?"

Kleppinger's own position was cautious. People constantly approached her at tournaments to ask about their child's future. She did not paint a glowing picture for most of them.

"I tell them the realities are that it's not such a glamorous lifestyle out there. It's probably glamorous the first time out, and then it gets difficult, and more and more demanding as time goes on. A lot of these kids play well, and there's no pressure on them. And then they lose and they have to face reality: are they really performing on a par with being a pro tennis player?

"Tracy didn't turn pro until she had won so many junior titles that it was just obvious. She was ready for the next level of competition. If people have to ask a lot of questions," she said, with a wry smile, "then maybe it's not so obvious for their child."

Minutes later, Tracy descended the wrought-iron staircase and struck a pose in front of her agent. From the neck up, she was made up and coiffed for a fashion layout. From the neck down, she was dressed for a match. If she had really been playing tennis, sweat would have destroyed the curls and smudged the mascara. But Tracy would not have to chase a single ball today. The action shots for the calendar would be posed, according to Kleppinger, "so she looks good."

"Tracy, let's see," said the lawyer. "Turn around. Oh. You look beautiful." Then she told her client about the producer from "Hart to Hart" and Tracy's elegant façade dissolved into almost childish glee.

"Are you kidding?" she squealed. "That's my favorite show." When she learned that she would have to turn down the offer because the show was scheduled during her self-imposed Australian exile, she pouted for a moment. Then she cooperatively trotted out to the court where the photographer was waiting.

Some of the young girls who took lessons at West End knew Tracy, but for the most part she kept her distance. It was her image, and its inherent challenge, that presided over the club. Robert Lansdorp still tended to evaluate the girls' work in comparison to Tracy's performance, even though she had not been able to sustain her game, even though it would be three months before anyone knew if she would be able to return to the circuit.

That didn't matter, because everyone assumed that she would return. The tennis world surely was about to witness the long-awaited second coming of Tracy Austin, a happy ending to a story that had put starstruck notions into a lot of girls' heads.

USTA Junior Indoor Championships

I

The first national tournament of the 1984 USTA junior season was the Indoor Championship, which was held during the five-day Thanksgiving 1983 holiday. The girls' 18-and-under competition was in Kansas City—not the Missouri one, with the tantalizing distractions of Arthur Bryant's world-famous barbecue and the vintage-1929 Country Club shopping center, but the Kansas one, which was essentially a bedroom community forty minutes and a state line away. The significant landmark here was the Overland Park Racquet Club, a long, low building, an oddly menacing presence that sat behind one of two small shopping malls at the intersection of Ninety-first and Metcalf.

The other residents of the intersection included a Wendy's hamburger franchise, Bud Brown's Chrysler, the Glenwood fourplex movie theater, and the Regency Park Resort and Conference Center, a set of two-story buildings surrounding a pool; in an earlier, less linguistically inflated decade, it might have been called a motel. There wasn't much to do here but play tennis and wait to play more tennis—and wistfully talk about what could be done if anyone had the excess energy to make a round-trip to the city.

While their families prepared for, and recovered from, their Thanksgiving feast at home, 128 girls, most of whom were staying at the Regency Park, would compete in singles and doubles at the Overland Park Racquet Club. Every morning they trooped down to the hotel's coffee shop, the Garden Coffee House, to consume what might be the only full meal they ate all day, a whopping breakfast served on top of place mats that announced, "Each day is a new beginning. Enjoy Yours." Then they trudged across the street, or piled into somebody's mother's rental car, or were ferried by a local volunteer who did nothing but drive back and forth all day.

The players faced a grueling schedule: two singles matches and one doubles match per day until the weekend semifinal and final matches. Even the early losers were expected to be good sports and thrash their way through consolation rounds with as much energy as the girls who had beaten them.

The surroundings did little to relieve the strain. The Overland Park Racquet Club, a private club with 1,300 members who paid between $200 and $500 per family per year for the luxury of playing tennis year-round, was built with an eye toward socializing. A long hallway led to a small lobby, bar, and snack bar which were clustered at the hub of four sunken sets of courts. Only one set was separated from the spectators by a plate-glass window; otherwise, fans could lean on a wooden ledge next to the courts and stare right down at the players.

It might be a nice place for friends to meet, but now it seemed an architectural pressure-cooker. The club was crammed with girls, parents, college coaches scouting scholarship candidates, the official USTA registration and information table, and bulletin boards that held the draw charts. The lobby was littered with all the equipment necessary to play tennis, complete homework assignments, and fend off the wet winter chill.

Players and parents also carried their own personal weapons against anxiety, an assortment of tiny tape players with earphones, books whose words would likely be forgotten, needlepoint kits, cigarettes, and chewing gum. By the second day of the tournament the club would resemble some nightmare version of a suburban living room: girls sprawled with their feet on the furniture, clothes flung everywhere, half-empty cans of soda perched near open textbooks, abandoned bags of potato chips, and more than a few hovering mothers exhorting their offspring to play their best, eat better, and study more.

The USTA ran eight such tournaments in cities across the country over the Thanksgiving break from school—national indoor championships for boys and girls in the 18-, 16-, 14-, and 12-year-old-and-under age groups—scheduled with an eye toward public relations and promotion of the junior program in places like Kansas City where, thanks to the weather, tennis was less likely to flourish than in Florida or California. The scattered locations also guaranteed that travel expenses would be shared evenly by member families—this time the families from the West Coast were faced with costly plane fares, but in August, when the hardcourt championships were held outside San Francisco, East Coast families had to bear the travel burden.

The plan broke up families at those times of the year when families tried to be together, over school holidays and during summer vacations. Between the big USTA tournaments, the international junior events like next month's Orange Bowl, and the privately promoted Easter Bowl, girls like Debbie regularly missed Thanksgiving, Christmas, and Easter at home. But the USTA was not about to ask parents to take their children out of school to compete. Officially, the organization took a strong stance in favor of higher education and frowned on the trend, among top junior players, to ignore college and often give only glancing attention to high school.

The USTA had almost 100,000 players in its junior programs, close to double the starting membership, in 1974, of 50,677. Very few would ever have a pro career. By the time a girl reached the oldest amateur category, she had a fairly clear idea of her chances; the majority of the girls in Kansas City knew that their best hope was a college scholarship. There was no need to dismantle their lives to accommodate the game. They might have had early fantasies of stardom—good fuel for the kind of effort required—but at some point the reality of rankings and records intruded and they began to see tennis in a different perspective, as a means to an end.

The USTA's primary responsibility was to those players, the bulk of its membership, especially since the exceptions, the probable pros, had a vast network of people eager to facilitate their careers. The one-million-dollar 1983 junior tennis budget went to the tournament schedule, the college-level Junior Federation Cup team, and the Junior Davis Cup for boys and Junior Wightman Cup for girls, which subsidized deserving

18-and-under amateurs on the international summer circuit.

But the USTA also understood that the exceptions—Debbie Spence, Marianne Werdel, Melissa Gurney, Shawn Foltz, Stephanie Rehe—had needs, and if served well would be goodwill ambassadors for amateur tennis. The problem was that their very excellence made a joke of the junior tennis program. They blithely skipped ahead of their age group, and chafed at the regulations for required tournaments and ranking eligibility.

They wanted to move more quickly, and with more freedom, than the USTA allowed—and if the USTA wanted to keep up with these players, to bask in their reflected glory, it had to be more flexible. The organization did not want to face another internal rebellion like the one in 1973; the formation of the WTA had severely undercut the USTA's power. No one wanted a new generation of disgruntled players. In the past year, the USTA had begun to experience growing pains of its own, as its officers worked to keep up with the times.

At this time of night back home in Indianapolis, Pat Foltz would have been putting dinner together. She worked hard to make nutritious meals, presenting steamed vegetables and fish to her sometimes reluctant husband, son, and daughter as often as possible; she gave in to the populist desire for red meat infrequently and under protest. After years of suffering from a severe back problem, Pat had recently discovered running, which seemed to relax her and ease her pain. Running led to a new, overall interest in health, which led to a revolution in the Foltz kitchen.

She was prone to radical action when it came to taking care of herself and her family. If running was good, lots of running was better: no matter where she was, she usually managed to run at least six miles twice a day, to keep in shape for the marathons she now entered. If eating right was good, she wanted to toe the line, to make up for the inevitable days like today, when the nutritional choices were limited to what the tennis-club snack bar had to offer.

She had the same attitude about raising her children—there

was no such thing as too much opportunity. Pat, more than any of the other parents, had simply given over this period in her life to her daughter. She was intensely caught up in the business of helping Shawn develop her potential, and believed fervently that no sacrifice was too great if it helped Shawn to excel. Other mothers often expressed amazement at the Foltzes' willingness to live apart during the school year. Pat told them what she had told her husband Wally two years ago: The time a parent has with a child is really very brief. She and Wally would have the rest of their lives together. For now, she wanted to concentrate on Shawn. Pat intended to ferret out all the available opportunities in Shawn's areas of interest— not just tennis, but acting and modeling as well—to ensure that Shawn could progress, in any direction, as far as her talent would take her.

Had Pat Foltz been born ten years later, she confessed, she might have put this kind of energy into building a career of her own. But when she was growing up, the only women who worked were women who had to. She envied her daughter, she said, for growing up at a time when it was permissible for a girl to be ambitious and career-minded. For both their sakes, Pat was determined to help Shawn figure out what she wanted to do.

As the wife of a wealthy businessman—Wally, a former semipro football player, had made liquor stores and real estate into a lucrative career—Pat had the means to put her plans into action. The Foltzes were able to maintain two separate households, send Pat to travel the international junior circuit with her daughter, and have composite photographs taken to further Shawn's fledgling modeling career. Pat always appeared at tournaments in tailored, tasteful clothes, or a rainbow assortment of coordinated running ensembles, complemented by a selection of gold jewelry.

Even more important than the financial assets, though, were the mental resources Pat Foltz seemed to have for the task. If Francine Spence often seemed awed by the outside world, Pat Foltz saw it as an invigorating challenge. She had not been cowed at the prospect of a year in Florida: it had taught her that she had to make a life for herself or she would end up a glorified chauffeur. When she had to move cross-country again this year, she insisted on a semblance of normal life. While she ran her daily twelve miles, she dictated her thoughts into a tiny tape recorder for a book she wanted to write about running while traveling. She began to explore the beach cities near her new southern California home. By the time she and Shawn returned from Kansas City her car and belongings would have been delivered to the apartment, and she could start making it into a more livable home.

With her environment in order, Pat went to work for Shawn. Wherever they went, Pat was sure to meet the right people, have the productive conversations, and make contacts who could help Shawn. Just in case some new acquaintance wanted to know more about her daughter, Pat had what she called a press packet back in the hotel room. The legal-size manila folder held press clippings about Shawn's tennis and her role as a tennis player in the movie *Spring Fever*, and a copy of the modeling photo composite.

Pat managed to keep all avenues open. On Wednesday, the first day of the Kansas City tournament, she consulted with a USTA official about whether Shawn was better off playing an upcoming tournament in the 16-and-under category, where she might win more easily but would receive less attention, or up in the 18s, where a good performance would get her noticed. Just in case things did not work out as they hoped, Pat encouraged Shawn to think seriously about going to college, and talk to some of the college coaches who were at the tournament.

In the afternoon, Pat sat at the bar and chatted with Parkes Brittain—the tall, bookish young man who was in charge of women's tennis for Advantage International—about which tournaments Shawn might play in the coming months, and whether he knew of a good traveling coach. Shawn and Debbie sat next to Pat, working on what would be the first of two orders of nachos and the only dinner they would get to eat. Shawn turned frequently to toss comments at girls who walked by, but Debbie concentrated on eating—oblivious to the fact that what would have been an order of fresh tortilla chips and jack cheese, at home, was, in its Midwestern incarnation, oversalted prefabricated chips and a bright orange cheese sauce reminiscent of melted Velveeta. This was not the best meal for someone who still had another singles match and a doubles match to play, but it was something to occupy her while she fretted.

Debbie had come to Kansas City expecting to play doubles with Marianne Werdel, only to find that Marianne had signed up with Anna Ivan, another student from Nick Bollettieri's academy. The move rattled her, especially since neither Marianne nor her father, Tom, gave Debbie a satisfactory explanation for the last-minute switch. Luckily, many girls who did not have regular doubles partners paired up at the last minute, so Shawn was available to be Debbie's doubles partner.

But Debbie felt rejected and defensive: did this mean the Werdels didn't think she was good enough anymore? She made worried comparisons between the quality of Marianne's game and her own sorry performance in the first round. She had won, but she did not feel that she had played her best.

"Well, Marianne's got so many people helping her," she complained aloud, to no one in particular. "Nick's helping her, *and* somebody else. The girl I beat this morning wasn't very good, which is good, because I played awful."

Her evaluation had little to do with her actual performance. Debbie was feeling the pressure of playing her first national junior tournament as the reigning queen of the eighteen-year-olds and the number one seed, and she was struggling under the weight of her crown. This was not a local tournament like Anaheim, where she could lose unexpectedly without drawing too much attention.

All the other girls were hungry for an upset victory over Debbie Spence—and Debbie only wanted to get on with her plans for turning pro. She had lost the excitement she felt last year, her first year in the 18s, when she got to the quarterfinals of this tournament. Without that edge of desire, she was going to have trouble defending herself.

She was in danger of becoming her own worst enemy; the

frustration she had felt ever since she became number one was now mixed with a fear that perhaps her game was starting to slip. She tried to recall how she had felt as she worked toward her top ranking, how each victory increased her confidence until she was "zoning," placing each ball with marvelous accuracy, playing commanding, aggressive tennis.

Now it felt more like survival tennis. She played in self-defense, rather than being able to take charge of a match. As soon as she got to the club today, she had grimly considered the draw, to see how far she could progress before she got into serious trouble. She was confident that she could get through the first few rounds on bravado and basic skills, but the quarterfinal and semifinal matches scared her. First she would have to beat Stephanie Rehe, who was intimidating because she appeared so aloof and composed on court. A loss to her would be a disgrace because she was only fourteen, playing in the 18s for the first time. If Debbie survived that match, she would face either Melissa Gurney, another fourteen-year-old newcomer to the 18s and the source of her recent humiliation in Anaheim, or Marianne Werdel, whom she felt had snubbed her, and had won this tournament last year.

The logistics of the situation only compounded her distress. To save money, her parents had arranged for her to share a hotel room with Carolyn and Melissa Gurney, which meant that Debbie could not even talk to her parents on the telephone without being overheard. She would have no time to herself to blow off steam, and no one to whom she could confess—friends were also potential opponents, who would try to take advantage of her vulnerability. Debbie had to maintain the illusion of being the best. It was as much a part of winning, and as exhausting, as an early morning practice session.

II

Shawn, who was seeded twelfth, felt a little queasy right before her Thursday morning match, but she chalked it up to minor-league nerves and headed down to the court. Pat moved a chair right in front of the plate-glass partition that sealed off this bank of courts, and settled in for the duration with a rectangular piece of needlepoint and a roll of wild cherry Lifesavers, which she would methodically devour during the match. The needlepoint was going to be a pillow for Shawn with her name spelled out in a floral pattern. Pat had already finished a similar pillow with her son's name, Brett, spelled out in baseball bats, basketballs, and other pieces of sporting equipment.

Watching a daughter play a match was a solitary vigil. Friendships came to an abrupt, if temporary, halt. Another parent might make a passing inquiry about the score, or offer a quick partisan comment on how a player looked, but the exchanges were brief. Sometimes Pat listened to music while Shawn played, as much to shut out the rest of the world as anything else.

It was agony, especially for parents who were used to doing so much for their children. During a match they were suddenly impotent. There was no way they could help. If Shawn was in trouble, Pat was limited to a pantomime of support—smiles, determined expressions, and hands held high, clapping. She muttered words of encouragement that Shawn could not hear.

If Shawn was doing well, Pat could only pray that nothing distracted her. Midway through the first set she leaned forward and peered at her daughter. The hem of Shawn's white Ellesse tennis skirt was starting to come down in back. Pat cursed poor workmanship, dug a safety pin out of her bag, and dispatched a young boy down to the court. He delivered the pin to an official, who ambled onto the court and gave the safety pin to Shawn. She smiled up at her mother, fixed her hem, and went on to win the match 6–3, 6–3.

Parkes Brittain made sure he was on hand as the match ended to congratulate Shawn and Pat—just as he would appear at Carolyn Gurney's side when Melissa played. He was working under luxurious conditions, since the competing sports management firms had not sent representatives to Kan-

sas City. Instead of jockeying for position with IMG or Pro-
Serv, he could work the room in his own subdued style.

This suited Brittain fine, since his approach was as understated as the rep ties, pinstripe shirts, and dark suits he favored. He had left ProServ earlier this year as part of a splinter
group that moved down the block to form Advantage International, Inc. Although a legal agreement prohibited members
of either agency from discussing the split, one distinction was
clear: ProServ, like its rival, IMG, was something of a corporate octopus, involved in broadcasting and tournament promotion, as well as more traditional management services like
long-range investment counseling and contract negotiations.
The two big firms also had what one parent called "an under-
ground railroad" for talented kids—IMG now depended on
Robert Lansdorp for the early, inside word on a future star, as
ProServ depended on Nick Bollettieri. ProServ and IMG
could, and did, imply that they would have an easy time ac-
quiring wild cards into their own tournaments for clients and
potential clients, a controversial practice whose proponents
argued that any effort to promote professional tennis was a
good one, and whose critics, like Advantage International,
considered it a conflict of interest which impaired the sport's
credibility.

Advantage International had no tournaments of its own and
no exclusive connection to a top coach. Parkes Brittain's task
was to convince parents and young players that there was an
advantage to signing with a smaller, less diversified agency,
and to taking the slower, more cautious route to professional
success that it often preached. He tried to position himself as
the realist of women's tennis, a pragmatist who understood the
lasting value of a reasonable pace. Maybe he couldn't make
the big promises the other agents made—but he argued that
his promises, while less thrilling, were more sincere.

"Now, other people in my end of the business have said to
girls, 'You're worth a hundred thousand dollars. What are you
waiting for?' But I'd never say that. I've never said that," he
said. "What I can say to somebody like Shawn Foltz is that we
can look to independent tournaments, match play, and pro-

moters. I say, play those USTA satellite tournaments. You get used to the idea of winning, of playing Monday through Saturday instead of Monday and Tuesday and getting your socks taken to the cleaners in the first round. That's really how Tracy started. She won a whole lot of junior titles and then went to small tournaments and won.

"My viewpoint—the countervailing viewpoint—is that a wild card in the main draw is potentially damaging to a girl's ranking. If she plays way above her head and keeps getting blown away, the tournament counts but she doesn't get any points. If she wins, she's golden; if she doesn't, she's way down in the ranking."

Some agents believed that pursuing the one "local" wild card, awarded to a player who lived near a tournament site, was a good idea for a young girl because it enabled her to compete without spending much time or money on travel. It wasn't as disruptive as having to fly cross-country to play days of qualifying rounds; a girl could have a semblance of a normal life.

But Brittain still wondered about the psychological price of such an attractive shortcut, about whether a girl would pay later for having gotten too many favors too soon. The shock of being just another pro working her way up could be rough for a player who had come to expect special treatment.

He had carved out an oddly schizophrenic niche for himself: he traveled the circuit to establish relationships with players that would eventually turn into profits for the company—his very presence, and expressions of interest, implied that a girl had a future—and then talked about the virtues of patience and hard work. He had to go after wild cards, just like any other agent, but, since he had less access, he tried to convince the girls that they might be better off without them.

He was in a potentially dangerous position, since players were under no obligation to sign with agents who gave them good advice. At any moment ProServ or IMG could swoop down on a player Parkes Brittain was courting and try to steal her away. He had to be prepared to step up his pace if his competitors suddenly became interested.

In the meantime, he had to sell the work ethic at tournaments like this one. It was not easy. Under the crowded, nerve-wracking conditions of this Thanksgiving weekend—and given a teenager's normal predilection for hyperbole—being singled out for special treatment seemed a life-or-death issue. These girls thought themselves quite sophisticated about the process of turning pro. They knew that wild cards were a way onto the fast track and would undoubtedly lead to more favors, like a free coach or a big endorsement. They believed that reasonable conversations about alternate routes were a polite way of saying that a girl's career was at a dead-end. No one wanted to hear Brittain explain that she'd be better off, in the long run, for having worked her way up through the ranks. All she wanted to know was why *she* couldn't get the wild cards.

It was the sort of plaintive, naïve question that any adult hated to hear from a child. The answer was either an evasion —Brittain's discourse on the benefits of not taking wild cards —or a reminder, however delicately put, that tennis was not just a sport, but a business. The people who made money from that business took many elements into account when they decided which girls they wanted to pursue, and promote, and raw talent was only one of their considerations. One player could play as well as another and still not receive an equal amount of attention. The process of turning pro was, in part, a process of abandoning notions of fairness. A girl had to accept the frustrating fact, usually faced a bit later in life, that rewards were not always doled out in perfect proportion to accomplishments.

If Parkes Brittain was cautious on the issue of turning pro, Ruth Lay was a hardline conservative who clung to traditional values despite the current trend toward adolescent celebrity. A fifty-eight-year-old USTA official whose only souvenirs of a high-school tennis career were two bum knees and the bills from five operations, Lay had been involved in junior tennis since the early 1970s, and she didn't like what she saw today. Things were moving too quickly. A fifteen-year-old shouldn't have to think about career strategies and a marketable image. She ought to be thinking about college, like a normal teenager.

As the chairman of the Junior Wightman Cup and Junior Federation Cup committees, Ruth Lay saw too many junior girls ready to give up their education, and too many agents talking to fourteen-year-olds. Until two years ago, college coaches couldn't compete for attention with the agents because they were barred from recruiting at tournaments. Now, in part because of the agents' aggressive scouting tactics, college coaches were allowed to attend tournaments. Formally, they weren't supposed to talk to any girls except the high-school seniors, but Ruth Lay didn't care about that restriction. She was thrilled that they were here, period.

This year she estimated that the ratio of college coaches to agents at the Overland Park Racquet Club was about twenty to one. "We ought to line up all the coaches in an auditorium and make the girls march through and talk to them about college," she gloated. "I think we're going to win this battle. Get the girls to take time to mature. Learn concentration—and conversation."

She wanted the top junior girls to keep going to school and try out for the Junior Federation Cup team on the college level. "This year we had fourteen players," she would tell them, "the very best at the collegiate level, and we coach them, chaperone them, travel with them, work out their tournament schedules, and pay all of their expenses. We see that they get on the computer; we work with them to break in on the computer, so that by the time they turn pro they are already ranked."

Obviously, a girl like Debbie Spence, who had been on the 1983 Junior Wightman Cup team along with Marianne Werdel, was too far gone to respond to Lay's entreaties. She was hanging on to high school by a thread; nobody was going to get her into college. The problem was to keep such players from giving up amateur tennis prematurely, and setting a bad example for the younger girls. So Ruth Lay, ever the pragmatist, had pushed for revisions in the Junior Wightman requirements, to meet the needs of girls who were getting ready to turn pro.

There had been a time, just a few years ago, when members of the Junior Wightman team were required to play junior tournaments exclusively during the summer season. But then the girls and their families began to complain that the schedule restricted the players' progress and actually encouraged early defections to the pros. They wanted help playing the pro tournaments as well, and felt that the USTA should help with that transition. If a girl was already overseas playing Junior Wimbledon, why couldn't she play one of the foreign pro tournaments at the same time?

So the USTA revamped the team's schedule, reducing the number of required junior tournaments, covering team members' travel expenses to certain pro tournaments, and helping them obtain wild cards. The idea was not to help a girl turn pro, but to keep her from having to make that choice too soon.

Ruth Lay understood that such changes were essential to keep the USTA from becoming a dinosaur bureaucracy, but she was not particularly happy about it. She still thought college was the best choice, and whenever she could she pigeonholed a parent or a player and made her case.

Her basic argument was this: Only a few women players, the ones who collected endorsement money as well as prize money, could make enough as pros to guarantee their financial independence once their careers were over. Some girls would never make it to the top; some would be waylaid along the way by injury, illness, or psychological problems. The more education a girl had, the more prepared she would be to make a life for herself outside of tennis.

"I just don't think the figures, right now, are healthy for a young girl to turn pro, unless she's a superstar," said Lay. She ran her finger down the list of top women prize-money winners for the first half of 1983, and stopped near number forty. The women in that range had made about $18,000 in six months; by December, they would have earned about $36,-000. And that was all they would earn, because, at that level, they probably did not have additional income from product endorsements.

"If a girl makes forty thousand dollars, she's not really making any money," said Lay in a loud voice, hoping that players sitting near her in the snack bar would overhear. "I keep coming back to the hard figures. How much money is it going to cost you in plane tickets, and meals—and then would somebody *please* explain to me how they can afford a coach to travel with them? And they're too young not to be chaperoned. Tell me how they can do all that for even twenty-five thousand dollars."

Twenty-five thousand dollars was the accepted minimum cost for a girl to spend a year on the pro tennis circuit, between transportation costs, lodging, shoes, clothes, and racquets. But prize-money figures were published without adjusting them for expenses, a fact that irritated Ruth Lay. She didn't like the idea that impressionable young girls were looking at the list and thinking that $40,000 was an awful lot of money to earn —not realizing that the fortieth-best woman tennis player in the world was actually making less than half that amount after expenses, hardly enough to provide for her old age, which, in this line of work, started in a woman's mid-thirties.

The deceptive prize-money figures were a small part of a much grander illusion, as far as Ruth Lay was concerned. What really upset her were the promises the agents made. Contracts were tricky documents designed to protect the corporate client, and there was usually a performance clause: a huge endorsement fee could simply dry up if a girl hit a slump. But these wide-eyed kids—and their often equally unsophisticated parents—were easily misled. Ruth Lay reserved her real venom for the agents; she felt that even the most civilized ones were hustling the players. The very thought of it made her Georgia drawl tighten and her eyes get narrow.

"These agents go in there and sell the girls all this bill of goods about how they can get all these endorsement contracts," she said. "Now, in some cases you can; you can capitalize on looks. . . . But otherwise they are incentive contracts, where you're paid by the round reached. Or you're given some upfront money, but in some cases it might not be but a thousand dollars. Some cases it might be twenty thousand dollars, but not everybody gets those fat upfront contracts.

"The bulk of the contracts are performance contracts, and

I don't think the kids understand it." Agents might protest that not all contracts penalized the girls for losses; some guaranteed a base figure and then paid bonuses based on ranking or the round reached in a given tournament. Still, a flattered teenager could not be depended upon to consider the discrepancy between real and potential earnings, or to believe that she might have a bad year.

Presumably, parents understood that an incentive contract was only as good as a girl's performance, but, in Lay's experience, parents were often more obsessed with sports stardom than their offspring were. "I think parents are looking for money," she said. "Quite often maybe some of the parents have got stars in their eyes. So often it's the parents more than it is the children. So it's our problem to educate the girls so they make the decision for themselves."

Having played in the days before women's pro tennis, Lay was delighted that the sport had developed from an expensive, elite sport into a money-making endeavor. And she never denied that the best pros—the ones who consistently progressed to the big-money rounds, and perhaps had endorsements as well—could end up set for life.

But with profitability came ulterior motive, from the obvious influence of business interests to the more subtle, often subconscious proddings of parents who hoped for a payoff on their emotional investment. As Ruth Lay saw it, even the enviable young player with the impressive entourage—a parent or two, a coach, an eager agent—was essentially alone, more depended upon than dependent.

She worried that the girls made decisions for the wrong reasons. At fifteen or sixteen, it was easy to mistake an adult's enthusiasm for some sort of guarantee that everything would work out fine. It was too soon to comprehend the possibility of disappointment, and the consequences lurking beyond it. Not every girl would end up in the top ten or twenty, despite all her desire and dedication. Ruth Lay believed that education would cushion that blow.

"I say to them, I think it's great that you love the game this much, and I identify with your ambition. But I want you to make sure that you're doing it the right way. Before you rule out having a normal life *plus* tennis. Make sure *you're* going to be happy, that you're not going to have regrets when you're twenty-one.

"My point," she said, over and over, "is not *not* to turn pro, but to turn pro at the right time. Make sure you have taken advantage of life. That's all."

She wandered the club, as she did various other clubs on the junior circuit throughout the year, with the prize-money list in her hand, a proselytizer seeking converts to an increasingly unpopular cause. A stocky, middle-aged woman who once had been the Georgia state high-school tennis champion, made a brief comeback on the thirty-five- and forty-year-old circuit, and could no longer play, had trouble competing for the attention of teenagers who were told, on a regular basis, that they faced a future of limitless possibilities. Lay's position was the equivalent of entreating a child to eat her vegetables while somebody else offered her pie in the sky, and she knew it.

More and more, Lay found herself preaching to the converted. The girls who played tennis for the chance at a college scholarship—girls who were thrilled at the chance to buy a bachelor's degree, or who were realistic enough to have judged their chances at a pro career and found they came up short—were happy to listen to Ruth Lay, who knew the college coaches and could provide the girls with introductions and advice. They accepted her word as gospel. The girls she really wanted to reach, like Debbie Spence, girls who would turn pro and become role models for even younger girls, as Tracy Austin had been a model for them, politely tolerated her sermonizing and continued to ignore it.

Ironically, the very qualities which might make a girl a great player were the ones which insulated her from recognizing the precariousness of her position. To reach the top a girl had to believe she was capable of being number one in the pros and would somehow avoid all the pitfalls that befell lesser players. In self-defense, the ambitious junior girl and her parents had to deflect what Ruth Lay said. They had to convince

themselves that her gloomy warnings were intended for someone else.

Denial—the saving grace of many a tennis family—pre-
vailed. Yes, Ruth Lay had the official earnings figures. And the
girls from southern California had to face the inescapable example of Camille Benjamin, number one in the 16-and-under
category in 1981, now trying to find her footing as just another
anonymous pro, good enough to keep going and not yet good
enough to make a financial killing. But the best juniors were
protected by a shield of self-confidence—or perhaps adolescent arrogance, the kind of bravado that comes from trying to
live up to an outsized talent. They anticipated wins, rational-
ized losses, and masked insecurity with a swagger. Mediocrity,
and the financial disappointment which would accompany it,
was a fate meant for other people.

III

The losers on Thursday were lucky: they got to head back to
the hotel in time for the special Thanksgiving dinner. The
winners—including Debbie, Shawn, Melissa Gurney, Marianne Werdel, and Stephanie Rehe—had to finish their second singles match of the day and play a doubles match as well.

Marianne Werdel shut out the world by listening to the
Romantics on her headphones. She felt relatively placid,
happy with her game and excited by the future. Marianne had
a big game—what one girl enviously referred to as "wail, wail,
wail"—and, at a broad-shouldered five-foot-eight, was an imposing figure on the junior circuit. She was still intimidated by
pro competition, and had not yet performed well on the circuit, but she believed she would grow into it.

Her parents were doing everything they could to prepare
her for a pro career, whenever it happened. Tom and Corinne
planned to send Marianne overseas in the spring to international tournaments in London, Hong Kong, Taiwan, and
Tokyo, so that she could gain experience against foreign players. They were also going to let her play in a few pro tourna-

ments. Marianne was still ranked in the low two hundreds on the computer, which was a poor showing for a girl who played so well in the juniors. Tom blamed it on nerves, and wanted to give his daughter opportunities to get used to pro competition.

On top of all that, the Werdels hadn't even complained when their straight-A student brought home a few B's for the first time. They seemed to understand that the private school she attended in Florida was more difficult than her old school in Bakersfield—and that tennis continued to be uppermost in Marianne's mind. They did balk at Marianne's suggestion that she be allowed to take correspondence classes, like so many of the other girls, and quickly sent her to visit her older sister Alyce for a football weekend at Stanford University. As her parents had hoped when they suggested the trip, Marianne had a wonderful time on campus. The notion of dropping out was blotted from her memory.

But she still regarded college as a distraction, and could not quite imagine completing four years while continuing to compete as an amateur. For her, it was not a question of whether to turn pro, but when. If she felt ready after her freshman or sophomore year, she intended to take time off from school and travel the circuit. "I've worked this hard," she said, matter-of-factly. "I'm not going to just stop. I'll know when the time comes, when I'm ready."

The alternative—to play through college and then become a civilian, a social player—sounded terribly boring to a girl who thrived on pressure and competition. Marianne was not about to slow down so soon. "Regular life? I *couldn't*," she said. "Sometimes after the summer I take a week off, but after three days I can't stand it. I go crazy. I guess I'm hyperactive. I can't sit still that long.

"You can't even compare us to people who aren't in sports," she said, with some pride. "It's like my mom said once. When I was twelve, for the nationals, she'd just drop me off at LAX and I knew how to get my ticket and where I was going. With my younger sister, who's twelve"—and would have a more traditional childhood, having been bitten in the eye by the

family cat and robbed of any chance to play competitive tennis—"she'd never dream of doing that. We're so much more
mature. You have to be, to go out there and fight and win. You
have to be competitive, and for that you can't be dependent
on anybody else."

Life after competition would require reversing direction:
after years devoted to cutting herself off from other people, a
girl would have to learn to work her way back in, socially and
professionally. To a youngster who had been raised to value
individual achievement, it was not an altogether enticing idea.

"It's kind of depressing to think about what you'll be doing
after this," said Marianne. "But it's not like your life is over.
You can have two parts. This'll be the *main* part and then
there'll be"—she hesitated, searching for the right words—
"the social part. Maybe you get married and have kids."

Tom Werdel, ever determined to remind his daughter of
that world outside tennis, rescued her immediately after her
match and took her to the Country Girl Kitchen restaurant for
Thanksgiving dinner. The other girls were not so lucky. Either
they got onto their courts late or became mired in three-set
matches, or both. Debbie and Shawn contemplated another
tray of tortilla chips and cheese with waning enthusiasm while
they waited for the match that preceded theirs to be over, and
Melissa Gurney sat off in a corner by herself.

Eating did not make Shawn feel any better, so Pat suggested
that the girls go back to the hotel for an hour to rest, joking
ruefully, "What kind of mother tells her kid to take it easy,
watch TV, and change her nail polish?" When they returned
to play their doubles match, they both wore eyeshadow, eye-
liner, and mascara. Earlier in the month Shawn had played in
the Lynda Carter–Maybelline Classic in Deerfield Beach,
Florida, where each player received a souvenir Maybelline
makeup kit. A good friend, she had grabbed an extra kit for
Debbie.

The only problem, Shawn complained, as she scrutinized
her friend's makeup, was that both the kits had exactly the
same shades of makeup. She generously insisted that Debbie

would look even better if Shawn had been able to find a kit for blondes. As if it mattered today, when the only spectators were the players and parents who couldn't get out in time for the holiday. Prettying up was just something to do while a very long day droned to a close.

By the time Pat Foltz, Carolyn Gurney, and the girls finally got back to the Regency Park, it was almost ten o'clock. Most of the employees of the restaurant had served their last Thanksgiving dinner and gone home to be with their families. The teenage boy who usually delivered room-service meals had the night off. Pat, Carolyn and their daughters stumbled blearily into the restaurant. Debbie, tired and fretful, had no dinner at all.

Even at this early stage, there were always two things to consider: how you did, and how the world perceived how you did. Friday morning Carolyn Gurney sat Melissa and Debbie down in the coffee shop, gave the waitress the breakfast order, and then slipped into the vending-machine room behind the hotel lobby to see what the local newspapers had to say about the tournament. She wanted to read the stories before she let the girls see them—or, if there was something upsetting, she wanted to keep the girls from seeing the papers at all. They had matches to play. She did not want them to be upset.

The coverage was irritating, but not distressing. The *Kansas City Times* ran a story on a Japanese girl, a member of the Bollettieri contingent who had already lost. There was nothing about the players from California. Miffed, Carolyn returned to the table, where the girls silently ate their breakfasts, offering no more than monosyllabic responses to whatever Carolyn said.

"They go into a trance," she said, as if they were not there. "They all have their own way of concentrating. Shawn listens to her Walkman. Melissa and Debbie get very quiet. It's like labor. At first you're gregarious. Then you go off into yourself."

The medical analogy was a reminder of the other half of Carolyn Gurney's overstuffed life. In addition to being the parent who traveled to tournaments with Melissa and

Lucinda, Carolyn had spent the last three years studying to be a registered nurse. In a little less than a year, she would be ready to look for a job.

She had been a nursery-school teacher, and grown tired of it, but she could not afford to stop working altogether. She had two daughters in junior tennis and a likely third candidate in her youngest daughter, Robyn. So Carolyn looked around for a new career that would both satisfy her desire to work with people and stave off the financial squeeze of being a two-, and maybe three-player tennis family on the salary her husband, Ram, earned from teaching high-school history.

For a while her decision to move into nursing made matters worse. Instead of bringing money in, she was spending it on nursing school. Ram's father, Ramsdell Gurney, Sr., an eighty-year-old practicing physician who lived in upstate New York, had begun to provide financial aid in 1979, and by now his contribution was up to an annual $20,000, but the expenses were still enormous and promised to get worse in the years to come. Carolyn's nursing income would offer some relief, but first the family had to make it through the coming expensive, tournament-laden season, to next fall.

This was a crucial year for Melissa, who was small-boned and slender, and still seemed to be growing into her hands and feet. To compensate for her size, she had learned to be a strategist—the word around the club was that Melissa Gurney looked like an easy mark but was, in fact, one of the smartest players around. She was ranked second nationally in the 16s last year, decided to play up in the 18s for 1984, and made an auspicious start by beating Debbie Spence in Anaheim.

As soon as she filled out a little, she'd have a real chance. Carolyn and Ram only hoped that the money would stretch far enough to keep her in tournaments, plane tickets, and motel rooms. At least Melissa got clothes and shoes from Adidas, and racquets from Wilson. And next summer she would try out for the Junior Wightman Cup team, to help cut costs.

But it continued to be a struggle. "I told Parkes yesterday," Carolyn said. "We're running out. We're not wealthy like the Foltzes."

Pat and Shawn, at that moment, were in the emergency room of a local hospital, where Shawn was being treated for food poisoning and/or flu after a night of diarrhea and vomiting. Pat worried that the Lomotil the doctor prescribed might adversely affect Shawn's game, but there was no alternative. If Shawn didn't start taking something stronger than the as-yet-ineffective Pepto-Bismol she had been taking since the night before, she simply wouldn't last through a match.

She appeared at the club, looking wan, just in time for her match against the number four seed, Mary Norwood, a rough opponent even under the best conditions. Pat, whose face was pinched and tired, started mustering her defenses against possible defeat. As Shawn headed for the court, and all during the match, Pat told onlookers how weak her daughter was, and described how she had been suffering since yesterday. If Shawn was about to lose, Pat wanted people to know it was not because she was the less able player.

Anyone who watched the match could tell that Shawn was suffering. She looked sluggish and uncomfortable, and when she lost in straight sets she shuffled miserably off the court for consolation and another slug of Pepto-Bismol. Pat sat her down, felt her forehead, and announced, "If Shawn were feeling well she'd have beaten Mary. I can see that."

Pat knew that the girls could agonize over an important loss until they blew it out of proportion. This was Shawn's first national tournament in the 18s, and it was going to be a long year. She needed evidence that she was not doomed to a life of mediocrity. So Pat quickly reminded Shawn of the three girls they had heard about, who had been sick at one of the national tournaments last year and still managed to be selected for the Junior Wightman Cup team. That made Shawn feel better. Perhaps her entire future was not in jeopardy. She nursed a diet cola and let Pat fuss over her while the other girls competed for the afternoon's quarterfinal matches.

Debbie was the first to earn a quarterfinal slot. She dispatched Friday morning's opponent quickly, 6–2, 6–1, and, buoyed by a decisive victory, shuttled between the other girls' matches, watching both as friend and as imminent foe. Debbie could talk nonstop during a match, analyzing a girl's game with a keen, quick eye. Tennis was the one thing that loosened her tongue. She was often awkward and distracted in social conversations, and her attention span for topics of general interest was minimal, but when it came to tennis she was hard to shut up. She had no memories about the city of Paris, where she had stayed during the Junior French Open, because she did not care for sightseeing. But she rattled on happily, and in detail, about the time she played doubles with Shawn there.

Late Friday afternoon, as Debbie changed for her second singles match, the club began to fill up with local tennis fans who wanted to see the up-and-coming stars. There were only eight girls left in the singles competition, including top seed Debbie Spence, Marianne Werdel, Stephanie Rehe, and Melissa Gurney. By the end of the day that number would be cut in half. These were the girls worth seeing, the ones whose names might be well known in a year or two.

The presence of civilians increased the level of noise, since this was, for them, a social occasion. By the time Debbie and Grace Kim, a Bollettieri pupil from New Jersey, began playing on a court at the edge of the lobby, the Overland Park Racquet Club looked and sounded like a cocktail lounge. People mingled and sipped drinks and generally drove the players crazy.

To make matters worse for Debbie, Grace Kim's relatives had taken position early, lined up across the viewing area that faced the court. From the start of the match, Debbie was bothered by them and their inevitable, predictable responses. She managed to take the first set, 6–2, but she started having trouble in the second, playing in the midst of such growing commotion that she looked up toward the crowd several times, silently entreating people to be quiet—only to meet the unresponsive gaze of a half-dozen of Kim's partisans.

The couple that was making the most noise did not notice Debbie because they were paying only peripheral attention to the match. They were here to watch tennis tangentially: their primary goal was to promote their pre-teen, ponytailed daughter, who had just begun playing junior tournaments. Mother, father, and daughter had ambushed a Wilson sporting-goods representative to ask about getting the youngster on Wilson's equipment list. The rep gave them the standard answer. The little girl was supposed to write a letter explaining who she was, and how she'd been playing, and the company would see what it could do.

At this, the parents' voices rose. Their little girl had already written in. Wasn't there something more they could do? Their words carried over the rest of the crowd, floated down onto the court, and got in Debbie's way. Grace Kim took the second set 6–1, and the girls took a ten-minute break before play continued.

Carolyn Gurney, whose daughter was suffering through a frustrating physical mismatch against Marianne Werdel—all the clever strategies in the world could not quite compensate for the difference in their size and strength—had wandered over to watch Debbie. She knew that the noise made it hard to concentrate, but she also knew that Debbie wanted particularly to beat Grace Kim, which made her more anxious, more sensitive to distractions. Both girls were what Carolyn called "the fifty-fifties. One foot in the amateurs, the other already in the pros." The girls were not just competing in the quarterfinals of a national junior tournament. They were competing for recognition on another level entirely.

When Shawn saw what had happened, she grabbed a can of diet cola and rushed downstairs to the locker room to give Debbie a pep talk. She reappeared as Debbie and Grace returned to the court and shoved in next to the Kims to watch. Although other matches were still underway, spectators drifted over to watch the third set. People smelled blood: the number one seed had split sets with the number nine seed. Debbie not only had to beat Grace, she had to beat the crowd, which rooted for the underdog.

Three courts back, Neil Brown started hitting balls to his daughter Melissa to warm her up for her match. It was impossible to hear anything they said over the din of the lobby and the grunts and squeals that emanated from Debbie and Grace; impossible to see the balls they were hitting because of the netting that hung between the courts. Neil Brown reached up and served an invisible ball and his daughter lunged in one direction, and then another, for her return. The only sound that carried was the intermittent thock-thock-thock of the ball.

Watching them, it was possible to imagine the same scene recurring, back through time. There was Neil Brown helping his daughter with her tennis two years ago, and then four years ago; there he was, handing her a tennis racquet on the day he started to teach her how to play. They looked like any father and daughter enjoying a game of tennis, he in his baggy bermuda shorts, pantomiming in slow motion how she should address the ball, she with her gangly legs and embarrassed giggles when she made a mistake. More remarkable, in this pressurized environment, they looked like they were having fun, playing an ancestral relative of the cutthroat game under way three courts closer to the audience.

While Debbie struggled, the other matches resolved themselves in much the way she had imagined when she first cast a worried eye over the draw sheet. Marianne Werdel eliminated Melissa Gurney, and Stephanie Rehe beat Mary Norwood to advance to the semifinals. Melissa Brown would advance without ever hitting a ball since her opponent had to default because of illness.

Shawn and Pat would go home happy, even with Shawn's loss, because a more highly ranked player had defaulted. Defaults were a sticky issue in junior tennis: they damaged a girl's ranking less than an outright loss did, so a player who assumed she was about to lose—who faced a difficult foe or was in less than top form—was tempted to default to protect her ranking. Now Shawn felt doubly redeemed. She had played her match ill instead of defaulting, which proved that she placed sportsmanship over self-interest, and a better player than she had succumbed, which proved that she was tough.

Pat was pleased, too. She had heard that other players were beginning to show symptoms of stomach flu. Perhaps the results of this tournament would not be taken as seriously as some others when the USTA formulated the year's rankings.

Although Melissa, like Shawn, had lost her match, she and

her mother were philosophical about the defeat—she needed six months and some added heft for an even match against Marianne. When Debbie came off the court, having salvaged her match with a decisive 6–2 third set, the Foltzes and Gurneys were waiting to congratulate her. But the one victor in this little crowd did not respond to the compliments and praise. Winning was small consolation for playing badly, and Debbie was still not satisfied with her game. Tomorrow she had to face Stephanie Rehe in the semifinal round, and she did not feel prepared.

She rode back to the hotel with the Gurneys and said, in a sarcastic singsong, "I get to play Stephanie. I get to play Stephanie." All she could think about was the awful possibility of being beaten by a fourteen-year-old who was playing in the 18s for the first time—the same humiliation that Debbie, who had just turned fifteen, had visited on a few older girls last year at this tournament, when she was on her way up.

That was how she saw it: she had been on the rise and then her father, with his insistence on playing the juniors to stay match-tough, had stalled her progress. Back in the hotel room, in front of Carolyn and Melissa Gurney, Debbie had a heated, unhappy long-distance conversation with her father about how trapped she felt in Kansas City. Any pretense of a winning attitude was gone.

The next morning, little things assumed cosmic significance. At breakfast Debbie pored over a newspaper article about her in the *Kansas City Times,* considered the accompanying photograph, which showed her pug face tightened in concentration, and moaned, "Why do they *always* take such awful pictures?"

Melissa Brown wasn't even seated at a table yet. She was waiting for her father, who stood at the hotel desk waving a plastic bag full of his daughter's clean, damp tennis underwear in the clerk's face. It was 9:15, Melissa had reserved a practice court for 9:30, and the hotel's clothes dryer didn't work. The clerk suggested a laundromat five blocks away, took one look at the contorted expression on Neil Brown's face, and quickly offered to throw the underwear in with the hotel's sheets and towels.

By the time they got into the coffee shop, though, it was too late for Melissa to have the pancakes she wanted. She had to settle for cold cereal with bananas. She ate her meal sullenly. A terrifying threat hung in the air, that anything—a bad photograph, pancakes denied—could upset a player's balance at this point and spell disaster.

Carolyn Gurney had taken measure of Debbie's tensions when they woke up this morning. Privately, she announced her verdict: she expected Debbie to lose. The combination of Debbie's self-pity and Stephanie's extreme confidence on-court was to Debbie's distinct psychological disadvantage.

"I'm preparing to do my consolation work," Carolyn said, as she walked to the parking lot with her daughter and Debbie. "I try to get the girls to talk about their feelings, not involve myself in it, just help them get it out."

For this match, Carolyn stationed herself close to the court and watched intently. Only two games into the first set, she shook her head and muttered, "Nope. You can tell the way Stephanie is playing. You can tell the way she *walks* out there. She's on a roll." Her words proved prophetic. Stephanie won the match quickly, allowing Debbie only three games in the first set and four games in the second.

Carolyn Gurney and Pat Foltz both approached Debbie as soon as she came up into the lobby, but she managed to avoid eye contact with anyone who might want to have a serious conversation with her about how she was feeling. She surrounded herself with other girls and started making plans for the afternoon. If she was going to take a plane out of Kansas City tonight, in accordance with her father's rule, she was going to keep herself busy until it was time to leave for the airport. She was not interested in empty moments, which tended to fill up with depressing thoughts.

There were responsibilities to fulfill, though, even for a loser, so Debbie lingered in the lobby to talk to a sports reporter. But she did not trust her composure long enough to watch the end of the match between Marianne Werdel and

Melissa Brown. She ducked into the locker room to change before Marianne won, so she missed all the praise being heaped on her former doubles partner, who would go on to win the indoor tournament for the second year in a row tomorrow. Debbie was out the tennis club door for a soothing trip to the adjacent shopping mall.

The top-ranked amateur in the girls' 18s had lost to a younger girl in her first major national tournament. To Ruth Lay, it was proof of what she always said. These girls were making premature decisions, sacrificing their education to an insecure future on the basis of one or two good years. She felt that a girl who couldn't prevail for a second year in the 18s lacked the consistency to make it as a pro. She had heard the argument, time and again, about having to move into the pros for a fresh challenge, and she dismissed it. The real challenge was to go back for another year of junior competition and defend your record against a new batch of girls. After all, the pros had to face eager young players every year. They didn't have the luxury of selecting their opponents.

"I want Debbie Spence and Shawn Foltz to look me in the eye and tell me that, in giving up a free college education and a chance to earn money the rest of their lives, I want them to tell me that they can be ranked in the top twenty," she said. She knew that they would. She'd heard the line: a girl had to think she could beat everyone to be able to beat anyone. But Ruth Lay, unlike parents, agents, and coaches, had no vested interest in the girls. She had no patience for self-deception disguised as healthy optimism.

"There's maybe one superstar here," she had said, even before the quarterfinals had been played. "That's a hot potato, because one thing about junior tennis is, I could sit here today and say, 'There's not but one superstar,' and in six months there may be ten. That's how fast they come up in the juniors. But I would say Stephanie Rehe, definitely. I'm looking at a mature young lady who's barely fourteen, who can carry on an intelligent conversation and who has a lot of poise. And I think her game is extremely mature.

"And I'm sure there are others. Marianne Werdel is a tremendous young lady. Very mature."

Debbie Spence was the best amateur in the country, according to the USTA, and had not yet lost when Ruth Lay made her appraisal. Didn't she have the motivation, and momentum, to successfully turn pro?

Ruth Lay picked her words carefully. "There are financial pressures," she said. "And in a lot of ways I think sometimes that's an awful lot of pressure on the child. I have seen players not make it because of that, because of financial strain. Because every time they played a match they were afraid to lose because of the money. And I don't think they could sometimes handle that. It takes a rare girl to be that tough."

It was hardly an unequivocal endorsement of Debbie's chances. It was an indictment of women's tennis as show business—the expensive beginnings, the expansive potential—which could cloud a family's judgment and push a girl onto the circuit before she was ready. Ruth Lay believed that Debbie Spence was in a hurry, in part because the rosy financial future she heard about was such an attractive alternative to her budgeted present.

It sounded like a bad reason to make a move—but then, Ruth Lay had to admit that she had never faced the lure of commercial tennis. When she had hit her peak, during World War II, it was hard simply to find tennis balls to play with; worries about when to cash in were admittedly foreign to her. And the desire for recognition and wealth was certainly a standard motivation in life. The only difference here, perhaps, was the awful compression of time.

Ruth Lay rolled it over in her mind for a moment. Maybe some girls rose to the challenge when they were playing for financial autonomy, for the chance never to have to work like other people did.

"I don't know," she said, finally, with a wry grin. "Maybe you're a little hungrier that way."

7
Strategies

Much of the money in women's tennis was generated in the General Motors Building, at the corner of Fifth Avenue and Central Park South in midtown Manhattan, where International Management Group had its East Coast office. IMG, with a home office in Cleveland, Ohio, was founded in 1960 by lawyer/sports buff Mark McCormack, and now employed four hundred people in fifteen offices around the world. The agency represented between four hundred and five hundred clients—including almost a dozen women tennis pros—and grossed between $100 million and $200 million annually. It was also involved in the promotion and TV broadcast of tennis tournaments.

Chuck Bennett, a thirty-one-year-old account executive, had worked at IMG's Manhattan office for three and a half years, after a stint as public relations director for the Women's Tennis Association. He described his job as "working in client activities and corporate marketing" under racquet sports division corporate vice-president Bob Kain, who was based in Cleveland. Bennett worked with the agency's roster of women players, which now included the two best players in the world, Martina Navratilova and Chris Evert Lloyd, as well as Billie Jean King and Andrea Jaeger. He also kept an eye out for the next generation of winners. Although junior recruitment was handled primarily by Jim Curley in the Cleveland office, Bennett was the mastermind behind IMG's ongoing wild-card campaign for Stephanie Rehe.

Like his counterparts—Sara Kleppinger at ProServ and Parkes Brittain at Advantage International—Chuck Bennett gave the impression of a slightly overage jock, trim, fit, and full of enthusiasm. Only the dark shadows under his eyes hinted at his growing disaffection with what he did for a living. On

104

a good day he looked like he had been awake for a week.

He was troubled by the girls' junior tennis scene and his position in it. An agent was basically a corporate flirt: he engaged in a protracted courtship with a talented player, all the while glancing over his shoulder to make sure a competitor wasn't trying to steal his girl away, and keeping an eye open for other girls he might want to approach. The good agent-as-suitor did everything possible to woo a potential client, since excess in the name of affection was certainly not a sin. Tournament wild cards and talk of multiple-endorsement contracts replaced flowers and candy in the vernacular of a tennis romance. It was true love as long as the girl continued to be as wonderful—as commercially viable—as she was today.

But all that attention had its disadvantages. Chuck Bennett looked at the lucky girls, the ones who were chosen for special treatment, and was ambivalent about what he saw. Sometimes it seemed to him that the more they got, the more they expected to get. Gratitude was just one more favor down the line. If he was going to give himself credit for helping players start their careers, he had to blame himself for his complicity in spoiling them rotten.

"They've come through the system where, from the time they're eight, manufacturers are all over them giving them free stuff. They're treated unbelievably at such a young age," he said. "And then you have people like us that are saying, 'Hey, we'll get you a tournament!' They're taken care of from the time they're so young. By the time some of them turn pro, they can be such prima donnas. And it's not their fault in a lot of ways. They have no sense of reality."

Chuck Bennett's problem was that he was starting to think about the consequences of what he did, and those thoughts— like any good player's momentary doubts—slowed down his game. More and more, he felt pushed from behind, forced, in the interest of good agenting, to focus on finding the next young star.

"I think what happens," he said, in an office littered with promotional posters for various clients, "and it is an unattractive part of the business, is that, with the pressures there are to get the next superstar, unfortunately, you have to do something about it. *Early.* Or someone else will.

"It gets a little ridiculous," he said. "I don't like things rushed like this because there are so few people who can make that transition from junior player to pro player. A few of the really special ones can do it and there's nothing wrong with them going out and doing it. I think that's fine. But what happens is that then everybody else thinks of themselves in the same light, and the parents start to call, and I think they're rushing it."

It was a vicious cycle: the better the agents were at ferreting out the young talent, the more anxious girls and their parents became. The side effect of IMG's success at isolating exceptional junior players was a pervasive fear of being left behind. If an agent talked to one family, a handful of others worried about whether, or when, they might be contacted. Chuck Bennett got to convince the luckier girls that they were God's gift to tennis—although he admitted that it was really impossible to know, at such an early age, if a girl would fulfill her potential—or he got to break the heart of a less fortunate girl, and dismantle a family's hopes and dreams, simply by choosing not to pursue her.

But Chuck Bennett's personal discomfiture had no place in a business decision, and he knew it. He comforted himself with the knowledge that he hadn't created the situation—he was just doing the best he could under the current rules. If the marketplace wanted a new young star, IMG was going to try to find one. But privately, Bennett wondered about a selection process that, more and more, rewarded girls who had not yet proven themselves, and often prized novelty over consistent achievement.

Basically, women's tennis was starting to emphasize entertainment value as much as, if not more than, playing ability. With Martina Navratilova and Chris Evert Lloyd firmly entrenched in the top two spots, the purely athletic aspect of women's tennis was beginning to get a little boring; there was not a lot of suspense about who would win the major tournaments. If one of the other top-ranked women pros played

Martina or Chris, and lost as expected, it was not news. But if a youngster managed to take a few games, or, miracle of miracles, a set from either of those players, it was a great story. A girl on her way up could get media attention for a good loss, because everyone could speculate on how she would do in another year or two.

That attention translated into marketability, and drained profits away from some proven players. Women ranked in the top twenty-five were suddenly having trouble getting endorsements because companies preferred to spend money on starlets. Chuck Bennett was blunt about what he saw: IMG's clients wanted to invest in tomorrow's dreams. Everyone was on the lookout for a fourteen-year-old All-American blonde. Whenever a coach or agent strung three adjectives together to describe a junior girl, two of them applied to her game and one, invariably, referred to her appearance or poise.

"Right now the business is such that the companies, when they're signing people for endorsement deals, the only people they're signing are number one, two, three in the world," said Bennett. "Then there's this drop-off. You can be number eleven in the world and not be making any great money— while a young kid who's just turned pro, who's made the big impact so that people are willing to bet she's the next superstar, will be paid a ton of money. For everyone else in between it's really hard.

"It's fairly recent. The young ones have always had a darn good opportunity to make some real money. But generally, if you were in the top fifteen in the world, it wasn't a gigantic problem. But now they're really just looking for the top ones and the next superstars. It's incredible."

A younger girl, a potential star, was worth more than an older girl; a pretty girl worth more than a less attractive girl who might be a better player. Women's tennis might be a revolutionary concept, on one level, simply because it allowed women to make money for being athletic. But as a popular diversion, as an entertainment, it had rather traditional criteria for stardom.

With a slight squirm, Bennett confessed that Debbie

Spence, at sixteen, was too old to qualify as a young phenomenon. She had missed her chance at an all-out recruitment campaign. "I think she's a heck of a player," he said, "but age has a lot to do with it." If she had shown consistency at an earlier age—or if Tom and Francine had had the money to show her off, by sending her to more national and international events when she was younger—perhaps one of the agencies would have pursued her.

But there were the more delicate issues of appearance and attitude, which would have hurt her chances no matter what her age. Word of Debbie Spence's passing shots may have preceded her onto the national juniors scene, but so had word of what Bennett referred to, with a pained expression, as her "weight problem." It was tough to sell a sportswear client on a girl who constantly battled an extra ten pounds, and was not a classic beauty to begin with.

Debbie also lacked the kind of image the clients looked for. She was emphatically not a cool, poised personality. By the time she got done scrapping her way through a set, she rarely had a promotable appearance. A man was expected to give his all, to come off the court drenched in sweat, his hair plastered to his head, his clothes soaked. A woman player was supposed to work just as hard without looking as though she had. She had to contend with women like Chris Evert Lloyd and Tracy Austin, who somehow managed to win without wilting, and had set an aesthetic standard for the sport. The world still liked its women pretty.

Debbie didn't quite meet the industry's requirements. The consequences, as Bennett well knew, were that she would have "a hell of a time" moving forward, and Bennett, bound by the rules of the game, would not, could not, help her out. Certainly, no one was going to write off the number one junior girl in the country completely; Bennett kept track of her progress, and Parkes Brittain, over at Advantage International, had paid attention to her in Kansas City. But these were merely bet-hedging moves, in case Debbie suddenly started winning everything in sight, became a sylph, and acquired the cachet of a young Grace Kelly.

For now, she was on her own. IMG had passed her over and invested in another girl's future, the junior recruiters were already looking at younger girls, and Chuck Bennett was burning out. By the spring, he would with some relief move to a new job working for IMG's television arm, Trans World International, a position that did not require him to deal directly with aspiring tennis players.

In the weeks that followed the Kansas City tournament, the Spences had to face exactly how isolated they had become. Marianne Werdel's decision not to play doubles with Debbie continued to upset Francine, who liked to believe that the two families were good friends, despite the fact that they did not see each other socially. The Werdels had always been so nice to Debbie. In August, Corinne Werdel had taken Debbie out for a sweet-sixteen dinner on her birthday, when the girls were in Memphis, Tennessee, for the USTA National Junior Championships tournament. She had tried to get Debbie to eat some decent meals, instead of starving herself, at the U.S. Open.

Since Francine had been unable to travel with Debbie, she was very grateful for the Werdels' attentions. She planned to invite them to her daughter Terri's wedding, but now, after so many years, there was this business about the girls not playing together. It was a mystery, and Francine wanted to clear it up. Despite Tom's entreaties to let the matter drop, she called the Werdels and got Corinne on the phone.

Within minutes Francine was crying, and when Tom came into the room and asked what was wrong, she couldn't answer him. He took the phone away from her and asked Corinne to put Tom Werdel on the phone so that they could straighten the matter out. However enlightened it might be to encourage a daughter to pursue a career, men still took care of the serious business.

Tom Werdel insisted that there had been a simple misunderstanding. Marianne had arranged to play doubles with another girl in Kansas City because months earlier, at the U.S. Open, Debbie had told her that she did not plan to play any more junior tournaments. He and his daughter accepted Debbie's announced intention to become a pro as soon as possible, and made plans based on the assumption that she could no longer be Marianne's doubles partner on the amateur circuit.

Tom Spence hung up, repeated the conversation to his now sobbing wife, and then confessed his real fear—that the true cause of all the trouble was the letter he had written to the USTA this past summer when Debbie was left off the Junior Wimbledon recommendation list. The Werdels had admitted that they'd heard about the letter, and Tom worried, now, that they had taken offense.

Marianne Werdel's name had been at the top of the 1983 Junior Wimbledon list, even though she would end the year ranked third. All that Tom had done, in his letter, was to review his daughter's record, which happened to include wins over Marianne. He had been uncomfortable writing in the first place—he felt pushy calling attention to Debbie, when she should have been invited without his having to say a word—and now he imagined that the Werdels might be resentful of his effort.

Tom Werdel would continue to insist that there were no bad feelings, and Tom Spence would swear that he never intended for Debbie to profit at another girl's expense, that he only wanted her to have the opportunity she clearly had earned, but the damage was done. And, in truth, one girl could never move forward without pushing ahead of another. As the process narrowed down, at the end of a girl's amateur career, relationships with other players and their parents had to change. Families eventually realized that their individual goals exerted a stronger pull on their loyalties than did their common experience. They retreated, and regrouped, behind their budding celebrities.

For the Spences, that meant havoc in the weeks right after Thanksgiving. The center of activity in their house, a big U-shaped kitchen that opened onto a family room, was even more deserted than usual on weeknights. At eight in the evening the plaid couch and easy chairs that faced the big color television set were still unoccupied, and Francine had begun a dinner that would be eaten in shifts as Tom, Debbie, and Rhonda straggled in from various practice sessions. For Debbie was about to get another chance to play the pros, and in anticipation she was training with a vengeance.

The business with the Werdels had reminded Tom of something he would just as soon forget: that he had intervened on his daughter's behalf, over the invitation to Junior Wimbledon, and failed to get results. He had to figure out how to help Debbie. He called Parkes Brittain to inquire about wild-card possibilities at upcoming Virginia Slims and Ginny tournaments, but Parkes suggested instead that Debbie play in three USTA Satellite tournaments in Chicago, San Antonio, and Delray Beach, Florida. The satellite circuit started at Christmas, and, since the tournaments offered little in terms of prize money and computer points, Debbie would have no trouble getting in. She was good enough to win a satellite tournament, which would give her a psychological boost. Why sit around and wait for wild cards, and risk running out of time?

Tom offered Debbie a deal. He would let her play in all three satellite tournaments if she would enter two international junior events in December—the Maureen Connolly Brinker Continental Cup in Tarpon Springs, Florida, where she, by virtue of her ranking, would be one of two players to represent the United States, and the Orange Bowl in Miami Beach, a privately promoted event. She would have to go to Florida alone, but Tom would send Francine to meet her in Chicago.

It meant leaving Cerritos almost immediately, on December 9, but Debbie didn't care about the holidays. In Kansas City, she had forgotten all about Thanksgiving until someone pointed out to her what day it was. Her memories of Christmas were of a brief celebration squeezed in between tennis sessions. "I used to always have to play tennis on Christmas Day with my dad, so that wasn't fun. We'd wake up, open the presents, and then it was, 'OK, ready for tennis now?'" she said. She preferred the idea of spending Christmas at a tournament. "It's a relief to be on my own. It's like my vacation; nobody's going to be there."

But Francine believed in families being together for the holidays whenever possible, especially on Christmas, and she was not going to let tennis tournaments get in her way. She informed everyone that this year the Spence family would celebrate Christmas with a traditional party on December 8.

Aside from the timing, she was thrilled that Debbie was getting a chance to collect three pro tournaments, which meant she only needed one more before next fall. Although Francine had always been the one to stress patience, she disagreed with Tom about the need to have Debbie play junior tournaments to keep her match-ready. As usual, in matters of tennis, she had deferred to his judgment. But since Kansas City her attitude had changed. She was outspoken, for the first time, about Debbie's right to play the pro tournaments. Francine knew she had an edgy, headstrong daughter. Her first concern was keeping Debbie's interest engaged.

"Tom feels there's some good that comes out of losing," she said, laughing. "I sure can't see the advantage. I mean, I just don't feel it would help your morale any.

"Besides, whatever she's doing, if it's keeping her interest and she's not bored, that's good. If she's doing something that's boring her or depressing her, then that's not good."

While Debbie trained, Francine did her own, more internal preparations for her trip to Chicago. She didn't want to be nervous, the way she had been in Bakersfield—the way she had always been, to a degree. Her daughter faced a new challenge on the court; Francine aspired to a new level of behavior, befitting the mother of a young professional. She was determined to be less of a wreck and more of a stalwart companion.

It was difficult to be detached, though, when she was so wrapped up in her daughter's life. The boundaries of Francine's future had been drawn early—she would probably never be wildly rich, or a world traveler, or an independent career woman. But Debbie faced infinite possibilities. Francine felt a vicarious thrill whenever she thought about her daughter's future, and took Debbie's disappointments personally. A mother's dreams and a daughter's hopes overlapped.

To get ready, Francine thought about losing. She was staring down a foe: if she concentrated on it, perhaps she would be able to master the way she felt about it.

"I hate to say it, but you really feel like it's the end of the world when you've lost," she said, folding her own feelings in with her daughter's. When Debbie and Maria La Franchi lost their doubles match last year at the Orange Bowl, we drove over to the mall and it was like, 'Well, what do we do now? The world's over! Everything's ended!' We sat in the car composing ourselves, deciding, 'What do we do now?' You really don't feel like a movie because you feel down. . . . And anything I say isn't really helpful, except I still do say things."

She drifted for a moment.

"When Debbie lost in Anaheim to Melissa she was really down and out. I think you have to cry. There's a lot of emotion going on out there on the court. And you have to hold that emotion if you're good, hold it back, because the goal is to play well and you can't fall apart on the courts. So you hold it back, and after the match it's like, 'Uuuuhhhh' "—she exhaled deeply—"you let it out."

Francine hadn't realized how deeply Debbie's matches affected her until that day in Florida, when she suggested sightseeing to cheer up the girls. There they were, sitting in a car in a parking lot at a shopping mall, when they could have been driving around, having a good time. The girls didn't want to budge. Francine, sure that they would all feel fine if they just found something to do, kept on about sightseeing until Debbie and Maria said they'd rather wander around the mall.

"So I let them out of the car and they went in," recalled Francine, "and *I* sat in the car and cried. You do have that emotion. When you're watching them in a match it's almost like you're playing. When it's over I guess you feel like *you've* lost. I don't really feel that close to the game, but you do want them to do so well. Ahh. You do feel low."

A teenager who thinks she has a particular talent can be a potent force in a family. If she thinks she has a timetable as well, she can become an emotional blackmailer, accusing any-one who questions her pace of trying to trip her up. Debbie was not yet truly confident about herself—a lot of what passed for confidence was really 'pose, or mimicry, or bravado—but she knew she was exceptional when it came to tennis. If any-thing, the misgivings that accompanied adolescence, the awk-wardness of suddenly being neither child nor adult, only hard-ened her desire to move into the pro ranks, to pursue the one thing she did reassuringly well.

She knew, with a certainty peculiar to all teenagers, that her parents and their contemporaries were incapable of under-standing her. Under normal circumstances a teenager tended to regard her parents with world-weary condescension; par-ents were too old and too settled to know anything at all. With someone like Debbie, who believed that her career was at stake, parental sluggishness became life-threatening. Turning pro was an escape from what a sixteen-year-old saw as paralyz-ing cautiousness. The fear of being held back was as strong a feeling as the desire to succeed.

The satellite tournaments were just what she needed to break out of the juniors, and she took her father's willingness to let her play them as an indication of a shift in their relation-ship. He wasn't giving up on the juniors entirely, with the two Florida tournaments, but his position clearly had eroded. He hadn't insisted that she play the two Florida junior tourna-ments; he'd had to bargain with her, and offer her the entice-ment of the satellites, to get her to agree.

There was a change in Debbie, too. She began to assert herself, as if she were on the court and suddenly sensed an opponent's fatal weakness. When she got home from practice that night, in between bites of a late dinner, she talked non-stop about where she was going to play and when she was going to turn pro, almost daring Tom to contradict her. Just in case he tried, she peppered her comments with "like," "y'know," and various strings of vowels, a typical enough teen-age defense against being interrupted while she took time to think.

It was, she insisted, time to move on. "I've been in the

juniors a long time," she began. "I just want to get up there and see where I am. I'm kind of anxious.

"There were supposed to be four satellite tournaments, that's how many there were last year, but this year there's only three, so I'm going to play all three and that'll be five. Then, if you get to, like, the semis or finals of one of the three satellites you get to move up into the Ginny tournaments. Like, there's a Ginny of Indianapolis and there's a Ginny of Houston. Like, a couple of weeks after that in February. Then if I get to the semis, y'know, I get right into that. And that could be the sixth one.

"Then after I get on the computer it'll probably be around, you know, February, and I'll see where I am. Hopefully I'd like to get to the top hundred and forty because then you can get into the main draw of, like, the Italian Open, the French Open, and Wimbledon, all the main tournaments coming up. The main draw's a hundred and twenty-eight players and some people don't play. So that's what I'd like to do.

"Then I'll go to the Italian, and if I go two or three rounds, then that's a good sign. Maybe turn pro. . . ."

She hesitated for an instant, to see if her parents would challenge her, but the plan met with no resistance. She started talking again, quickly, before they could think of an objection.

"Even if I do *bad* in the Italian and don't turn pro, I go to the French, see how I do. Then Wimbledon. After Wimbledon comes the U.S. Open. I'll have a couple of months to decide what to do. Maybe turn pro then."

A million things could go wrong between now and then, but having a strategy was a great comfort. It provided the illusion of control in a situation that was absolutely beyond control. Debbie often sat in the car before a match flipping the radio dial until she found a song she liked, "a good song, so when I go out on the court I'm singing a good song." It couldn't guarantee a win, but it did make Debbie feel better—and that could make a difference in the outcome of a match.

Coming up with a plan was like having a good song playing in her head all the time. If she repeated it to herself often enough, like a mantra, perhaps she would come to believe in it, and then, perhaps, it would come true. For her problem right now was not her physical game. Her problem was the game going on inside her head. She needed to concentrate on all the good things that were about to happen and block out any anxious thoughts about what had gone wrong recently. And she needed to feel that she was moving forward, instead of struggling to keep from falling behind.

Now that she was about to have a chance to get within one tournament of a computer ranking, she could confess how badly she wanted to turn pro.

"In the pros you get treated a lot better," she said. "I don't know how exactly. It's just *better.* You're just up there. I mean, in the juniors you still have another step to go. You're always a step behind, whatever you do. In the pros, that's it. You can't get any higher. You're there."

She also imagined that life would somehow be easier as a pro, because she would not have to be proving herself all the time. In her fantasy of the future, the pressure was magically gone, the jostling for position nonexistent. As a junior, she had been under constant pressure to compete, to show that she was capable of taking the next step. As a pro, she would essentially be working for herself, and she intended to be a reasonable boss. She believed she would be able to earn a good living and take some time off—and did not realize that this was a rather unrealistic prediction, the work of a tired mind.

She insisted that life would be less hectic. "Once you're in the pros you can pick your tournaments, you can sit there with the sheet of all the tournaments and figure it out, what you want to play," she said. "It's so much better that way. You know where you're going to be, what you're going to do. . . . If there's a tournament in a month, you could take, like, four days off. Or a week."

Which would give her time, she said, to "spend the money," on a teenager's catalogue of delights: "Shopping, tapes, little things like that. Cassette tapes. Walkmans. It's relaxing." Her parents did not point out that the list was predicated on the notion that they would continue to house and feed her. There was plenty of time to talk about money—and they understood that this rumination about the pros was really a protracted pep talk. The family's immediate concern was getting Debbie into a position to turn pro. If her daydreams about the easy life helped to motivate her, there was no reason to talk about economic realities.

Tom and Francine did what they could to bolster Debbie's confidence. Francine told Debbie how proud she was to have a daughter who could think for herself, who was starting to grow up instead of depending on her parents to make decisions for her. Tentatively, Francine talked about what a good idea it was for Debbie to get her ranking established, and she gently took Debbie's side on the issue of turning pro. Tom's problem, she joked, was that "fathers just don't want their daughters to grow up."

Tom contacted Jack Sharpe, who lived in a suburb outside Chicago and coached Michelle Torres, the promising amateur whom Debbie had beaten back in October, at the Florida Federal Open. Sharpe offered to let Debbie and Francine stay in his apartment during the Chicago Satellite tournament, while he stayed with his parents, so that the Spences could avoid a big hotel bill. He would arrange practice time at the courts where he worked.

And there was the car, Tom's extravagant gesture of good faith, meant to show Debbie the extent of her father's support. Tom was not the type for emotional declarations, so instead he put a down payment on a $14,000 dark brown Mazda RX-7 GSL sports car with automatic transmission, air-conditioning, power windows, a sunroof, and a tape player. It was not a gift; it was a loan. He and Debbie agreed that she would pay him back out of her first pro earnings.

The Spence family, July 1985: *(left to right)* mother Francine, Debbie, Terri, Rhonda, father Tom. Francine and Tom teach junior high school—and Tom holds down an extra job as a tennis coach to help subsidize his daughters' tennis.

Opposite Debbie Spence *(left)*, just turned sixteen, and doubles partner Shawn Foltz, fifteen, take an aerobics class between matches at the Florida Federal Open in Tarpon Springs, Florida, October 1983. Debilitating injuries on the women's tour have led to a new emphasis on overall fitness.

Below left Wearing her Walkman to block out distractions, Debbie Spence competes at the Virginia Slims tournament in Delray Beach, Florida, February 1985. In early 1984 she was an amateur player struggling to recover from mononucleosis and establish a Women's Tennis Association computer ranking; by the fall of that year, just after her seventeenth birthday, she began to travel the professional tennis circuit. (PHOTO BY MELINDA PHILLIPS)

Below right Debbie Spence, five months into her pro career, suffers a second-round loss to highly ranked Zina Garrison at the Virginia Slims of Washington, D.C., January 1985. (PHOTO BY CAROL NEWSOM)

Below left Fifteen-year-old Debbie Spence is the top-ranked player in the national girls' 18-and-under singles category; summer 1983. (PHOTO BY JANET ZAGORIA)

Below right Debbie Spence, playing "up" in the 18-and-under category at fifteen, wins the girls' singles title at the USTA Junior Hardcourt Championships in Burlingame, California, July 1983. (PHOTO BY JANET ZAGORIA)

Nine-year-old Debbie Spence *(left)* and eight-year-old Marianne Werdel, first- and second-place winners in the girls' 10-and-under singles competition at the 1976 Whittier, California, junior tournament.

Below Nine-year-old Debbie Spence works on her forehand at the public tennis courts in Cerritos, California, 1976.

The Gurney family, Christmas 1984: *(left to right)* Cinda, mother Carolyn, Melissa, father Ramsdell, Jr., and Robyn. Carolyn is a part-time nurse, Ram teaches history and coaches tennis at a private school—and Ram's father, a practicing physician in his eighties, provides financial aid so that his three granddaughters can travel the tennis circuit. (PHOTO BY CHERYL A. TRAENDLY)

Below Fifteen-year-old Melissa Gurney *(left)* takes Chris Evert Lloyd *(right)* to three sets before losing in the Virginia Slims of Los Angeles, October 1984. The match sparked controversy over whether young girls had the physical stamina to survive on the pro tour without risking injury—and fueled the argument that there should be a minimum age for turning pro as well as restrictions on the number of pro tournaments a young player could enter. (PHOTO BY CHERYL A. TRAENDLY)

Opposite Top amateur player Melissa Gurney competes in the Virginia Slims professional tournament in Los Angeles, October 1984. Junior players compete on the pro circuit for experience, exposure, and computer ranking points before they turn pro. (PHOTO BY CHERYL A. TRAENDLY)

Fifteen-year-old Melissa Gurney, who shared the number one ranking in the national 18-and-under singles category with another player in 1984—her last year as an amateur— with her dog Fritz, on the beach in southern California. (PHOTO BY CHERYL A. TRAENDLY)

Nine-year-old Melissa Gurney *(right)* and seven-year-old Cinda, Rancho Palos Verdes, California, 1978. Melissa began playing tennis when she was four years old.

Above Thirteen-year-old Shawn Foltz *(left)* and Carling Bassett, stars of *Spring Fever,* a Canadian film about the pressures young tennis players face, which was financed by Carling's father, John. Shawn played the rich girl who got caught in a lie; Carling was the sweet, hardworking kid who beat her.

Left At sixteen, aspiring model Shawn Foltz had her picture taken by entertainer—and tennis aficionado—Kenny Rogers at his farm in Athens, Georgia, late in 1984. She sported a much different look, **opposite**, as she progressed in the Lipton International Players Championships in Delray Beach, Florida, February 1985. (PHOTO BY CAROL NEWSOM)

Right Shawn Foltz *(right),* decked out in old-fashioned tennis clothes for a publicity photograph, and her mother, Pat, at Wimbledon, July 1985. Pat travels with her daughter— she spent one school year living in Florida and another in California, where Shawn was training, while her husband, Wally, and son, Brett, stayed home in Indianapolis. (PHOTO BY CAROL NEWSOM)

Marianne Werdel, summer 1985. Marianne's father, Tom, is an attorney, and her mother, Corinne, is a member of the wealthy Chandler family, whose media empire includes *The Los Angeles Times;* they have always stressed the importance of a college education and imagined that Marianne might one day follow in her father's professional footsteps. Despite the current pressures to turn pro early, Marianne decided to accept a full tennis scholarship to Stanford University.

Fifteen-year-old Marianne Werdel *(left)* with her sisters Alyse *(center),* a member of the Stanford University women's tennis team, and Hilary *(right),* Bakersfield, California, 1983. Marianne was ranked number three nationally in girls' 18-and-under singles that year. (PHOTO BY ROXANNE)

Eight-year-old Marianne Werdel, Bakersfield, 1976. She and Debbie Spence dominated southern California junior competition until they graduated from the ranks—Debbie into the pros in 1984, and Marianne into international junior competition and then college in 1985.

Coach Robert Lansdorp, whose past pupils include Tracy Austin, once the top-ranked woman player in the world, has worked with Debbie Spence, Melissa Gurney, Shawn Foltz, and Marianne Werdel. He is the West Coast guru for young players who want to turn pro. With his daughter Stephanie Michelle at the West End Tennis and Racquet Club, summer 1985.

8
USTA Satellite Circuit— January 1984

Women's professional tennis was too young and volatile to be steeped in tradition, so its value system was based, instead, on superstition. There were personal fetishes—when and whether a girl called home, what she listened to before, and drank during, a match—and there was a body of folk wisdom about the various tournaments. A player knew which pro tournaments she needed to win for the sake of statistics, but she also believed that certain amateur victories would bring her good luck.

The thirty-seventh annual Orange Bowl International Junior Tennis Championships, held in December at the Flamingo Park Tennis Center in Miami Beach, Florida, was considered an important win. Women who had gone on to become tennis celebrities had won this tournament—Chris Evert Lloyd in 1969 and 1970, Andrea Jaeger in 1978, and, in 1982, Carling Bassett, a wealthy, attractive player/model /actress who was quickly dubbed "Darling Carling" by the media. That qualified as a trend. Players believed that the victor here was guaranteed attention as the latest in a string of players who won the Orange Bowl on her way to bigger and better things. For a girl like Debbie, who was having trouble generating her own self-confidence, a win would be a welcome boost. Feeling flattered was a decent interim substitute for feeling sure.

Debbie came into the tournament flying. She and Caroline Kuhlman, representing the United States in the 18-and-under category, had just defeated two girls from the Soviet Union in the finals of the Continental Cup. Debbie was tired, as she always was by the end of a tournament, but she was exhilarated. The Continental Cup victory had settled her nerves somewhat. If she could keep her momentum, and win the

Orange Bowl, she knew she would do well in the USTA Satellite Circuit tournaments.

Her state of mind was further enhanced by the fact that she faced a fresh set of foes, instead of the girls who had witnessed her recent lapses. Marianne Werdel, Stephanie Rehe, and Melissa Gurney had chosen not to play the Orange Bowl; Debbie was one of sixty-four girls from all over the world, most of whom she'd never met before. Shawn Foltz was here with her mother, Pat, but she posed no threat, having decided to play in the 16s instead of the 18s. The Foltzes were staying in the same hotel as Debbie—almost as good as if Francine were here to keep a watchful eye on her daughter.

The two girls played marvelous tennis, marching in tandem toward the finals. On Saturday, Christmas Eve, Shawn Foltz won both the singles and doubles titles in the 16s, and prepared for her triumphant return to Indianapolis on Christmas Day. Debbie had a semifinal match against Austria's Petra Huber on the morning of Christmas Eve, which she won 7–6, 0–6, 6–0.

Afterward she complained about a mild sore throat and decided to spend the rest of the day in her hotel room, taking it easy. That night she got about four hours of sleep, and woke up Christmas morning feeling weak. The pain in her throat seemed to have congealed into three knots in her neck. Luckily, the players had Christmas Day off, so Debbie hung around the hotel, alone, talked to her folks long-distance, and tried not to get nervous about her final match.

On Monday morning, still not feeling up to par, she got dressed and headed down to the courts. Her opponent in the final, Anna Maria Cecchini of Italy, was ranked number two in the international juniors, 18-and-under. Debbie didn't have an international junior ranking, because her parents couldn't afford to send her to enough international tournaments to qualify. But she did have the edge with the crowd, which could be just as intimidating to an opponent as a high ranking.

American fans were aggressively patriotic about their tennis, and American tennis parents could be the loudest spectators of all. They often were resentful of foreign players, who were given berths in international tournaments like this one at the expense, many parents felt, of their children's progress —as if tennis were an American sport and outsiders tolerated only as a favor, conveniently forgetting that American girls played in all the European junior tournaments.

Financially strapped families looked at the Eastern European players in particular, who benefited from strong tennis federations which administered government-subsidized training programs, and rooted even more enthusiastically for the hometown girls. The pretense of pure amateurism in the United States—the "loaned" equipment and clothing, the convoluted system of reimbursements—put the burden of support on parents, setting them against each other in a competition based on money. Whoever had the most could do the most for their child. In many European countries, a girl's talent was a more important asset than her parents' bank accounts. Under these circumstances, it was often difficult for an American parent to maintain a sportsmanlike attitude.

The combination of envy, resentment, and defensive pride could make an American crowd rowdy. When Debbie lost the first set 6–2, a wall of sound rose from the stands, encouraging her not to give up. "I wasn't feeling well," she would tell her mother when they met in Chicago, "and I was starting to get nervous. But I didn't want to let everyone down."

She didn't. Debbie outlasted Cecchini in close second and third sets, 7–5, 6–4, the crowd went crazy, and the latest Orange Bowl star headed back to the hotel to pack for the trip to Chicago. Despite the increasing soreness in her throat, she felt great. She had won the tournament under less than ideal conditions—feeling tired and a little achy. Imagine what she would be able to do after a few days' rest. She would meet her mother in Chicago, collapse, and let Francine wait on her. By the time the USTA Satellite Circuit tournament began, on the following Monday, January 2, Debbie would be ready to go after her computer ranking.

Francine arrived at O'Hare International Airport in Chicago late on Monday and waited for Debbie's flight to arrive at 10:00 P.M. When Debbie got off the plane, Francine thought she looked terrible. But then, Francine *always* thought Debbie looked terrible after a tournament. She asked Debbie how she felt, and Debbie described symptoms that sounded like the beginning of a strep throat, which was easy to fight with antibiotics. Francine decided that the first thing on their agenda was to get Debbie's illness under control.

Jack Sharpe, the coach Tom had contacted, met Francine and Debbie at the airport. He loaded their things into his car and headed for his parents' home, hoping that they would have some medicine to relieve the pain in Debbie's throat. Sharpe's parents gave Francine a bottle of ampicillin, which would knock out a strep infection almost immediately, and Francine and Debbie drove over to Sharpe's apartment and went to sleep. Tuesday morning Debbie was no better, so Francine got the name of a doctor from the coach and made an appointment for later that morning.

Her primary concern was to alleviate the symptoms so that Debbie could compete. It was not unusual for a player to come up with a physical complaint before a big match. Since the girls on the circuit were under such pressure, every now and then the stress overflowed into a sniffle, or a stomachache, or a sore throat. The ailments rarely lasted very long.

After the doctor examined Debbie, Francine explained their predicament. "We told the doctor: 'We want this kid to get better in two days. What've you got?' " she recalled. He told her to have Debbie continue taking the ampicillin. "So we went home and she took it."

The next twenty-four hours were frightening. Whatever this was, it was clearly more than a fleeting physical manifestation of nerves. Debbie didn't improve; in fact, she got worse. She said she was having trouble breathing, and her glands were swollen. Still, neither Debbie nor Francine was willing to entertain the notion that Debbie was too ill to compete. They acted as if they could will Debbie's mounting complaints to be inconsequential: they would pretend nothing was wrong, and so nothing would be wrong.

Francine insisted that more rest and good nutrition were

the answer. Debbie only need to relax, eat right, and give the medicine a chance to work. But Debbie couldn't seem to sleep for more than a few hours at a time, and she had no interest in food. So Francine closed all the blinds in the apartment to keep it dark and make it easier for Debbie to sleep—and Francine began sleeping fitfully, getting up whenever her daughter did, catching a snack every now and then, until she lost track of whether it was day or night.

Then, in the middle of the night, Debbie woke her mother with a new complaint: her jaw hurt. Francine, who had woken up a few times and not known where she was, was overtired and disoriented. She panicked.

"I think, *lockjaw*," said Francine. "What am I going to do if she actually stops breathing? I've heard of reactions to medicine where everything tightens up. It was two o'clock in the morning, and when I called the doctor's answering service I got the emergency doctor."

He advised Francine to give Debbie ice water to drink and a couple of aspirin, and offered to come over in an hour if she did not feel better. "I think he said that," she said, later, "to relieve my mental state."

But he also said the one thing Francine did not want to hear, since he understood only symptoms and diagnosis, and not their career ramifications. " 'Don't be alarmed,' he told me, 'but it could be mono.' "

Francine still hoped to stave off disaster. She spent the early hours of Wednesday morning swabbing Debbie with a cold washcloth, giving her glass after glass of ice water to drink, and trying to calm her down. When the doctor's office opened, they were there. Debbie took a blood test and got the bad news. The test showed an abnormally high white-blood-cell count. She had infectious mononucleosis.

The doctor explained that the best way to get over the disease was to give in to it. Debbie needed bed rest—and she had to avoid physical exertion. Two months of recuperation might be a good idea.

As Francine and Debbie left the office, the nurse asked if Debbie needed assistance out to the car. Francine, who seemed suddenly to have focused on exactly how weak her daughter was, urged Debbie to accept the offer of a wheelchair rather than walk the distance to the parking lot, but Debbie turned them down and slowly made her way outside.

Her plans, and the happy dreams that rode on them, were ruined. There was nothing to do but give up and go home. Francine and Debbie left Chicago the next night and flew back to Los Angeles, where Debbie, after only two days of complete bed rest, began complaining. Francine, desperate for ways to entertain Debbie at home, tried to interest her in the plans for her sister Terri's wedding, which was less than six weeks away, but the idea backfired. There had been a time when Francine had joked about having to schedule the wedding during a hole in Debbie's tennis schedule. Now there was a gaping chasm. Debbie should have attended her sister's wedding after playing in Chicago, San Antonio, and Delray Beach; she should have been within one tournament of a computer ranking. Instead, she was an invalid. Talking about the wedding did not cheer her up.

Undaunted, Francine bought two tight-fitting plastic caps with tiny holes in them and spent an afternoon adding blond highlights to her daughter's hair, and lightening her own, by pulling strands of hair through the holes and painting them with dye. She tried to get Debbie excited about her bridesmaid's dress, a long, dusty-rose gown with thin shoulder straps and a short vest. Debbie observed that her tennis tan—which ran up her arms to the place where the short sleeves of a Fila tennis shirt began, and down her neck to the V of an open shirt collar, and had gotten darker thanks to the weeks she had just spent in Florida—would look ridiculous with the dress.

There was no way to distract or console her. She knew the pro schedule for the coming months by heart, and the three satellite tournaments had been crucial to her plan to be on the computer in time to qualify for the European tournaments, which began in May, and improve her ranking over the summer. The alternatives were all either more expensive or more difficult, or both.

She could try some of the pro tournaments in Mexico and

South America, but that would mean asking her father to finance an awful lot of travel, just because his daughter was in a hurry. Or she could struggle through a Virginia Slims tournament, but the competition would be extremely tough—if she got in at all, and that was doubtful.

Four months into the new 1984 ranking year, her 1983 number one ranking a bit tarnished by her defeats in Anaheim and Kansas City, she had little chance of being invited to a pro tournament just because she was a top junior. Being the best had helped get her started at the U.S. Open and the Bakersfield Ginny, but too much had happened since then. To get a wild card she needed an agent behind her. Not someone like Parkes Brittain, who exhibited sporadic interest in Debbie's career, but someone who aggressively wanted to recruit her.

She was at an impasse. Unless she did something, soon, she faced a particularly unattractive choice: she could back up and play enough junior tournaments to get a 1984 ranking in the 18s, which would surely be lower than number one, given her performance in junior tournaments so far, or she could give up on Europe, try to find some more satellite tournaments to play over the summer, and get onto the computer by fall. Then, if her ranking wasn't high enough, she might have to spend months working it up to an acceptable level to turn pro.

Any way she looked at it, she saw months of delay. Meanwhile, the other girls made progress. Marianne Werdel's parents were sending her to Ginny tournaments and then, later in the spring, to international junior tournaments in the Far East and a pro tournament in London. Melissa Gurney was playing the USTA tournaments in Chicago and San Antonio that Debbie had missed.

This was agony. All Debbie wanted was to get back on the tennis court, but Francine kept talking about taking it easy. Debbie nagged incessantly. Her initial symptoms, the sore throat and swollen glands, had disappeared almost completely. Why should she have to stay in bed if she felt better? She admitted that she tired easily, but being tired was nothing new to a junior player who was used to jumping time zones, getting off a plane, and playing a match. After less than two weeks at home, she started talking about catching the last USTA tournament in Delray Beach, during the third week in January.

The family doctor put an end to that notion. He took another blood test, confirmed the diagnosis of mono, and advised Debbie to take at least four more weeks off, which meant skipping Delray Beach. He explained that the disease could show up in a patient's blood as long as six months after its onset. Debbie might feel fine, but she might still be sick—and she would definitely start to feel sick as soon as she exerted herself.

She hung around the house for another week and then ventured out for a couple of practice sessions. "I feel *much* better today," she said, to anyone who would listen. She might confess that she still felt weak to Shawn Foltz, who often drove out to Cerritos to visit her friend, but she couldn't afford to waste any more time.

Neither Francine nor Tom had the heart to insist that she stay at home. They worried about psychological, as well as physical, damage. A bad loss called a girl's very being into question, at least until she won her next match. Mono was that kind of disappointment multiplied many times over. The challenge, for Debbie, lay in maintaining a healthy state of mind while her body got better. If hitting balls for an hour improved her attitude, no one had the heart to tell her to give it up.

Francine and Tom were determined that Debbie not return to competition until she was well enough to play her best—but they also wanted to get her back on her feet before she began to doubt herself. Tom judged his daughter on a rather simple scale: either she looked good on the court or she didn't, and if she didn't she wasn't ready to compete. Francine—who, like her daughter, had been full of adrenaline, ready for that month-long series of tournaments—felt torn in two. As a mother, she wanted to keep Debbie home until the blood tests were completely clear. As a *tennis* mother, she was all too aware of her daughter's addiction to forward motion.

Deprived of the chance to compete and progress for too long, Debbie could lose her mental edge—be entirely cured and insufficiently confident. Francine found herself watching Debbie for hopeful signs. She wanted to believe that her daughter's exceptional physical condition would enable her to beat the medical estimates of recovery time, which were, after all, for average children.

There is a fine line between encouragement and unyielding pressure, as every parent and player knows. Over the past few years, some girls had found that they couldn't handle the stress of constant competition and never-ending scrutiny. They had to walk away from tennis because the tension was ruining their lives—making it impossible to think about anything else or survive a match without becoming physically ill. Some, terrified that they would not catch the corporate eye because they were a pound overweight, became borderline anorectics.

At first, tennis families dismissed the horror stories as isolated cases, and assumed that there must have been something wrong with the girl, or her parents, in the first place; she was not sufficiently dedicated, or they were the sports version of stage parents. But in the last year, two of women's tennis' shining lights, Andrea Jaeger and Tracy Austin, had short-circuited. Jaeger was quickly earning a reputation as the distaff John McEnroe, a petulant, difficult girl with a loud mouth and a brash attitude, while Austin, still the sport's sweetheart, remained unable to compete because of her physical ailments.

Parents of a top teenage player had to look into the future, see the spectres of two disabled players, and wonder whether their child would suffer a similar fate. Tracy's agent, Sara Kleppinger, believed that a lot of today's precocious juniors were going to crash-land before they were twenty, victims of having moved too far, too fast.

Part of the problem was that any child who had been well trained would pressure herself, internally: Debbie Spence's desire to get right back on the court, despite her illness, was in line with the way a top competitor was supposed to behave. If she hesitated for a moment, someone else would step in front of her and take her place. Even if Francine and Tom took it easy on her, Debbie would still push herself. That was what they had always taught her to do.

Andrea Jaeger, who started out in 1980 as pro tennis' pig-tailed fourteen-year-old darling, had done what she was supposed to do, and it almost finished her career. People who had seen her play recently thought she was simply being an uncooperative brat, playing poorly, losing interest in the middle of a match—suffering, the word was, from mental burnout.

In fact, she was being the epitome of the hard-driving pro. She was playing injured, and not telling anyone about it because she was supposed to play, and that was that. Her emotional outbursts on court, she would admit months from now, were because she was in pain and didn't know where to turn for help. She was afraid to break down and tell people about her problems, afraid to take time off to heal—only to find that the longer she kept quiet, the more people accused her of malingering. She was keeping a rather large secret—and the pressure she was under, from her parents and herself, was making her miserable.

"I played so long injured it looked like I was tanking matches," she would confess, referring to the practice of giving up and deliberately losing a tough match. "But really, I was just confused about what to do, whether to default or what. It took me a long time to make a decision. The doctors had to just about hit me across the face to get me to listen.

"I go out there with the right attitude and give a hundred and fifty percent. But when I feel bad and people are giving me a hard time and my shoulder hurts, then I *don't* have the right attitude. I mean, I'll go out with my shoulder hurting and I can't serve and it'll get worse during a match. So I'll get irritable. But people don't know how much sleep I've lost over that shoulder, how upset I am. They just look at me and say, 'Oh, mental burnout.' "

No one, in this souped-up race for stardom, had ever figured out how to take a rest. Andrea Jaeger was headed for an enforced rest, later in 1984, when, debilitated by a catalogue of physical complaints, she announced that she was taking a break from pro tennis. Still, players and parents—who had a career to consider—would continue to discount what happened to her, insist that they were not pushing as hard as some families were, and persevere.

Tracy Austin didn't scare them, either, although she was becoming more vocal on the subject of crime—pressure-cooker tennis—and subsequent punishments, like being incapacitated for years on end. She was blunt: in a blind rush to get back into tennis before it passed her by, she had done herself considerable harm.

When the sciatic nerve in Tracy's back first acted up, in 1980, she gave herself what she thought was enough time for an exceedingly fit young woman to recover. Her estimate turned out to be wrong. She stayed out long enough for her back to heal, but did not spend enough time getting into shape before she returned to competition. She continued to have trouble with her back, and then her hip, and her shoulder, a terrifying series of ailments that had kept her from playing a complete year's circuit in the four years since.

Now she sat on the sofa in her parents' home in Palos Verdes Peninsula, a wealthy community overlooking the Pacific Ocean south of Los Angeles, and blamed impatience for her problems. Her mother had answered the door in a tennis outfit, but Tracy wore a jogging outfit and running shoes, symbols of yet another exercise regimen designed to get her body back into tournament condition. The three months she had spent in Australia had not quite done the trick, so she had embarked on another overall exercise program, to try to compensate for the early damage she had done herself.

Tracy considered her impeccable manicure and spoke, softly, of how foolish she felt she had been, and how fearful she was for the young players today, who were under even more pressure than she had been. "The back injury was a freak thing, and then basically because I was out so long it was a vicious cycle," she said. "I was out of shape and I was so eager. Probably like Debbie. You don't see that a month is important at that point. You can't wait a month. Even though you can play till you're thirty-five, a month, at that point, is like *fifteen years*. You've got to do it *now*. You can't wait a month.

"That was my problem." She stared out the window. "That's why, finally, I have to strap myself down and say, 'You've got to be patient and you've got to be totally fit and strong again before you go out on the court.' I was so eager to get on the court—I was so out of shape—things were hurting and I was still going out there, just because I wanted to play tennis."

Hindsight analysts tended to think that Tracy would have recovered more quickly from her initial back trouble if she had been in better overall shape to begin with—a convenient interpretation, because it implied that a general fitness program would protect other children from her sad fate. When worried parents confronted Robert Lansdorp, wondering if they were pushing their children too hard, too early, he prescribed running, jumping rope, lifting weights, and aerobics classes. Training was the best defense against having to wait out an injury.

That theory made Tracy's eyes flash with resentment. The player who personified the youth movement in women's tennis was beginning to bridle at people's attempts to label her as an exception, a girl whose body had let her down. She believed that junior girls today were in just as much jeopardy, stood as much a chance of wrecking themselves, as she had been. Certainly, a girl who wasn't in shape would never survive—but even the fittest could end up a casualty of the accelerated schedule of women's tennis.

When Tracy turned pro, the only pressure she felt was internal: she had been ranked number one in the 18-and-under category when she was only fourteen, and again at fifteen. She had progressed to quarterfinal rounds of major professional tournaments as an amateur. She turned pro because it was the logical thing to do, and yet she did so with more ambivalence than most people remembered.

"I thought if I changed something, then everything would be pulled out from under me," she said. "Why should I change if I was happy the way I was, just playing juniors? It was hard for me to change. But then I finally realized there was really nothing left for me in the juniors—and also, I had been up there in the pros and played a while."

Tracy had the lonely luxury of being the only fifteen-year-old in a position to turn pro in 1979, and even then she had felt rushed. But over the last few years, the nuances of Tracy

Austin's transition had been forgotten. In the mythic recounting of her rise to celebrity status, the only things that mattered were that she had turned pro at fifteen and made a bundle of money. No one stopped to contemplate what had happened to her—whether she had made mistakes, in the name of adolescent enthusiasm, that she was paying for to this day.

There was no time for careful reflection. The current crop of junior girls was doubly hurried, because there was a new level of competition, beyond the literal one—the jostling to be the next potential star. Five years ago Tracy Austin could decide to compete in the 18-and-under category for a second year, to make sure she was ready for the pros, without worrying that another girl would step in front of her and grab a lucrative endorsement. Today there were more girls fighting for a finite number of deals. Tracy felt badly for today's junior girls, who were, she thought, "pushing and shoving to get their contracts."

It was not an atmosphere conducive to reason, or caution. It was not a time when a girl like Debbie Spence could afford to stay in bed for very long.

In late February the blood test still showed that Debbie had mono, but she was out practicing several nights a week and hitting with her father on the weekends. They had a new goal. There was a $150,000 Virginia Slims tournament in Dallas on March 19, and Parkes Brittain, sympathetic to Debbie's plight, had written a letter requesting a wild card on her behalf. If that didn't come through, there was a southern California junior tournament in Long Beach at the beginning of March —a depressing alternative, to Debbie, but an opportunity to test herself in competition.

Suddenly the house was deserted again. Debbie and Tom were back on a tennis court. Terri Spence had gotten married, and she and her husband were living with Tom's parents temporarily while they finished out the school year. Rhonda was at her tennis lesson. Things were back to normal.

Francine was home alone, with the oven timer set to ring when it was time to pick up Rhonda. She opened two bulging scrapbooks on the big rectangular glass table that divided the kitchen from the family room. "I'm just a proud parent," she said, laughing. "I have about ten copies of everything."

There were articles, ranking sheets, photographs, even a cardboard sign from some long-ago doubles tournament identifying one set of partners, "Werdel/Spence," in stenciled letters. There was a picture of ball girl Debbie Spence and a bunch of other kids with Chris Evert Lloyd in 1976, and a 1974 photo of Debbie with Billie Jean King. There was a 1977 picture of eight-year-old Marianne Werdel and Debbie wearing matching tennis outfits with appliquéd racquets on the front, and another, later photo of the two girls posed with Mickey Mouse and Goofy at a Sport Goofy Tournament at Disneyland. And there was one of Francine's favorite pictures—of a very young Debbie Spence asleep in her seat during a Chris Evert Lloyd match.

"Debbie was such a little twerp. Even Terri was very young. We were so excited about Robert taking them on," she said softly, recalling the time, almost eight years ago, when Robert Lansdorp had agreed to give the girls lessons. "We were basically the bottom of the line at the time. They played one hundred percent. It was like playing with the pros."

There were fuzzy home movies, too, from Debbie's earlier days: Debbie scurrying at a charity exhibition match in Calabasas, California, Debbie and Tom playing doubles together, and Debbie playing an exhibition at the opening of the West End Tennis and Racquet Club in 1978. Her opponent was a big, blowsy brunette—coach Robert Lansdorp in drag.

The pictures and movies stopped abruptly that year, when Debbie started to complain that her mother was embarrassing her with the constant attention, and did not pick up again until the summer of 1983, at the National Sports Festival tournament in Colorado Springs, Colorado. Debbie maintained her own, private collection of photographs and articles which she would not allow to be shown, and Francine intended to put these books away before her daughter returned home.

She tried to be considerate of Debbie's feelings these days. Although Debbie did not like to talk about her illness, and the missed tournaments, Francine knew that her daughter was terribly upset.

"I think she's nervous about getting enough tournaments, and about how she'll do," said Francine. "She was *all* geared up when she got sick. She was so ready, psychologically. She doesn't talk about it a whole lot, but I know she wants to do well. She's anxious. It's like something you want to hurry up and get over with, so you can see how you did."

Francine wanted to see Debbie get into the Dallas Virginia Slims, and, although she was grateful for Parkes Brittain's attention, she was not content to sit around and wait for him to get results. He had written to request the wild card almost a month ago, and had heard nothing. Francine encouraged Debbie to get on the phone with the Virginia Slims people herself and push for the wild card. It might not make a difference, but at least Debbie would have something to do. Francine wanted her daughter to feel that she could begin to make progress again, that she could take steps to control her future.

She also wanted to help Debbie avoid the junior tournament in Long Beach. In her own way, Francine had begun to push Debbie more than Tom did. He continued to define progress in purely physical terms: his goals were for Debbie to regain her health and her game. Francine evaluated Debbie's mental state and decided that the last thing her daughter needed was to slide back into the juniors. The best medicine, right now, would be the stiff challenge of a pro tournament, because that was what Debbie wanted. It would be hypocritical to contradict her.

Francine believed that Debbie's determination was a mark of maturity, proof that she and Tom had succeeded in teaching their daughter the virtues of independence and dedication to a task. Tennis parents often talked, with some pride, of the point in a player's development when she began to exhibit her own, internal desire to excel and no longer needed outside motivation. They began to defer to their offspring, and they interpreted what might only be an adolescent's dogged pursuit of a stable identity as something far better—the first signs of adulthood. The first week of March came and went, and no one suggested driving down to Long Beach for the junior tournament.

There were so many requests for wild cards into the Virginia Slims of Dallas that the promoters were forced to invite eight girls, including Debbie Spence and Melissa Gurney, to compete in a special three-match qualifying round for a wild card into the main draw. As far as time spent and risk taken, the arrangement was no better than the usual qualifying round setup, and Tom Spence was reluctant to spend the money to send Debbie to a pro tournament where she might not even get to compete.

Then, to everyone's surprised delight, Parkes Brittain called. He had been able to get Debbie a wild card into the $150,000 Virginia Slims of Florida, which was held at the PGA National Resort in Palm Beach Gardens, starting March 12, a week before the Dallas tournament. Francine thought it was a wonderful opportunity. "It's a matter of life and death," she said, with a gleeful laugh. "No. . . . But it really is."

Instinctively, Tom knew she was right. Debbie would be spared the rigors of the qualifying rounds, an important consideration, since her stamina had not been tested for almost three months, and she would be competing in a tournament that awarded more computer points than a Ginny or a USTA Satellite contest. As long as he was paying for a sure thing in Florida, he could even let Debbie take a chance on the wild-card qualifying rounds in Dallas, on her way home.

Still, he held back, worried that she was not in good enough shape to play two Virginia Slims tournaments back-to-back. He had already told Debbie that sending her to Dallas seemed extravagant to him. He was in a position to assert himself. He could stand fast and only let her play in Florida.

But that would be a pose—that was just authority for its own sake. Either he thought she was ready or he didn't, and if he did he had to support her. He tried to convince himself that it was all right to let her go to Dallas. Perhaps there was a hidden advantage. She would be one tournament closer to a ranking, which would alleviate some of the pressure she felt.

She might end up playing better. Tom thought it over and decided to let Debbie go, but he didn't tell her right away. He wanted a day to make sure the move felt right to him.

To assuage his doubts, he hired Chris Boyle, whose father ran the Chuck Boyle Tennis Academy in Santa Ana, as a traveling coach. It was better than sending Francine, at this point. Debbie needed someone with her who could pay attention to her game and help her practice, so that she would feel she was playing her best when the matches began. If Chris Boyle boosted Debbie's confidence and she advanced one round further than she otherwise might have, the expense was worth it.

As soon as Debbie left for Florida, though, Tom began to worry about what he had done. His options were not as clear as they used to be, and he disliked ambiguity. It wore him out. If he sent Debbie to Palm Beach and Dallas, he had to worry that he was endangering his daughter's health; if he made her stay home, he had to wonder if he was damaging her tennis.

On Monday night, March 12, the first day of the Palm Beach tournament, Tom talked to Debbie on the phone, learned that the day's matches had been rained out, and then collapsed into the recliner chair in the family room, looking deflated and vague. Francine bustled around the kitchen and Rhonda positioned herself in front of the television, while Tom stared into space, seeming not to notice all the activity that surrounded him.

Francine tried to draw him into a conversation. "I think Debbie will continue with her tennis until she drops," she announced proudly. "Her goal is to turn pro. If she were number two hundred for a year she'd hang in there. She's a fighter."

Tom grimaced. "*I'd* give up. She wouldn't be making any money."

"But that won't happen," insisted Francine. She thought about the difficult events of the past months. "I predict that Debbie will do very well. If she loses, she'll get right back in there. The kid hangs in there because her parents don't say 'Oh, take a month off.' You say, 'Keep going.' Because if you say, 'Hang on, take a rest,' then you have a kid who starts saying that too."

Tom winced, hearing his wife spout his own "always give a hundred and ten percent" philosophy. He'd worked his daughter right into an enforced layoff, and was beginning to wish he'd been less doctrinaire about Debbie's training schedule. "I've started praying for rain a few times this year, so I'd have an excuse to give her a rest," he joked, with a wan smile.

While Francine's confidence seemed to be increasing—possibly because she saw that Tom and Debbie needed her to be confident—his was at a low ebb. He talked about the confusion of being a tennis parent, of not knowing how to navigate the tournament schedule. He blamed himself for not contacting agents at the right time, and not knowing exactly what to ask for when he did.

He continued to berate himself for letting Debbie go to two pro tournaments. "Sometimes, you give up in frustration and just go with something. It's so hard to know what to do." As he so often did these days, he began to debate himself: "I think turning pro could be put off for too long—but at this young age, not really. I think the girl who steps out too soon runs the risk of not having developed her game sufficiently to go pro —but on the other hand, what if she loses as a junior? How can you ask somebody for a wild card then? Still, I believe in deferred payoff. You can defend your position as a junior even if you lose, and when you're a pro you're going to have to keep facing younger juniors."

It all came down to timing. Tom was uncomfortable because he believed in moving more cautiously than the pace of women's pro tennis, or his daughter's desire, seemed to allow. He did not want Debbie to be making the transition to pro quite so quickly—so far, haste had only gotten them in trouble —and yet, like his wife, he felt that it would be wrong to stand in her way.

Francine tried to tease her husband out of his depression. In a flirtatious tone of voice, she asked: If Debbie were a student instead of a tennis player, what grade would Tom give her? When Tom didn't respond, Francine straightened up and said,

"C'mon. Where's your confidence?"

Finally, he confessed the source of his current despair. When Debbie had called earlier in the evening she admitted, with some fear in her voice, that she was really tired. The conversation frightened Tom, and made him defensive. For a while he fell silent, satisfied to watch his youngest daughter watch TV and listen to his wife talk about how well things were going to work out.

Then, slowly, he began to talk himself out of his bad mood. A tennis parent had to maintain an even psychological keel, just like a player did. A negative attitude would only slow him down. So Tom Spence did exactly what Debbie Spence did when she felt herself floundering: he fixed his attention on some point in the future when things would be better. He reminded himself, as she did, that there was a long-range plan, a panacea for all of his short-range woes.

He started talking about the summer, by which time, he was sure, Debbie would be completely recovered and ready to tackle the European circuit. He knew she had had her heart set on having a ranking that would have gotten her into the main draws by then, but Tom had concocted an appealing alternative plan.

He hoped to take small revenge on the USTA for the slight, last year, when they omitted Debbie's name from the 1983 Junior Wimbledon invitation list. As the top-ranked junior in the country, Debbie had a good chance for an invitation to the 1984 Junior Italian Open, in May. And she undoubtedly would be on the list for the 1984 Junior Wimbledon, in July. The USTA paid travel expenses of girls who were invited to represent the United States at European tournaments and at Junior Wimbledon. Tom could send Debbie overseas a week early to pick up another pro tournament, both times, if he wanted to, without spending a penny.

His face brightened at the thought, even though he had not yet figured out how Debbie would get into the pro tournaments once she got there. Maybe someone would finally reward her with a wild card, or maybe she could play the qualifying rounds. Something would work out. In any case, he had figured out how to get her into one, and maybe two, more pro tournaments. If Debbie did her part and won the wild card next week in Dallas, she might have her computer ranking in early July.

Tom was pleased with his plan. Debbie would be on the computer before her year was up. He would have spared his daughter the indignity of settling for another junior ranking, and saved himself the expense of chasing more Virginia Slims tournaments.

Francine, relieved to hear him speak positively of the future, eagerly echoed his position. "The USTA was embarrassed once, on Wimbledon," she said. "They wouldn't want to overlook her again."

The next day, Debbie lost her first-round match at the Virginia Slims of Florida. She won only one game in each set and missed a lot of drop shots because she wasn't moving fast enough. She had to face the fact that she still wasn't in peak condition—and she wasn't enthusiastic about the mental stress of having to play other juniors for the chance to compete with the pros in Dallas. It seemed like an opportunity for a high-profile defeat, and she was wary enough to suggest to Chris Boyle that she might prefer to go home.

Debbie did not call her father to consult with him. She thought it over herself, decided not to take the chance, and flew home. Since her ticket had been written with a stopover in Dallas, her one act there was to get off the plane and call her parents to inform them that she was on her way. Tom wasn't there. Debbie told Francine what she'd done and got back on the plane.

When Tom found out, he was furious. He and Debbie had disagreed, ever since the U.S. Open, on the correct strategy for this year, but at least they had talked to each other. This was the first time she had openly ignored him, after he had paid for the plane ticket and the traveling coach.

He announced that Debbie would have to compete in the Easter Bowl, a major junior tournament held in Tucson, Arizona, in mid-April. He didn't want to hear about how much she hated playing the juniors. She had to prove herself to him.

Courtships

Melissa Gurney, who was still three months shy of her fifteenth birthday, won the wild-card qualifying round for the Virginia Slims of Dallas, and won her first-round match in the main draw, losing to Helena Sukova, ranked seventeenth in the world, in the second round. Parkes Brittain of Advantage International started thinking about which European tournament promoters he could contact for wild cards for her, while Jim Curley, the IMG account executive who did a lot of junior recruitment, wrote to the Gurneys to offer whatever assistance they required.

Melissa was exactly the kind of girl they were looking for. She was fast and decisive on court, possessed of a graceful, imperturbable style. She was young enough to qualify as a phenomenon, a more dramatic, and so more marketable, commodity than an older girl who had worked her way up. On top of that, she was pretty: she had shiny, honey-blond hair that she wore in a ponytail, perky bangs, and her once-gangly form was taking on a trim, long-legged shape. If Melissa Gurney lived up to her potential, she would be easy to sell.

The response from the agents pleased and startled the Gurneys, who suddenly realized that Melissa's moment might be upon them. The race in the girls' 18-and-under category in southern California had shifted since Thanksgiving, when Melissa was eliminated in the quarterfinals of the USTA Junior Indoor Championships in Kansas City. Debbie Spence's illness put pressure on her to ignore amateur tournaments in favor of the pro circuit, and Marianne Werdel was concentrating on the international junior circuit and the pros. Melissa had won a southern California tournament in Whittier, in January, and lost to Stephanie Rehe in the finals of another tournament in Fullerton, in February. Thanks to a combination of player defections and the natural growth process, which was adding inches and pounds to Melissa's frame, she had a clear shot at being number one in the 18s nationally in 1984.

Ramsdell Gurney, Jr., sat on the deck behind his house and savored the situation over a glass of white wine. At fifty, he was a circumspect man who enjoyed philosophizing, a Ph.D. in Russian history who had spent a year out of work in northern California before moving to Palos Verdes Peninsula to take a job at the private Chadwick School, where he taught history and coached the boys' and girls' tennis teams. Aside from a slight bitterness about the uncertain rewards of the academic life, and a case of nerves which prevented him from watching his daughters compete, he kept his emotions in check. He was a careful, modulated man, very much the teacher, who was devoted to telling the plain truth.

Ram Gurney, Jr., supported three daughters and a nursing-student wife on a teacher's salary. They rented a house on school grounds, provided by the Chadwick School, in a neighborhood Ram could not have otherwise afforded. In the interest of honesty, he informed his daughters of the practical financial consequences of their performance. "If we had a lot of money and this were a plaything," he said, "that would be one thing. But it's been a tremendous sacrifice and there would be no way we would do it if the children weren't successful. The priorities would be shifted." He and Carolyn were willing to forego certain comforts to support their daughters' tennis, but Ram Gurney made sure the girls understood that tennis was one of the reasons he had never taken his wife to Hawaii.

He also apprised Melissa and her younger sisters, Cinda and Robyn, of his father's continuing financial contribution, which would reach a total of $100,000 in the coming year, now that Robyn was beginning to compete and there were three players to support. "Melissa knows her grandfather is helping out. These kids are not stupid: even if I didn't tell her she'd know. I think it makes things easier with us if she knows. I've said to her outright, over the last couple of years, 'Melissa, if your tennis slips we cannot support it at this level.' She knows, and

Cinda and Robyn do too, that we do not have the kind of money we can throw around. . . . I couldn't afford to send a child across country to play a tournament for the first, second round.

"There's no point in denying the fact that this is an enormous financial sacrifice, and it absolutely demands a certain level of performance to continue it."

His attitude was in sharp contrast to the tremendous wealth and self-indulgence he saw in women's tennis—and in Palos Verdes Peninsula, which was quite a change from the small college town of Santa Clara, where he had taught Russian history at the University of Santa Clara for seven and a half years. He recalled how pleased he and Tom Spence were to find, in each other, a kindred financial spirit: "Once we were looking for a motel," said Ram Gurney, with a short laugh, "and I said, 'I don't think I can afford this.' And Tom Spence said, 'I don't think I've ever *heard* that phrase out here.' "

He had raised his daughters to value personal achievement, not the profits that might accompany it, only to find himself surrounded by money and the promise of more. As proud as he was of Melissa, Ram was frightened that success would warp her perceptions. He did not want her to forget that there was a world outside the comfortable, even seductive world of professional tennis and private school. He worried that the attention she had begun to receive would blot out his teachings.

They were already involved in something of a struggle. "Every once in a while we have a little squabble about clothes," said Ram. "The girls feel they should have their five outfits for the week because all their friends do. And I say, 'I'd love to drive you down to Watts and put you out in the street for a day or two. You'd be so happy to have your one outfit for the *month.*' I think it awakens a sensor somewhere in me. I feel very strongly about it.

"One trait I absolutely detest is arrogance. I've made it very clear to the children not to put this out of perspective. They've got talent, but more important is how they are as individuals. There will be no spoiled brats in this family. They know that we take a great deal of pride in their accomplishments, but they've got to keep certain values in perspective."

What kept him from watching his daughters compete was not the anxiety of a stage father, then, but of a historian who feared that the game his family had always shared would break that family apart, now that a commercial element had been introduced. Ram Gurney revered tennis. His father had taught him the game when he was eight years old, and he had been the captain of his high-school tennis team. "It was," he said, "a very important, happy part of my life." When he met Carolyn Jones, whom he described as "an all-around athlete," he wooed her over to tennis as her primary sport.

When Melissa was four he took her out on the court, and he would do the same with Cinda, and then Robyn. The game began to resonate, for him. It was the continuity that tied generations of his family together. As the girls got better at the game, and the question of a possible career began to intrude, he resisted the notion that one of them would eventually become a star. He continued to stress that this was a group activity. "It's been a family endeavor," he said, "that has perhaps brought us closer together—not that we were ever not close—but it is a common struggle. We're all headed toward the same thing; namely, to do the best we can."

With a smile, he admitted that his wife was "thrilled" at the attention Melissa was beginning to get. But Ram insulated himself from that aspect of junior tennis. The closer Melissa got to the kinds of decisions Debbie Spence had had to make this year, the more Ram Gurney tried to keep his daughter's feet on the ground.

He was determined to be the constant in her life, to provide a reference point; he recommended books to Melissa, and encouraged her always to take something to read when she traveled to a tournament. Lately, he had stepped up his efforts to make her speak properly. The sloppy language he heard from her peers—which had begun to creep into her comments —was an affront to his sensibilities, as grating and crude to him as the current emphasis on selling his favorite sport.

"Correct English, to me, is more important than all the

millions of dollars people make," he said. "I told the girls, 'I don't want you walking around speaking like a dumb jock, because you're not that. If I ask you how you played, I don't want to hear that you played real good. *Real good.* You played *really well.*'

"They'll rebel a little bit against that, as I did, and actually take pride in speaking poorly in front of you. But I remind them. I cherish traditions—not to the point where they make you inflexible—but it's an evolutionary process, and language is so critical in understanding where you come from. Just to throw up a whole heritage, whatever it is . . . There are still standards that have to be maintained."

If Ram was the family's civilizing influence, Carolyn, who was almost ten years younger, was the family's manager. She was better equipped, emotionally, to handle the daily demands of junior tennis. She remained eerily calm during Melissa's matches; a slight tightness to her mouth was the only clue to her level of anxiety. And she had a wry, understated sense of humor. The requirements of the tournament circuit, from the travel arrangements to the record-keeping to the conversations with USTA officials, agents, and coaches, didn't seem to faze her.

She quietly went about her business without complaint. The family had a common goal, as described in Section III, Item 2 of the tennis biography they had composed for Melissa, which read, "Is definitely considering a future professional career." Carolyn might be flattered when the agents called, but she was not distracted. She continued to get up at five in the morning to study for her nursing classes. She got ready to take Melissa and Cinda to Tucson, Arizona, in mid-April for the Easter Bowl.

Robert Lansdorp had four girls playing in the 18s at the Easter Bowl—Debbie Spence, Melissa Gurney, Shawn Foltz, and Stephanie Rehe. He had a month, after Debbie skipped the Virginia Slims of Dallas, to get her back into shape.

He was ambivalent about working with her. As far as he was concerned, Debbie had started playing too soon after she came down with mono, and her inability to play two pro tournaments in a row was conclusive evidence that she needed to take more time off. But she and her parents seemed convinced that she needed to recover her old form, not to waste more time resting, so Lansdorp went along.

Much to Debbie's dismay, he sided with her father on the issue of whether she should play the Easter Bowl. Lansdorp believed in leaving the juniors on a high note, the way Tracy Austin had, full of self-confidence and eager for a new level of competition. Debbie acted like she had to escape from the juniors before the younger girls trampled over her and left her in the dust—and the more she complained, the more Lansdorp was convinced that she needed more junior matches, to remind her that she had nothing to be frightened of. She had to start acting like a top player again.

"Once a kid thinks she can get hurt, she's scared," he said. "If you don't want to play a certain person, you go out and play them until you've mastered the feeling, and you can walk out there without it bothering you. If you are afraid to play the juniors, you should play the juniors. It'll catch up with you otherwise. Being afraid to play juniors is not a good reason to turn pro. A good reason is, 'I've played enough juniors and I'm going to turn pro.'"

He could see how self-doubt was affecting Debbie's game. "Debbie's very negative about herself," he said. "Tears herself down and builds up the other person too much. That's when she loses. She's mentally very tough, so she has it on the inside, but the negative stuff starts to become subconscious. She needs to start talking more positive about it.

"I think Rehe is mentally superior, and Melissa is mentally superior. Debbie is very good, and she might prove us all wrong and go right to the top. But there's one thing. Melissa will work at something to improve. Debbie doesn't work on something to improve it.

"I just had a long talk to her about it," he continued. "She doesn't practice a certain thing, she just hits balls. There are things you can work on instead of just standing there and hitting the ball. Debbie tends to do six hours of practice, but never on certain shots. And it can take a year and a half to improve a volley."

Lansdorp was beginning to believe that Debbie's fate was to be ranked somewhere in the top twenty worldwide, which did not guarantee her either star status or endorsement income. He guessed that Melissa would land "at least" in the top ten, and Stephanie had a good chance of ending up that high as well.

He never made his estimates public; there was no reason to tell a girl who was paying him to make her a better player that there was a limit to what she would be able to accomplish. Besides, Lansdorp continued to think that it would be best for Debbie to turn pro before the other girls, despite the setback of her illness and what he delicately termed her "attitude problem."

He took a practical position: while he did not expect her to make a big splash on the pro circuit, he did understand that, at sixteen, she had no real choice left. In the pursuit of a goal she might never realize, she had narrowed her choices down to one. "She doesn't like school and she loves tennis, so I think for Debbie, 'Give it a shot.' She's going to do fine. She might not become great, but even if it didn't work out, there's nothing lost."

Debbie spent a lot of time at the West End Tennis and Racquet Club before the Easter Bowl. Shawn Foltz had been in Johannesburg, South Africa, representing the United States in a tournament sponsored by South African Airways, and the two girls were glad to be reunited. When they weren't practicing, or having a lesson, they sat at an umbrella table and gossiped. One afternoon, after a prolonged did-you-hear, did-you-see, didn't-she-say conversation about an anonymous boy who may or may not have been interested in Shawn, Debbie brought her friend up to date on her social life. Debbie was "constantly together" with the boy she knew who played tennis, she confessed, although she still insisted they were "just friends."

She had started to go out on weekend nights, too, which gave her something to think about besides tennis and gave her father an opportunity to assert himself. "On Friday night I'd want to go out, and my dad's, like, 'Who are you going with? Where are you going? What's going to happen with your car? What time are you going to be in?' " She laughed and rolled her eyes at the hassles he gave her. "He'd make me come in at ten, eleven, eleven-thirty all the time. But I get home from a workout at eight or eight-thirty. He says, 'Just leave by nine and you could be in by eleven.' Well. What do I do, go in my tennis clothes?"

She and Shawn dissolved into giggles at the thought of going on a date in sweaty, disheveled tennis clothes. And then Shawn noticed a rather large, reddish-blue bruise on Debbie's neck, which had been covered by her hair. Shawn started laughing uncontrollably and questioning Debbie, loudly, about what looked like the result of a rather passionate kiss.

Debbie blushed, and screamed, *"Don't.* You'll ruin our image."

Actually, the opposite was true. Enthusiastic displays of heterosexuality were integral to a junior girl's appeal. Robert Lansdorp might tease Debbie about paying attention to boys, but it was affectionate kidding. The man who insisted that his girls wear skirts to their lessons and preached a return to femininity in women's tennis saved his serious criticism for gay women on the tour.

He griped about them loudly one afternoon, sitting in the TV room surrounded by players, so that everyone would know how he felt. "I say thirty percent of the women on the tour are lesbians," he announced. "I would never let my daughter travel alone on the tour. Look, the women's tour is so lonely. These girls get depressed. They lose and they think they're down the tubes, and they get enough offers—and none from men. There are no men groupies like the girl groupies on the men's tour."

One young girl shot back, "Their egos can't take it."

Lansdorp ignored her. "The girls want companionship. So they say yes. That's why you see so many moms now traveling with their girls."

His moral objections aside, Lansdorp had trouble on a

strictly business level with the gay public image of women's tennis. How could anybody hope to make money off what he saw as rampant homosexuality? Although he had a provocative, brash style that put some people off, no one could dispute the validity of his concern when it came to the topic of sex and commercial appeal. The business community had made itself quite clear: it liked its public spokespeople to be happily— overtly—heterosexual.

Billie Jean King had learned a grim lesson in 1981: the news of her homosexual affair with Marilyn Barnett cost her one clothing-endorsement contract that she was just about to sign, and blue-jeans and hosiery endorsements that were being discussed when the story broke. Her total loss in income was estimated at over $2 million. In contrast, Tracy Austin, a disabled player with a boyfriend, continued to collect endorsement checks even though she wasn't playing much professional tennis.

As women's tennis became a more profitable sport—and as the agents, coaches, and promoters who made money from it became more sophisticated about what sold and what didn't —a new emphasis on a rather old-fashioned notion of femininity emerged, reflecting traditional values that predated the women's tennis rebellion of the early 1970s.

This year, for the first time, the WTA would introduce a ten-dollar full-color calendar that featured thirteen women pros in fetching off-court outfits, including cover girl Chris Evert Lloyd in a bathing suit and jacket ensemble. Even Martina Navratilova, who spent an inordinate amount of time fending off questions about the nature of her relationship with her female traveling companions, and would, in her 1985 autobiography, make public her affairs with several women, was posed in a silver lamé evening gown with a plunging back. Whatever the reality of some players' sexual preferences—and despite the objections of WTA members who felt that the calendar promoted "sexist stereotypes," according to one WTA official—the new public image of women's tennis was going to be "tasteful and glamorous," and appealing to men.

The complete woman pro was encouraged to be exceptionally aggressive on the court, and typically feminine off of it. It was a neat, salable combination of qualities, which allowed a young girl effectively to ignore the question of what life would be like after her early, enforced retirement from competition. She could simply shift from her on-court to her off-court persona, from being a player to being dependent on a man. Debbie Spence, for one, had a very clear backup plan.

"I've always looked at it as if, if I just make it, I'll be rich and I won't need to do anything else. Now I don't really know; I have to wait and see if I will be rich and won't have to worry. If not? I'll marry a rich man. If I play tennis, I've *got* to meet some guy with money."

A week before the Easter Bowl Debbie and her father had an argument about her Mazda sports car. Tom complained that her insurance premiums were high, and he wasn't pleased about paying them when she couldn't even be bothered to keep the car clean. He was thinking of selling it, he said. That night she had a dream that something awful happened to the car and she was afraid to tell her father because he would blame her and make her get rid of it.

10

Easter Bowl

As the sun set on Monday, April 16, 1984, the lobby of the Sheraton Tucson El Conquistador Golf and Tennis Resort, a 440-room hotel set into the side of Pusch Ridge outside Tucson, Arizona, filled up with guests. There were wincing city dudes in their wobbly cowboy boots, ready for a week of horseback riding; middle-class Orthodox Jewish families from Tucson, the men in dark suits and the women in bright silks, here for a Passover *seder* being held in one of the banquet rooms; and 290 children under the age of eighteen who were competing in the seventeenth annual Easter Bowl.

It was hot, even this late in the day, and so dry that warning signs had been posted near the tennis courts reminding players to drink a lot of liquids, to protect themselves against dehydration. One blond boy, stripped to the waist, hurried across the lobby with his tennis racquets, without looking where he was going. Suddenly he found himself surrounded by three generations of a family heading for the *seder*. They stared uncomprehendingly at each other: a boy cut off from everything but his sport, a family unaware, for the moment, of anything but family.

The moving force behind the Easter Bowl was Seena Hamilton, a gravel-voiced, myopic, middle-aged ex-tennis mother from Manhattan who was obsessed with family, and with what junior tennis was doing to it. A blunt woman with a preference for frivolous hats, Hamilton believed that the pressures on junior tennis players and their families were immense. She doubted that most families had the situation under control, no matter what they said, and had alienated her share of tennis parents by suggesting that people who talked about how much their child enjoyed the game were indulging in extreme self-deception.

"You only play for fun," she was fond of saying, "as long as you're losing."

Seena Hamilton might be difficult for some parents to take, but she was impossible to ignore. She had been the promoter of the Easter Bowl for sixteen years. This year, for the first time, she had lured Head Racquet Sports and Sports Wear into being a corporate sponsor and moved the tournament from Florida to the plush El-Con, which was how the hotel was known to anyone who, like Seena, had more important things to do than pronounce the whole five-syllable name.

In addition to the tournament itself, Seena was also managing two days' worth of workshops for junior players and their parents. Her son had been a promising junior player in the late 1960s and early 1970s, and she had always been disarmingly frank about her own shortcomings as a tennis mother—she was disorganized, she was confused, she was nervous. She had talked to other parents about their troubles on the circuit over the years, and this year had vowed to do something for them.

The tournament presented a perfect opportunity for a little education: she had a captive audience holed up in the middle of nowhere for a week. So she gathered together all the experts she could find. Tonight, Arthur Ashe, who had been the Easter Bowl honorary chairman for the last five years and was the chairman of Head's advisory staff, would be the featured speaker at the opening-night forum, entitled "Surviving Junior Tennis."

About three hundred people showed up to hear Ashe's opening remarks and meet the workshop leaders. It was a strange sea of faces, mostly in sets of two, the parent and the strikingly similar child, along with a handful of reporters and a TV crew from KQED-TV, San Francisco, which would televise the finals over public television.

Ashe was an enduring star. He had twice been ranked number one in the world, in 1968 and 1975, won the first U.S. Open in 1968, was ranked in the top five for ten years in a row, and then came back from injuries to regain a position in the top ten. Since his retirement in 1980—following a heart attack and quadruple bypass surgery—he had devoted himself to working with young players and expanding junior tennis through his National Junior Tennis League, a public-parks program designed to get inner-city children involved in the sport.

He was a man made rich by tennis, and yet he was a cautionary figure who warned that the promise of big money did "funny things" to people. Ashe asked parents to stop thinking about their children striking it rich, and think, instead, about the players who were stuck between 70 and 120 on the computer, who barely made enough money to get by but were afraid, and ill-equipped, to walk away from the game.

Then he introduced the workshop leaders. Dr. Jim Loehr, a sports psychologist, talked about how he'd like to play a videotape of the mental "casualties" who came to him for help, for those parents who thought that being a competitive tennis player was easy. Emilie Foster, the women's tennis coach at Trinity University, in San Antonio, Texas, said that making a decision about college versus the pros "is really the first step toward adulthood for the child," and a group of players sitting toward the front of the room began to nudge each other and snicker.

Seena Hamilton had stacked the deck. All the speakers favored a slow, methodical approach to tennis, and a skeptical stance when it came to wild promises of professional glory— a position few parents were willing to take as long as their children were winning. Debbie and Francine Spence missed the opening speeches. They chose to go out to dinner instead.

Debbie and Francine skipped the Tuesday morning workshops on the "Junior Tournament Scene" and "The College Scene," as well, since Debbie had a match at four that afternoon and wanted to get in a practice session at a nearby high school before lunch. They were staying at the Westward Look, a less expensive hotel five miles from the El-Con, so Francine dropped Debbie off at a practice court and wandered up to watch some of the other matches. She kept a wary eye on the sky, which was dotted with clouds, and worried about the breeze. Debbie was ambivalent enough about being here without having to face a rain delay.

Debbie appeared at noon and insisted that they find a place to have lunch right away. She was a little hyper—she was willing to admit that—and the best antidote was having something to do every single minute of the day. She wouldn't even let Francine drive, because being a passenger was too boring.

Debbie folded herself into the driver's seat of her mother's Datsun 280Z, the windshield still riddled with squished freeway bugs from the eight-and-a-half hour drive from Los Angeles, and roared onto East Speedway Boulevard. She turned up the car stereo, and then she turned up the bass even further. The inside of the sports car pulsated with rock and roll, just loud enough to drown out her mother's entreaties to turn it down. To a sixteen-year-old—and sometimes to Francine, temporarily sprung from the usual, endless responsibilities of being a teacher, wife, and mother—this was part of the lure of the tennis circuit. It was like playing hooky. There they were, in the middle of a weekday, roaring down a smooth street in a strange town, having an adventure.

Driving was a good way to waste some time, so Debbie refused to consider any of the nearby restaurants. She drove for miles, happily chattering about so-and-so's game, taking her hands off the steering wheel and turning to her mother when she wanted to make a point. Francine kept suggesting restaurants—it should have been an easy choice, since Debbie's only rule was, No Mexican food before a match—but Debbie ignored her.

Then, after about fifteen minutes of cruising, Debbie spied a Hobo Joe's in a shopping mall on the other side of the street.

Nothing else would do. The mall reminded her of the night she and three friends drove from mall to mall, movie theater to movie theater, in Los Angeles, looking for something to do. They were in the fast lane on the freeway when Debbie's Mazda ran out of gas. The boys had to get out and push the car across the other lanes toward an incredibly complicated exit with a dangerous downhill slope, while they all prayed that no other cars would come along and get in their way. Debbie laughed hysterically at the memory while she steered

Francine's car toward a turn pocket and got ready to make a U-turn. Francine implored, "Why don't you turn left and *then* finish your story?" but Debbie didn't listen. She made the turn, shot across another lane, and rolled up a driveway to the restaurant parking lot.

The restaurant was almost empty. Debbie and Francine took a booth in the back, away from the noise of the counter and kitchen, and studied the menu, which offered a dizzying array of sandwiches, soups, and salads. It was too much of a choice for a girl who was already thinking about her match, and Debbie had trouble making up her mind. She couldn't decide which sandwich would provide her with the most energy three hours down the line. Francine suggested the patty melt on rye.

"But isn't that the stuff with seeds?" Debbie whined, as if caraway, foreign to her standard diet, would spell her doom.

Francine quietly suggested that Debbie ask for the sandwich on plain bread and tried to change the subject to what a lovely place Tucson was, and how lucky they were to have found a restaurant with such an extensive menu. Debbie responded to most of her comments with a blank stare. The only time she came to life was to complain about how difficult it was to get into the pro tournaments.

But Francine was determined to keep Debbie's spirits up, so she refused to sympathize. Instead, she recounted a conversation she'd had just that morning with another girl's mother, a conversation which only pointed up how fortunate Debbie had been so far. The woman had gotten a call last October because there was an unexpected opening in the draw of the Bakersfield Ginny. Her daughter could compete if they drove out right away. The woman and her daughter jumped into their car and drove two and a half hours to Bakersfield—only to arrive five minutes too late, to learn that the slot had been filled by another girl.

Francine had meant to remind Debbie that she was better off than some girls—after all, she had played in the Bakersfield tournament, and done well there—but as she finished her story, she faltered for a moment. She mused about how nice it would be to have a lot of money, so that Debbie could fly to various cities where tournaments were being held. Girls always dropped out of the draw at the last minute because of illness or injury. If the Spences were rich, they could take advantage of that kind of opening.

But they weren't rich, and she was skating dangerously close to self-pity, not the proper mood for the mother of a player who was short on optimism herself right now. Francine turned her yearning into a joke. Maybe she and Tom would borrow some money to buy Debbie the chance to chase opportunity. "After all," said Francine, trying to recover her happy mood, "payments on ten thousand dollars *couldn't* be much worse than on five thousand dollars." When lunch arrived, she congratulated Debbie on her good-looking sandwich and went back to talking about how much she liked Tucson.

On the way back to the El-Con Debbie twirled the car-radio dial until she found a station that was playing Kool & the Gang singing "Tonight" ("Toooo-night's the night/Everything's gonna be all right . . ."). She turned it up so loud that the bass began to buzz. "Aw-*right,*" she yelped. "A good song to psych me up."

She still had an hour and a half until her match. She and Francine didn't want to go back to their hotel—with the driving back and forth there wouldn't be much time to relax. So they settled into an acquaintance's room at the El-Con to wait. Debbie leafed through an issue of *Mademoiselle,* but she didn't have the patience to read any of the articles. She tested the perfumed blow-in card that was stuck between the pages, and then she sprawled on the floor in front of the color television set and tried to find "General Hospital."

Forty-five minutes before the match was to begin, Francine went off in search of ice for Debbie's thermos. Debbie waited until she left the room to confess, to the near stranger whose room she shared, that she felt awfully nervous.

She tried to cheer herself up by recalling her Orange Bowl victory, back in December. Even though it marked the beginning of her illness, it had been an emotional, exciting win. It was proof that she could win under adverse conditions. She lay on her back and stared at the ceiling, hoping that the memory would make her feel better.

"I was down. I lost the first set, I was down 4–0 in the second, and then I finally got my first game," she said. "You should have heard the crowd yelling. I think they felt sorry for me. Anyhow, I started feeling like I *had* to win. I mean, I was down 4–1, second set, how was I supposed to come back that far? No way I should've won. But I just worked real hard. Real hard. And it was great. Even though I felt bad it was great. I couldn't believe it. I just felt like I had to win for the crowd. The fans."

She stood up abruptly and started to pull her hair back into a ponytail for the match. It was getting harder and harder to stay psyched up: since she got sick and missed the three satellite tournaments, Debbie had lost the energy to fight back, which had always been a key element in her success. Now she felt defeated before she ever began, by insecurities she had been able to conquer in the past. Her illness and her losses loomed much larger in her mind than her victories did.

"Y'know, it's been so long since I've played a tournament," she said, as she studied herself in the mirror. "The last one was Florida, last month, and before that it was with Mom in Chicago, at Christmas, and I got sick and didn't play, and the one before that was way back at the Orange Bowl. I'm just not confident of my shots. I mean, I used to go out and if I was playing badly I'd think, OK. I can do this, and this, and this, and I'll be OK. Now I think, I'm not playing well, and I get out there and think, Oh my God. *What am I going to do?*"

Several other girls who competed in the 18-and-under category wandered by the court where Debbie was playing her second-round match—her first performance here, since, as the top seed, she had gotten a bye in the first round. Whatever her personal misgivings, which she tried to keep to herself, she was still number one, an important girl to beat, and people came by to take her measure.

Robert Lansdorp paced the aisle between the courts. First he watched Debbie for a few minutes, then he turned to a court across the way to watch Stephanie Rehe. One mother of a top 18s player eyed Debbie critically for a few minutes before she pronounced judgment: Debbie was possibly heavier than she had been at the 1983 U.S. Open, and, worse, she wasn't getting any kind of a proper education. The woman's daughter might not be ranked in the top five, but at least she was trim, fit, and in school. Satisfied, the woman moved on. In her private, personal rankings, her girl was clearly the victor.

Debbie won her match in straight sets, and she and Francine headed back to their hotel to clean up for dinner. As usual, of late, Debbie was not satisfied with her performance. She carried an ideal in her head—the way she had played to earn her 18s ranking, the way she had played in her first two pro tournaments, last fall—and judged her current game far below it. The edge she needed to get through the finals was gone. She felt slow and uncertain, and worry cut through her concentration. It was only a matter of time before the other players passed her up.

She considered the draw for the rest of the tournament and threatened, "If I lose to Cathy O'Meara"—her next opponent —"I'll just quit." A moment later she said, "If I lose to Shawn, I'll just quit." Francine didn't say anything.

Finally, after about ten minutes, Debbie announced, "I *refuse* to let them beat me."

"That's what I want to hear," said her mother.

It was a tentative expression of confidence, but not enough to get Debbie through the players' dinner tonight. She was too "embarrassed," she said, by the way she'd played today to spend an evening socializing with the competition. More and more, she kept to herself, sure that the other girls would be able to read her vulnerability if they spent any time together. Francine had tried to get Lansdorp to have dinner with her and Debbie—she thought it would give Debbie a boost—but he had already agreed to go out with Carolyn and Melissa Gurney.

Francine put on a white dress with a matching eyelet jacket, Debbie donned jeans, a sweater, and white leather pumps, and they drove up to the El-Con to pick up Cinda Gurney, who had decided she would rather have dinner with them than with her mother, older sister, and coach. Francine had spied a necklace in the hotel gift shop that she wanted to buy, so she darted in while Debbie sat in the car in the hotel driveway. When Cinda appeared, having checked out the players' dinner, Debbie grilled her—Were a lot of the girls there? Was the food any good? Are we missing something?—and was gratified to hear that the answer to all three questions was no.

There was a manic energy to Debbie that evening—not the happiness of a confident victor, but an edgy, speedy sort of delight, tinged with the fear that tomorrow might be horrible. She insisted on driving again, and, since her match was over, she insisted on Mexican food, at a restaurant she and Francine had been to before. She parked the car, slammed the door, and then shrieked in dismay. The car keys were locked inside.

Francine ignored her and headed for the door. This was one of Debbie's favorite practical jokes, and she had played it once too often to be believed.

Francine managed to keep the girls at the table long enough to place their order, but then Debbie and Cinda darted out to play the video game they'd seen when they entered the restaurant. They were up and down all through dinner, but Francine did not reprimand them. She was determined to meet her primary responsibility, which was to keep her daughter feeling good about herself, and if Debbie needed to blow off some steam Francine was not going to make manners an issue. She ate her dinner and, whenever the girls returned to the table, talked about what fun they were having.

The picture projected on the screen was a frightening one: an eighteen-year-old girl, a college player with a computer ranking in the nineties, sat with ice packs on both knees and one shoulder after a match. According to Dr. Jack Groppel, who billed himself as a biomechanist and had become something of a fixture on the tennis circuit, the girl's career was in deep trouble. Why? Because she hadn't been brought along very well.

He and Seena Hamilton's husband, Dr. S. K. Fineberg, conducted a Wednesday morning workshop on the care and feeding of the young tennis player, where they talked about bringing along junior players as if they were racehorses, skittish, delicate creatures who were capable of greatness if only they were cared for properly. Dr. Groppel told a group of twenty parents about overall fitness and the importance of an exercise program that would compensate for the uneven strain tennis placed on a young body.

Then Dr. Fineberg, an internist, talked about the latest fashions in athletes' diets—what kinds of carbohydrates and liquids to ingest, and how to schedule meals before a match. One father interrupted to point out that most families couldn't manage fancy diets—they spent a lot of time in places like Burger King and McDonald's because tennis stretched their budgets to the breaking point. Dr. Hamilton advised him to order his child pancakes, no syrup, no butter, but no one could explain how to get a child to eat an unappetizing meal like that.

After a morning of admonitions, warnings, and dire prophecies about the long-range effects of physical and nutritional irresponsibility, the workshop participants were much more eager to hear what psychologist Dr. Jim Loehr had to say. Jim Loehr was the guru of mental toughness, founder of the Center for Athletic Excellence in Denver, Colorado, and executive director of the Jimmy Connors U.S. Tennis Center in Fort Myers, Florida, where he regularly conducted Mental Toughness Clinics for adults and children.

Loehr believed that a child could be taught to win. He had built a profitable business around teaching players—among them, young pro Kathy Rinaldi—how to think to win, through the use of video analysis of a player's responses, on-court drills, and written personality tests. In the last few years, as more and more finely tuned adolescents started to spark and sputter, his specialty had become quite popular.

"All confidence is, is a feeling," he intoned, striding around the room like a preacher at a revival meeting. "You train for it. It is controllable, like any other feeling. You must create the state of enjoyment that makes playing well possible."

Debbie Spence, who at that moment was warming up for her second-round match, believed all of the things that Dr. Groppel, Dr. Fineberg, and Dr. Loehr said. She pursued over-all fitness with as much vengeance as her still-recovering body would allow, and proudly waved her jump rope at Robert Lansdorp today, to show that her heart was in the right place. She had begun lifting weights. Before she got sick, she had taken an aerobics class, and she planned to again, as soon as she had the energy.

She certainly understood how important a positive attitude was during a match. "It doesn't matter what I say before a match," she said, as she headed for her court. "As long as when I get on the court I think I can do it."

Debbie knew what she was supposed to do, physically and psychologically. What she didn't comprehend was how to bridge the gap between knowing and doing, how to turn infor-mation into improved action. Everybody told her what she should feel—Robert Lansdorp, who said attitude was the only thing that stood between her and great success; Francine, who told Debbie she had woken up at three in the morning think-ing about strategies to keep her daughter in a positive mood; and Tom, who said she'd do fine if she gave her all—but no one could tell her how to feel it.

Still, her talent had not diminished; only her appreciation of it had. Sheer ability got her past Shawn Foltz in the quarterfi-nal round, 6–1, 7–5. She faced Melissa Brown in the semifinals, while Melissa Gurney played Stephanie Rehe.

Before the semifinals Debbie began to complain about a sore throat, and Francine, whose constant attempts to keep her daughter happy had worn her out, worried that they should have paid more attention to the blood test Debbie had taken only two weeks before, which still showed an abnormal white-blood-cell count. Debbie's glands did seem to be slightly swollen.

She played Melissa Brown anyhow, and lost, but Francine discounted the defeat. Of course Debbie had played poorly. She was ill again. Francine began to refer to Debbie's condi-tion as a "relapse" of the mono, which provided an odd comfort, mental protection against the possibility that Debbie was really in trouble. Debbie was as good as she'd ever been—but there was this obstruction, this relapse, which prevented her from displaying her talent. As soon as she was completely recovered, everything would be fine.

It was a fragile defense, but Francine clung to it tenaciously. The important thing, now, was to get away from Tucson, from what she would come to regard as the low point in her daughter's difficult year, and begin to think about the summer circuit—about Tom's plan to use an invitation to a European junior tournament in May, and to Junior Wimbledon in July, to buy Debbie a couple of European pro tournaments as well.

She and Debbie left immediately for Cerritos. Melissa Gurney beat Stephanie Rehe and then Melissa Brown to win the Easter Bowl, which confirmed Melissa's status as a strong new contender for the European junior tournament invitations. According to Seena Hamilton, it also meant that the USTA might invite Melissa to Junior Wimbledon.

A few weeks later, at the end of April, the USTA announced the names of the girls who were eligible to compete in the European junior tournaments that began at the end of May. Debbie Spence was not among them. She had informed the USTA that she was not interested in the Junior French Open —because of her illness, it would be hard to beat last year's success there, when she had reached the finals, and it conflicted with the tryouts for the Olympics tennis team in early June. She did want to play the Italian Junior Open, though— primarily for that expenses-paid trip to Europe. Both she and her parents had assumed that she would be invited.

But the USTA passed her over in favor of the younger girls, the ones who had played so impressively in the past few months and still had a strong commitment to junior tennis. Melissa Gurney and Stephanie Rehe were invited to the Junior Italian Open, and would travel with Robert Lansdorp. Shawn Foltz was going to the Junior Italian Open and the Junior French Open, and had gotten into the main draw of the German Open on her own. Those girls could now go to work to acquire wild cards for the main draws on the European circuit.

Debbie's old doubles partner, Marianne Werdel, was not on the list either, but it didn't matter as much to her, since she was scheduled to play a pro tournament in London that would have conflicted with the European junior tournaments. London was to be the last stop on a very successful tour for Marianne, which included victories at three international tournaments, the Hong Kong Open, the Kennex Cup in Taiwan, and the JAL Cup in Tokyo—a pleasant respite for the sixth-ranked player in the international junior 18s, from what had turned out to be a disappointing stay at Nick Bollettieri's Tennis Academy in Florida. The year so far had been tough on Marianne; too many players vying for attention and too much regimentation during her off-court hours. She had not been able to improve her computer ranking—she still clung to the bottom of the WTA list, in the 200s, below where she should have been. She was thinking of not going back to Florida next year.

From a practical standpoint, she did not need, or expect, European invitations from the USTA. For sentimental reasons Marianne did want to play Junior Wimbledon one more time. Traditionally, the girls who were invited to Junior Wimbledon by the USTA were reimbursed for their expenses and automatically asked to join the Junior Wightman Cup team, as Marianne had been in 1983. Since she didn't need the financial subsidy and didn't want to play the national junior summer circuit, her parents made a special request of the USTA. They asked that Marianne be put on the recommended players list for Junior Wimbledon in recognition of her past achievements, as a favor. The Werdels would pay her way, and another girl could have her slot on the 1984 Junior Wightman Cup team.

Tom Spence was not in any position to be so financially flexible, and he greeted the news that Debbie was not going to Italy with mild disgust. There seemed to be no consistent basis for the USTA's actions. Debbie would have to settle for Junior Wimbledon during the first week of July; she was a cinch for that invitation. She could catch a pro tournament the week before—and in the meantime she could get back into shape, to make sure there was no risk of another relapse. Maybe skipping Europe was a blessing in disguise. She would have May and June to build up her strength, with the Olympics trials in the middle to build up her spirit.

As soon as the USTA announced which junior players would go to Europe, the agents sprang into action. Parkes Brittain went to work to secure a wild card into the main draw of the French Open for Melissa, a difficult endeavor, for there was usually only one wild card for a non-French player. Since Debbie had chosen to compete in the Olympics and skip the French tournament, Brittain was off the hook with the Spences. He could pursue Melissa with all of his energy without seeming to slight Debbie.

His only problem was IMG, which proceeded apace with *its* plans to get Melissa Gurney a wild card into the French Open. All of Advantage International's groundwork—since Jeff Austin's initial contact back in October, and Brittain's first conversation with the Gurneys, that dank Thanksgiving in Kansas City, where he and Carolyn had talked about how long the family could afford to support three junior players—was suddenly in jeopardy. He could congratulate himself on his keen eye for talent, but he had to step up his efforts or risk being edged out by IMG, which had certainly displayed its wild-card muscle in the past year. It didn't matter that IMG had noticed Melissa Gurney months after Parkes Brittain had. He was suddenly involved in a corporate match with a flashy foe. The winner stood to collect a percentage of the millions of dollars a girl like Melissa could earn during her career, and, crucial to a young agency like Advantage International, a better shot at the girls who followed her, by virtue of that association.

11
European Circuit

In a year's time Debbie Spence had gone from being a rising star to being a questionable commodity. In May 1983, Ruth Lay had visited southern California to attend the eighth annual *Seventeen* magazine Tennis Tournament of Champions at the Marguerite Recreation Center in Mission Viejo. She strolled the grounds, stopping first at one court, then another, to check the progress of the 156 girls competing there. She surveyed the matches with a practiced eye and spoke knowledgeably about the players—she knew where they came from, what their folks were like, and whether they had the potential to make a name for themselves in women's tennis.

Then she pronounced judgment. She pointed at a teenager with a long blond ponytail and decreed that, of all the players in the country, Debbie Spence was the one to watch.

So much had happened since. In May 1984, Debbie Spence was at home in Cerritos, trying to figure out how to salvage a bewildering disappointment of a year. She chose not to compete in the *Seventeen* tournament, which some of the other girls had entered to sharpen their games before they left for Europe. Her enthusiasm for the upcoming Olympics trials had waned—she still wasn't feeling her best, and besides, tennis was an unofficial event. The players did not receive medals, get to march in the opening parade, or wear team uniforms. It was just another big junior tournament, really, so she decided to pass it up. With Europe out of the question, she had more important things to think about—like where she was going to find the three pro tournaments she still needed for her computer ranking.

There was a new set of starlets in Mission Viejo. The reigning ponytailed teenager at the 1984 *Seventeen* tournament was Stephanie Rehe, but the girl who was getting a lot of attention was Melissa Gurney, who had lost only six games in four matches to advance to the final against Rehe. Last year Melissa had won the 16s competition and the Most Promising Player award here, and this year she was doing her best to live up to that distinction.

Her victory at the Easter Bowl made an upset a real possibility, and the grounds of the club were crowded in anticipation of the match. Melissa seemed to take the attention in stride. When the match preceding hers ran long and caused a delay, she calmly set off for a practice court to warm up.

Carolyn Gurney wandered around the club distractedly. Suddenly, her daughter was in the limelight, and the glare was unnerving. This was like the match Debbie Spence had played against Grace Kim in Kansas City, over Thanksgiving: performances were being evaluated by people who could affect Melissa's future as a pro. She no longer functioned in the sealed world of junior tennis. Her auspicious entry into the 18s, with a victory over Debbie Spence in Anaheim, last October, had gotten her noticed, and since the Easter Bowl, whatever Melissa did seemed to cause reverberations in agents' offices around the country.

It made Carolyn jumpy. She was here alone with Melissa and Cinda, waiting, so she went looking for her younger daughter for no reason at all, and she worried. "Doctor Rehe just disappeared with Stephanie," she said, with a self-deprecating laugh, "and with my paranoia, I'm sure she's gone off to some secret practice session with a hundred-dollar-an-hour pro, you know, who can fix *everything* in forty-five minutes."

The two girls were fighting for more than this particular tournament title. One of them would end up the top-ranked girl in the 18s for 1984, and the other would be number two. They seesawed back and forth as Debbie Spence and Marianne Werdel had done in southern California in 1983. Melissa lost to Stephanie in two southern California tournaments, but then she turned around and won the Easter Bowl.

"Melissa grew up with Marianne and Debbie, who were *always* number one and two," said Carolyn. "Then, when they exited fast, it became Stephanie and Melissa. This could well be their last year in the juniors. There may be no virtue in staying. It's very expensive. And I have two more daughters to worry about."

Carolyn felt that Melissa would be ready to make the move up to the pros, after only one year in the 18s. "Graduating to the so-called 'big time,' the adult level, is exciting. But Melissa has always been ahead of herself, and she's had good wins. . . . When she started playing up in the 18s people got on us, saying that she should stay back and take the pressure. But that's stopped because Melissa's proved herself on her own. The backbiting is over."

Carolyn tried not to place too much importance on Melissa's junior ranking. She told both her daughters to play their best and let the numbers take care of themselves. And, although she would never admit it to a competitor's parent, Carolyn often thought that she would gladly settle for a close number two ranking for Melissa.

There were too many variables in junior tennis—a bad umpire, a wrong line call on a crucial point, a series of tough draws—to insist that a child settle for nothing less than number one. She could do her best and still be denied the ranking because of things that were beyond her control. Or worse, like Debbie, she could win the top ranking, only to learn that being the best for a year wasn't necessarily enough to make you a star. An adult might be able to comprehend that the world was unfair, and bad breaks often got in one's way, but a fourteen-year-old like Melissa still believed in a pure connection between effort and reward. A fourteen-year-old's mother was hard put to dismantle that notion. Carolyn knew how rough the last year had been on the Spences, and she could see that the source of much of Debbie's pain was simply confusion: she couldn't understand why there were so many obstacles in her path, when she had done everything she was supposed to do. She had been the best and gotten little for it, which made no sense to a child reared on the clean alternatives of winning and losing.

"It's very sad for Debbie, because it's affected her confi-

dence," said Carolyn. "Right now Debbie doesn't exist because of her illness, and because of bad luck, which is why I
don't want my kids to strive to be number one, necessarily. So
much luck is involved."

After the Easter Bowl, she and Ram had been told that they
should call the USTA to request that Melissa be invited to
Junior Wimbledon. But they declined when they found out
that Debbie wanted to go, because they felt that she deserved
the slot. Melissa could go, possibly as a pro, next year.

They were interested in getting her a wild card into the
main draw of the French Open, though, since she would be in
Italy the week before for the Junior Italian Open. Melissa had
been invited to compete in the qualifying rounds of the
French Open, but could not go because the early rounds conflicted with the end of the Junior Italian Open. A wild card
directly into the main draw was her only hope. Parkes Brittain
was working exclusively, and feverishly, on her behalf, but if
IMG got the wild card the agency would have to choose between Stephanie, who had been getting them for a year, and
Melissa, the new heartthrob.

Today's match could make a difference. The real prize here
was not the *Seventeen* tournament crown, but the free pass
into the French Open—which, for Melissa, would mean the
chance to start accumulating pro tournaments for her computer ranking. "I have a feeling," Carolyn said, with some
trepidation, "that whoever wins this will get the wild card."

The match turned out to be a primer in all of the things that
Carolyn worried about, the elements of a match that were
beyond a player's control. She moaned when one of the umpires walked onto the court, because she feared that the
woman favored Stephanie. The crowd seemed to be behind
Stephanie, to a rather dramatic degree—people not only applauded her good moves, they applauded when Melissa made
a mistake. After Melissa lost a long volley, the crowd clapped
enthusiastically, and Carolyn saw it, not as appreciation of
Stephanie, but as criticism of her daughter.

"They shouldn't do that," she whispered. "It's so cruel."

Melissa took the first set 6–3, only to lose the second set 6–2.

Carolyn rushed to her side and diagnosed her daughter to be suffering from heat prostration. She shepherded Melissa to the locker room and had her lie down during the ten-minute break before the third set, but it was no use. Melissa was so knocked out by the heat that she did not win a single game in the final set.

After weeks of calls, letters, and telexes to the promoters of the French Open on Melissa Gurney's behalf, Parkes Brittain finally emerged victorious, or so he thought. He got word during the third week in May that the wild card into the main draw would go to Melissa Gurney, despite her *Seventeen* tournament loss. Melissa was already in Milan for the Junior Italian Open with Stephanie Rehe and Robert Lansdorp, so Brittain jubilantly placed a transatlantic phone call to give her the news.

At which point she gave *him* the news. She already knew that she had the wild card. Jim Curley from IMG had called her parents and taken credit for the coup. It was a frustrating, but not entirely unexpected, development. Brittain tried to keep his sense of humor, since he had no choice but to hang in as if IMG did not exist.

"Last year I went with a girl and her mother to the French Open," he recalled, with a laugh, "and I ended up dancing with the mother and another company was there dancing with the girl."

Brittain was taking a flight to Paris tonight, and he went with a growing sense of anticipation. The same American girls had been trading victories in junior and pro tournaments for almost a year now—Spence, Gurney, Foltz, Werdel, and Rehe from southern California; Melissa Brown and Caroline Kuhlman from the East Coast; and Michelle Torres from the Midwest. Aside from Werdel and Kuhlman, it didn't look as though any of them had serious designs on a college education.

Somebody had to turn pro, and soon. The last wave of talented juniors had broken through a few years ago. After Tracy Austin came Andrea Jaeger, who turned pro in 1980, a few months before her fifteenth birthday; and Kathy Rinaldi, who was just fourteen when she became the youngest girl ever to turn pro in 1981. Now there was a new graduating class. Brittain felt that some families had hesitated, held their daughters back for an extra year when it seemed that some of the very young pros were encountering problems, but they couldn't wait forever. These girls were ready to make a decision.

Although Brittain was never one to encourage a girl to make the move too early, he had to be ready with a plan for any of the talented girls with whom he had built a relationship. If he wasn't, IMG or ProServ could sign her out from under his nose.

Brittain had begun to think about what he might be able to do for some of the girls, should they seem promotable to him when the time came. Melissa Gurney was an easy one, at the moment: a sunny fourteen-year-old from southern California was a very salable commodity. Shawn Foltz had a young model's self-assurance. All she needed was to prove herself a bit more consistently in the 18s.

Debbie Spence was more questionable, since she had not yet regained her stride, but Brittain recalled a client once who fell ill and took a year and a half to climb back. He was not about to write Debbie off. Perhaps IMG could afford to stand back, skeptical of her image, satisfied to represent world-famous players and hand-pick a few, select newcomers. Advantage International had to build a client roster.

"The solidity of this company," said Brittain, "is in its future. We have the best squad of young up-and-coming players, male and female." If Debbie proved herself, and if the agency decided to sign her, Brittain already knew the approach he would take.

"American top junior, tennis credits are all there," he recited. "Southern California, blond. Not an overwhelming personality, but you can't really call her soft-spoken. You could say, 'confident.' Debbie's the kind of player that really has a lot of guts on the court. She, more than almost all of her contemporaries, will chase down almost any kind of ball that's hit to her. That's her strength—she gets in there and covers the court.

"So you look for companies for endorsements who would want someone like that, who already have a lot of Europeans. You say, 'You need a young American to round out your profile.' If she's blond you turn to some Japanese companies, because tennis, and blond tennis players, are very popular there. There are some rules to go by. We deal with so many companies that we know basically what each company has to spend each year, where the bulk of their money is going, and what their needs are. Their corporate profiles. Once we come up with Debbie's identification as a player and a personality, we look at the companies for whom those qualifications match their needs.

"And that's the only way a sale can be made—because no matter how great she is, if she doesn't match a company's needs, they're still not going to sign her up."

For all its low-key style, Advantage International was quite the high-powered matchmaker. The agency might not be able to get girls into a lot of pro tournaments, but it would get a footnote in the commercial history of women's tennis for having made the best deal ever for a new pro. Although Kathy Rinaldi had not made the leap from tennis star to household word in the three years since she turned pro, she was clearly being groomed for celebrity status.

Before she did anything as a pro—when all the agency had to sell was her junior record and her potential—Advantage International had gotten Rinaldi endorsements for Lee Jeans, Prince racquets, Le Coq Sportif clothes, and Lotto tennis shoes. She had since replaced Le Coq Sportif and Lotto with Reebok shoes and clothes, and added a resort development in Florida to the list of companies that paid her to represent them.

Once an Advantage International agent had positioned his client in the marketplace, his responsibilities were, in a strange way, those of a parent. On the junior level, parents helped with schedules and provided financial support. On the pro level, the agents assumed those jobs. A professional woman tennis player who was represented by Advantage International still received an allowance out of her earnings, which went directly into an agency bank account. If she liked, the agency would even pay all of her bills for her.

In fact, Parkes Brittain used a family analogy to describe his approach to the girls and their parents. Not all parents liked to have the agents dancing with their daughters in Paris, and Brittain was careful not to push too hard. He was as willing as the next agent to entertain a girl or her parents if that was acceptable to them. But he preferred to think of himself more as a member of the family than as a suitor.

"What I try to do is become more like a big brother," he said. "If I take that attitude—and get off the recruiting bandwagon, and get off the flash bandwagon, and really try to relate to the person as someone, not as a prospect, not like a sorority or fraternity rush—I think, with that philosophy, I've been a little bit more successful."

Brittain could be a rather tough big brother, though, more of the Orwellian variety, who kept a watchful eye on all his charges and never let them stray too far from the future the agency had mapped out for them. One of the reasons for management companies like Advantage International, he said, was that young athletes never thought about what life would be like after their competitive careers had ended. They didn't want to take the time, now, to plan for the future. Somebody had to make sure they would be financially secure in fifteen years.

"We tell them exactly what they can spend and what they can't spend," Brittain said. "We have a complete viewpoint toward the rest of their lives. That's, if anything, one of the greatest strengths we have in this business."

That perspective included tax-shelter investments for the present, and long-term, equity-building investments for that inevitable day when a player stopped competing and needed a nest egg. "We present investment opportunities to them and say, yes, you can get involved with this group of limited partners, all of whom are other athletes, and here is the length of the term of the investment, here is your tax depreciation write-off, here is how much money you have to spend, this is what we recommend," said Brittain. " 'Get into it or turn it down.' We're in the saddle on those decisions."

A young woman making between $60,000 and $80,000 on the pro tour might be encouraged to buy shares in a limited partnership of Advantage International clients investing in real estate—so that she would have a write-off now, and, assuming that the value of her purchase appreciated, money down the road when she needed it. Laurie Baker Lawler, the agency's director of investments, spent much of her day hunkered down in front of a computer terminal in a spacious office down the hall from Brittain's. She was in charge of all real-estate investments for Advantage International's more than one hundred athlete clients, and the computer held information on who owned what, where it was, and what it was worth.

Lawler traveled about two months out of the year, hunting for profitable real estate and checking up on existing investment properties. On one wall of her office there was a large map of the United States, dotted with plastic push-pins of various colors. Each pin represented a different type of real estate—the red ones were shopping centers, the green ones were apartment complexes, the blue ones were office buildings, and the yellow ones were miscellaneous properties. The white pins were properties that the agency had sold recently. About 80 percent of Advantage International's clients were involved in real estate. Since 1975, when the agency was still part of ProServ, those clients had spent over $20 million on acquisitions.

Advantage International collected up to 25 percent of a client's endorsement earnings and 10 percent of her prize money for such services. "Becoming a client is easy," Brittain explained. "It's a matter of signing a document, opening a bank account, and getting an American Express card and hitting the road."

The hard part, once a girl signed, was the grueling schedule. Even Brittain, who only traveled to a select number of tournaments, felt the boredom of being in another city for another match. "I have to defend myself with my friends," he said. "They say, 'Ooh, you get to go to Paris.' But you're working. You might as well be in Cleveland." He might know how to protect his clients from a bleak financial future, but he could not offer them an emotional protection plan. He tried to warn the girls; his favorite, oft-repeated line was, "Every locker room is the same." Success carried with it the guarantee of exhaustion and loneliness. The girls had to develop their own defenses against that.

"This is not," said Parkes Brittain, "an easy life."

Nor was it a predictable one. Melissa Gurney and Stephanie Rehe, the current stars of the Robert Lansdorp Tennis Academy, both lost first-round matches in the Junior Italian Open and the main draw of the French Open, victims, they were told consolingly, of first-time European circuit nerves.

12

Wimbledon

Finally, while the other girls were in Europe, the Spences came up with a plan. Debbie would go to New Jersey for two USTA Satellite tournaments that were held, back-to-back, during the middle of June. Then she would go directly on to London for the 1984 Junior Wimbledon, which began July 2. She would arrive a week early, plenty of time to recover from jet lag. If she could pick up a pro tournament there, she would have her computer ranking by the time she got back home.

It was a smart idea on several levels. Tom knew that Debbie's mood would improve if she got to play in the pros, even on the satellite level—and, with the best players away on the European circuit, she actually had a shot at winning one of the tournaments. He also knew that he could ask the USTA to reimburse him for Debbie's plane fare to New Jersey, which was the first leg of her journey to London for Junior Wimbledon, so the plan had economic, as well as psychological, appeal. None of the girls had been formally notified, as yet, of their invitation to Junior Wimbledon, but the call would come any day. Debbie couldn't afford to sit home and wait for it while two pro opportunities passed her by.

Tom thought about sending Francine, but the plane fare overseas, and the expenses once she got there, were beyond him. Warren Rice, who had traveled to the 1983 U.S. Open with Debbie, was on his way to New Jersey, and he offered to fly out with Debbie and then go back to the Newark, New Jersey, airport with her when it was time for her to take the shuttle to New York for the connecting flight to London.

In the first satellite tournament, in Freehold, New Jersey, Debbie was defeated by the draw. She lost in the first round, in an 11–9 tiebreaker, to the girl who went on to win the tournament. The second tournament, in Chatham, New Jersey, was played on clay courts, where Debbie played well. She beat the eighth seed in the first round and won her second-round match in straight sets.

Then, on June 19, USTA Junior Competition Coordinator Nancy Arnaout called the Spences to inform them that Debbie Spence had not been invited to compete in the 1984 Junior Wimbledon. The USTA had sent a list of five girls to the Wimbledon Committee: Stephanie Rehe, Marianne Werdel, Debbie Spence, Melissa Brown, and Caroline Kuhlman. The Wimbledon Committee had taken Rehe, Werdel, and Brown, added Shawn Foltz—and dropped Kuhlman and Spence without explanation. Arnaout was chagrined and apologetic. This was the first time the Wimbledon Committee had ever deviated from the USTA's submitted list.

Tom Spence didn't much care how sorry anyone was. He had to call his daughter before her quarterfinal match and break her heart, tell her that she had been left out, for no good reason, for the second year in a row. His careful equanimity deserted him. He and Francine were frantic, suspicious, and angry. The bad news unlocked all their frustration.

"I'd sure like to know who in England is making the decisions," said Tom, barely able to control the quaver in his voice. "I just don't know if the USTA is telling me the truth. I think they're lying to me. I'd just like to have a name and number I could call." He would, in fact, get the number of the Wimbledon Committee office and call to inquire, but the response would be, simply, that the committee had made its choice. The explanation was that there was no need for an explanation.

In the meantime, Tom faced the more immediate crisis of how to handle Debbie. He gave her the news that night and she became "*real* upset," he said, so much so that she intended to call the USTA herself to complain.

Tom tried to raise the delicate subject of whether Debbie wanted to go to Junior Wimbledon as an alternate player. Nancy Arnaout had suggested it, since girls always dropped out of tournaments at the last minute and a slot would undoubtedly open up. She even said that the USTA would pay for the trip, as if Debbie were on the list with the other girls.

Debbie was insulted by the idea. "She doesn't want to do that," said Francine, after talking to her daughter. "She said to me: 'Why should I sit around watching them all play when I can beat them?' " Francine could hardly argue. This insult was more than even her normally generous nature could tolerate.

She grudgingly allowed that Stephanie Rehe deserved to go. But Marianne Werdel hadn't played any more national junior tournaments than Debbie had, did not intend to play the juniors next year—and had been having such a rough time in the pros that she had slipped off the WTA computer, which ranked almost three hundred women. To Francine, it made no sense for her to be invited and not Debbie. And what about Shawn Foltz, who hadn't even been on the submitted list? Nancy Arnaout had suggested that Shawn's performance in recent international events had impressed the Wimbledon Committee, but that didn't satisfy Francine. When was Debbie ever going to be rewarded for being the best in the country?

Last year Debbie had been overlooked because it was too early in the year to know how well she would do. This year, it seemed, she was being overlooked because it was too late to bother with her.

Or perhaps she had been ignored because the Spences didn't know how to maneuver. Francine was distraught. Debbie was as good a player as the other girls, but she lacked what was clearly a crucial element in a tennis player's success— money, and the insider's influence and exposure it bought. The Spences had thought, perhaps naïvely, that Debbie would succeed on the basis of her game alone. Now her parents were ready to abandon that notion.

"It just seems like it's all in who you know after all," said Francine. "It's all politics. I *know* other girls' parents must have made calls and put the pressure on. This doesn't make any sense.

"I guess it doesn't pay to be the nice guy. I think people must have put pressure on, and then the USTA comes up with an explanation that fits what they have done. They give in to people who have called them, and then they figure out what to say to the rest of us. But I think there ought to be one set procedure for this, to decide who deserves to go. Instead, it just sounds like they change the explanation to fit what they've done."

The phone calls flew back and forth for days, between Cerritos, Chatham, New York, and London. Nancy Arnaout sent a telex asking that the decision be reconsidered, to no avail. The Wimbledon Committee would not budge. Even Debbie called London, and got a tournament official on the phone. What do I have to do, she asked, to get into this tournament? The woman had no answer, and Debbie got irritated. I *should* be invited, she huffed, and *not* as an alternate.

Debbie's self-doubt gave way to a stronger emotion: she got angry. She was going to show the USTA, and Wimbledon, what a mistake they had made in snubbing her. She played in Chatham with something of her old fire, and was within a day of winning the satellite tournament, when Nancy Arnaout called the Spences again. The Wimbledon Committee, she said, "strongly advised" that Debbie come to London, because they were sure she would be able to get into the tournament. Tom and Francine decided to take the chance. After Debbie won her final match on Saturday, June 23, she immediately checked out of her hotel room and headed for Newark Airport.

As a young woman ready for a pro career, Debbie Spence was not supposed to succumb to emotional tantrums; as a young girl, she had to find a way to vent her feelings. The one sanctioned expression of a junior player's despair was an occasional, brief cloudburst after losing a match. Beyond that, once a girl got into the pros, she was expected to prove her maturity by remaining calm in the face of adversity.

But Debbie was under an unusual amount of stress. Going to Junior Wimbledon as an alternate was a humiliation, as she saw it, and worse, she was expected to grin and bear it. She tried to be calm. It wasn't that she consciously went looking for trouble; it was more that trouble found her when she was upset in the first place, vulnerable to some small crisis that would give her an excuse to go temporarily nuts. Distress always found an outlet, however strange.

Debbie managed to make her shuttle flight to JFK International Airport without any problem. She carried five racquets and a suitcase over to the British Airways gate where she would board the 9:30 P.M. flight to London's Heathrow Airport.

Then she opened her purse to take out her plane ticket and passport, so she could check in for the flight. After a frantic search, she realized that she had failed to bring the passport with her.

Debbie lugged all her belongings over to a phone booth and called Cerritos on her father's credit card, but no one answered. She panicked and started to cry. By that time on a Saturday night, the terminal was rather deserted, "with scuzzy men around," as Debbie recalled it. She was afraid to go anywhere. For an hour she stayed jammed in that booth, sobbing, dialing home over and over again, until Francine finally answered. Tom was up in their cabin in Big Bear— Francine was only thankful that she had not gone with him for the weekend—and Francine had been out running a couple of errands.

Francine's instinct was to be impetuous—grab the passport, head for Los Angeles International Airport, and fly to New York and on to London with her daughter. But that was an expensive reaction. She needed time to think, to figure out how to get Debbie to a safer location, how to get the passport to the East Coast, and how to get Debbie on a later flight to London. She instructed Debbie to leave all her belongings near the phone, except for her tennis racquets, which she was to take with her, and look for a phone in a better location. Once settled, she was to call her mother back.

By the time she did call back, Debbie had made a lot of progress. She was a seasoned traveler, and, once she got over the initial shock, she did have certain resources. "She'd befriended this guy who was in law school," Francine learned, "and he was getting on a flight, but he could see she was really upset. So he gave her the name of a friend, and a phone number, and said, 'Call these people. They're really nice. They'll help you out.' So she *did*. And they drove out to the airport and got her and took her back to their house for the night and then drove her back to the airport the next day," by which time the passport had arrived. Francine had driven to Los Angeles International Airport and put the passport on a plane.

The fact that Debbie had spent the evening with strangers bothered no one but her grandfather, who was furious with Tom and Francine for having been so disorganized. They were only relieved that a potential obstacle had been over- come, and sorry that Debbie's tournament victory had been eclipsed by such a silly problem.

Debbie left Sunday afternoon and arrived in London at 6:40 A.M. Monday, where she was picked up by one of the coaches working with the American players. She ended up sitting at a tennis club all day in her street clothes, watching other players practice, while she waited for a ride to the hotel. It was too late for her to pick up another tournament here; for the rest of the week she could only practice, and wait.

Wimbledon, more than any of the other major tournaments, practiced strict devotion to the rules of proper behavior. Women players still faced the Queen's box seats and curtsied after a match—and when Czechoslovakian player Hana Mandlikova, in a surly mood after losing a match, chose not to, the gaffe was a headline story in the next day's newspapers.

Debbie Spence felt cantankerous to begin with, and the formal atmosphere did not make her feel any better. Her presence at Junior Wimbledon should have been an honor and a compliment. Instead, it was a terrible embarrassment. The other four girls from the United States were officially invited guests—and then, a step down the ladder, for no reason at all, was Debbie. She wandered around the All England Club with a chip on her shoulder. She treated herself to a stylish shag haircut at the hotel, but even that did not improve her spirits.

She would refuse to take responsibility for what happened in the second round of the Junior Wimbledon competition.

Debbie was scheduled to play the second match of the day. The boys' match before hers ended early when one of the players hurt his ankle, and a call was sounded in the players' locker room—where, according to Wimbledon rules, players were supposed to wait for the duration of the match preceding theirs—for Debbie Spence and her opponent, Niege Diaz.

Debbie Spence was not there. UCLA women's tennis coach Gayle Godwin, who chaperoned the junior girls, ran to look for her, but the courts covered a vast area and there were players and fans everywhere. It would be almost impossible to find a single player. A tournament official, who happened to be the woman Debbie had spoken to from New Jersey about how she deserved to play at Junior Wimbledon, abided by Wimbledon rules and waited the appropriate fifteen minutes. Then she announced that Debbie Spence had been defaulted.

Moments later Debbie rushed up to the court—she had finally arrived in the locker room and heard about the boy's match ending early—and got the bad news. Rules were rules. The fact that she was here, now, and ready to play meant nothing.

She did not call her parents that night, nor the next night, by which time they had begun calling, looking for her. They had read about the default in the *Los Angeles Times* and wanted to know what was going on. Finally, two days after the default, her parents got her on the phone.

Debbie indignantly swore that she had been involved in the most altruistic of activities, warming up for her match on a distant court, when her match was called. She blamed the tournament official, who, she insisted, had disliked her from the beginning.

She also blamed the sheer physical size of the grounds at Wimbledon, which made it impossible for Gayle Godwin to find her quickly enough. And she blamed the boy who had been injured. Debbie had checked in at the court, seen that the boys were playing the first set, and assumed she had time to warm up. How did she know one of them was going to get hurt, causing the match to end early and her match to be called before she was ready?

If the whispered word among some parents and players was that Debbie had been buying souvenir T-shirts, not practicing, when her match was called, it hardly mattered. In a back-handed way, she had finally gotten what she wanted; she had effectively finished off her junior career.

Debbie had already made a commitment to play the Soisbault Cup in Le Touquet, France, as one of four junior girls representing the United States, so she was able to forestall a confrontation with her parents for another week. The U.S. beat the Soviet Union again, as it had in the Continental Cup almost eight months before. Debbie came home a winner, despite having been wronged by the Wimbledon bureaucracy. She had not given up. She was in a strong bargaining position.

Events had made Debbie's desire to turn pro a question of family loyalty. First she had endured the insult of not being invited to Junior Wimbledon; she had swallowed her pride and come as a second-class citizen. Then she had been defaulted because of some split-second rule. Not only that: Debbie said that the official had told her, "You don't belong in this tournament, anyway." Were her parents really going to continue to insist that she participate in junior tennis, when the bureaucrats who ran it conspired against her on a worldwide scale? Or were they going to support her in what she really wanted to do?

For the first time, the Spence family was a united front with a common enemy—the junior tennis establishment. To Tom, Wimbledon had been one huge frustration. To Francine, it was a slap in the face. She defended her daughter on purely humanistic terms. Francine didn't care where Debbie had been when the match was called. Even if she was off buying T-shirts, the punishment was out of proportion to the crime. The official could have bent the rule just a tad. Nobody asked her to break it, just to be a little flexible and allow the girls' match to proceed. But she had placed more importance on a regulation than on a human being, and that was something Francine could not comprehend.

"Now I have to say," she said, "that I bet this woman didn't *mind* defaulting Debbie. I have to say that. You have to wonder, after all the hassles, if this woman hadn't had it in for Debbie. I mean, a big, important tournament like Wimbledon. Couldn't they have sent somebody to look for her? I have to wonder. How hard *did* they look? Couldn't somebody be bothered?"

For public consumption, Debbie Spence was the sixteen-year-old injured party, and Wimbledon, the 107-year-old rule-bound bully. Privately, within the family, there was some conflict over the incident. Tom pointed out that Debbie would be considered an adult once she turned pro, and would have to watch out for herself. There would be no coaches to search for her if she was in the wrong place at the wrong time. He might complain about the treatment Debbie received, but he eyed her suspiciously and wondered whether she had, in fact, been goofing off. Francine wished, fervently, that she could have been there to watch out for her daughter, who still seemed to need surveillance. Debbie developed a sore throat and took to her bed for a week rather than travel to the West End Tennis and Racquet Club and have everybody ask her questions about what had happened.

There was no talk of Debbie playing another junior tournament, as there had been in the past when Tom was making the decisions. He had insisted that she play in Anaheim, Kansas City, and at the Easter Bowl, to convince him that she was ready to be a pro, but that tactic no longer worked. He agreed to let Debbie skip the rest of the junior summer circuit—she had already missed the beginning of the USTA Junior Hard-court Championships, where she won her gold tennis-ball charm last year, so she might as well skip the USTA Clay Court and National Championships as well, even though a victory at the nationals was usually a guarantee of a wild card into the U.S. Open.

Debbie had made her position glaringly clear, and if Tom opposed her now it would seem selfish. If he was ready to do what was best for his daughter, he would let her go.

For the disaster at Junior Wimbledon had overshadowed a significant, surprising event: the WTA notified Debbie Spence that she had appeared on the WTA computer for the first time on June 29, 1984, ranked 128 in the world. In all the confusion over which tournaments to play, and how to get in, the Spences had overlooked a pertinent detail: playing in the qualifying round of a pro tournament counted toward a ranking, even if the player did not advance to the main draw. Without realizing it, Debbie Spence had begun working toward her ranking back in August 1983, when she lost in the qualifying round of the 1983 U.S. Open—not, as she and her parents had thought, at the Bakersfield Ginny in September.

It was a decent ranking. With a little work, Debbie could raise it high enough to get into main draws—maybe even the main draw of the 1984 U.S. Open. She had done what she set out to do, and any hesitation on Tom's part now would look like a willful attempt to obstruct her progress.

In a strange way, the WTA letter was confirmation that sixteen-year-old Debbie Spence had begun to grow up, and away from her family. If Tom was having more than the usual amount of trouble letting go, it was because he felt that he had not done enough for his daughter. Debbie had not gotten the send-off she deserved. He still hedged about exactly when she would turn pro, and spoke vaguely about spending months working to improve her ranking before she made the move— as if something magic would transpire in those months to make him feel better, to erase the past year's confusion and make her leave-taking seem less like his failure.

13
USTA Junior Hardcourt Championships

On Wednesday, July 11, Carolyn Gurney and over 1,000 other nursing students arrived at the Pasadena Civic Auditorium to take their nursing exams. The review course for the test had been given the same week as the Southern California Sectional Championships, and now the test itself conflicted with the USTA Junior Hardcourt Championships, which had the rest of the Gurney family in northern California.

Melissa Gurney was competing in the 18-and-under tournament in Burlingame, California, a small town twenty minutes south of San Francisco. Cinda Gurney was at the 16-and-under tournament in San Rafael, a half-hour in the opposite direction, and Robyn Gurney was entered in the 12-and-under tournament in Mountain View, near Burlingame. Even Ram had been pressed into reluctant service. He stayed with Robyn until she lost and then went up to San Rafael to be with Cinda. Carolyn had hoped to get to Burlingame on Wednesday, but would not arrive until late Thursday afternoon.

She had not seen Melissa for over two weeks, because her eldest daughter had come to Burlingame directly from the annual Junior Wightman Cup camp at the University of California campus in Berkeley, where she had demolished the competition. The girls who competed in Junior Wimbledon were automatically invited to become members of the Junior Wightman Cup team, an invitation which only Shawn Foltz and Stephanie Rehe had accepted this year, since the other girls were not interested in playing the required six weeks of junior tournaments this summer. That left six slots to be filled by girls who attended the camp.

Melissa did not lose a single match at the camp, and arrived in Burlingame the strong favorite to take the hardcourt title. She had already won her early morning match today, and was wandering around the Peninsula Tennis Club, chatting with friends and watching the other players.

Last year Debbie Spence had been the young phenomenon here, the fifteen-year-old, playing in the 18s for the first time, who blitzed her way to victory. It was a measure of how quickly fortunes rose and fell that neither Debbie nor her strongest competitors, among them Marianne Werdel, Melissa Brown, and Michelle Torres, had come back for another shot at the hardcourts. They were already working their way out of the 18s—either into the pros or into international junior competition, to buy themselves a little extra time to make a decision between the pros and college.

The cult of youth perpetuated itself. A girl was better off to follow wild success with a hasty exit from the juniors than to face a new crop of whiz kids who could eclipse her record and leave her behind. Debbie's campaign to get out of the juniors since last year's U.S. Open might have been waged for questionable reasons—because she was impatient and insecure, and her flagging self-confidence couldn't withstand a possible beating—but it made good business sense.

Melissa was unruffled by the speed at which she was rolling toward a top ranking, and the decisions she would face because of it, but Shawn Foltz seemed to find her improved status unsettling. Although her game had picked up—over the last several months she had won the Orange Bowl in the 16s, and, in the 18s, reached the semifinals of the Junior Italian Open and the quarterfinals of the Easter Bowl and Junior Wimbledon—she had developed a rattlingly bad case of nerves for the first time in her brief career.

Earlier in the year, when she thought of herself as a good player working to get better, she had been in a relatively low-pressure position. Her defense against the tension she did feel was the notion that she could always do something else, like modeling or acting, if tennis didn't work out.

The better she got, though, the more seriously she had to think about whether this might be her career choice. She had to confront an elemental fear: what if she decided she did want to turn pro, gave tennis her all, and never really made it? The closer she got to a choice, the more vulnerable she felt. Her other interests no longer provided an emotional escape hatch.

She fixated on her seeming inability to take a match in only two sets as an indication that she might not be good enough. This morning, as she labored to a three-set victory, a tense Pat Foltz watched from the bleachers, worried that her daughter would choke and lose the match for no good reason.

"She just got a good tip from the Junior Wightman Cup coach," said Pat, referring to Betty Sue Hagerman, the thirty-six-year-old coach who had just been named to the team this season. "Shawn was saying that when she splits sets she gets so nervous she can't move. Her legs tighten up. So the coach told her to exaggerate all her motions, because usually you go so far in the opposite direction."

She leaned forward and said, in a voice her daughter could not hear, "Bend those knees, baby doll, and loosen those shoulders."

Shawn came off the court the victor, and sprawled on the nearest lounge chair. "I get *so* nervous. I don't understand. I've been here four days and it keeps getting worse." She was too wired to just lie there and relax, so she jumped up and headed for the clubhouse, looking for a distraction. Burlingame was like Kansas City at Thanksgiving, with better weather—it was still tennis all day and then back home to a string of motels along Highway 101, where it was almost impossible to eat a meal without seeing other girls and their parents. San Francisco was too far away to be a practical diversion. The setup was not conducive to a feeling of inner calm, especially now that Shawn was a member of the Junior Wightman Cup Team, an officially designated special player who drew a lot of attention. The last thing on earth she wanted to think about was how nervous she was.

"If I talk about tennis too much, I get really tight, which is what I've been doing lately. I've just got to keep my mind off it," said Shawn, gazing around the clubhouse and wondering if anyone here could talk about anything else. "I know right as I come off the court that I shouldn't talk about tennis. Take some time to wind down. Then maybe, *maybe* over dinner I might think about talking it over. I'm not the kind of person who can eat and sleep tennis. I've got to do other things—or I'll start not to like it so much."

She looked forward to Robert Lansdorp's arrival, since he was good at joking the girls out of their anxieties, and wondered, to get away from the subject of her nervousness, about where he would stay. Lansdorp never made room reservations. He simply arrived at a tournament and somehow managed to find a vacancy; he seemed to like the way his luck enhanced his image as a powerful guy. All the motels along the strip by the San Francisco airport were full, though, and Shawn had just learned why: "There's some convention coming," she said. "Democratic something or other."

When she was informed that the Democrats were nominating their presidential and vice-presidential candidates in San Francisco this weekend, she laughed.

"Oh yeah? Well, I bet Robert doesn't know that's what it is either."

By ten o'clock Thursday morning Shawn was into her second Diet Coke of the day, on her way to winning the first set of her match. When Shawn was playing well, Pat allowed herself small talk. It was only when Shawn appeared nervous that Pat focused all her attention on her daughter, as if she could communicate confidence by mental telepathy. She was happy with the way Shawn was playing this morning, and as she watched she laughed about her daughter's latest plan for independent living. Shawn and her friend Liz Costa, whose family lived in Las Vegas, wanted to get a condominium near the West End Tennis and Racquet Club in the fall with Liz's younger sister, who was also a tennis player. Pat could go back home to Indianapolis. They were ready to take care of themselves.

Pat had begun to look at two- and three-bedroom condos before she and Shawn went to Wimbledon. While Pat was not ready to give the girls complete independence—she planned to be "the resident mom, maybe one month on, one month off "—the idea of her fifteen-year-old living alone on a part-time basis didn't unnerve her. Everything was speeded up in women's tennis. There was something about the rush that was actually exciting.

"We flew in from Wimbledon and all of a sudden Liz is saying, 'Won't this be fun?' And I said, 'Won't *what* be fun?' I mean, I had so many things on my mind. They had brought up the condo and I said, 'Oh, that sounds like a good idea,' which people took as a confirmation.

"Maybe it's not such a bad thing, having to make up your mind so quickly," she said. "It jolts you into action. We'd been talking about it last spring. It'll be fine."

Shawn rolled to a fast 4 –1 lead in the second set, but then she slipped and her opponent picked up two games. Shawn came off the court for the changeover and tossed her racquet down. "I'm doing it again," she said, loud enough for onlookers to hear. "This is like a pattern."

When she lost another game, she addressed herself sarcastically: "That was just the most major tank of the three games. But that's OK. I do it all the time."

Pat stopped talking and faced the court, so that Shawn would see a familiar, encouraging face each time she looked in the direction of the bleachers. "This match is particularly important for her," she muttered. "To get her foot in the door, to take it in two. So she knows that yesterday was not a habit. It was just something that happened, and now it's over."

Shawn did take the second set 6–4, having regained the accuracy and speed that had temporarily deserted her. She ignored the frustrating line calls that went against her and made sure to coax the next passing shot just inside the line, and she scrambled, instead of missing a ball by a step. For the moment, she had conquered her fears of mediocrity. But there was no respite. If she managed to believe in herself, and play as well as she should, another hurdle—unfortunately, a familiar one—loomed in her path.

"What I would like to know," said Pat, as she walked away from the court, "is how you beat Melissa Gurney." Last year

Shawn had gotten to the finals in the 16s hardcourt tournaments, and Melissa Gurney had robbed her of the title.

Coach Betty Sue Hagerman thought that Junior Wightman Cup team member Melissa Gurney was an exceptional player —but more important, she thought Melissa was a good example to the other junior players of the way a girl should behave. Hagerman's first few weeks on the job had been a rude awakening. Between what she'd seen at the Junior Wightman Cup competition camp and what she'd been told by Glen Herb, who'd chaperoned the girls in Europe, Hagerman had reached the bemused conclusion that these kids needed to work a lot harder on their personalities than on their games.

She was particularly mortified at Glen Herb's tales of how the girls behaved when they traveled. Herb had been a volunteer USTA chaperone for eleven years, and she still couldn't get over the way some of the players acted. She and Hagerman sat at an umbrella table between the courts at the Peninsula Tennis Club and commiserated.

"They say, *'I want'* just like a baby when they're home, and everybody jumps," said Herb. "They're so demanding. And they're oblivious to how to ask for anything politely. It was embarrassing in Italy. I just put my head down in restaurants while these kids are yelling, *'With cheese! With cheese!'* at the waiter."

Hagerman, who had led a rather sheltered existence as a college coach until now, blamed the immaturity she saw on two things—pushy parents and youthful indiscretion. Everyone seemed to forget that these girls were very young. They still had to be taught how to act, and if their parents were too busy weaving success fantasies to teach them proper deportment, Betty Sue Hagerman had the time to do the job. She did not feel that talent exempted a youngster from having to learn decent manners.

"I think the girls are pretty level-headed. . . . But the parents. A lot of them like the idea of their kids making money. I still think way too many parents are using their kids to achieve things—to do what they were not able to do, in terms of money, fame, glory, newspaper headlines," she said. "Now, the camp was only a week, so the girls don't unload a whole lot about their careers. But I had three who talked about the pressures they feel to perform. A lot of the time they play 'to win.' One thing I try to get them to realize is that they should think in terms of playing their best, because it goes hand in hand. You play your best and you end up winning more, because you're relaxed."

Hagerman had already determined that it would be her job to put on the skids. She wanted to stress college, and demand certain social niceties, to balance the pressures the girls often felt from parents, private coaches, and agents. From her perspective, the advantage to the new Junior Wightman Cup program, which subsidized some travel to pro tournaments, was that it helped a girl get out on her own. She could start to make the distinction between her desire to succeed and her parents' emotional investment in that success. Instead of traveling with her family, a girl could travel with Betty Sue.

"It gets them away from their parents, which can be good," said Hagerman. "Having a parent around can be an advantage, because there's always someone around to help, but it can be a thorn in a kid's side, too, to always have a parent tugging at their sleeve."

Besides, a girl who always traveled with a parent could start to think that the world revolved around her needs and whims, a rather prevalent attitude that rankled the Junior Wightman Cup coach.

"One drawback to the parent going is that the kid gets the idea that they're the center of attention. Everything gets done when they want, the way they want. But when they travel with us there's a valuable lesson to learn—that they're a team and they have to mesh," she said. "My role is to take care of everyone and to be consistent, so no one gets preferential treatment. Most of the time the parents have got the kid so starry-eyed that I've got to help them unlearn their behavior. Like some of them don't know how to talk to adults. They're rude."

There were plenty of people eager to regale the players

with stories of the marvelous future, but few were willing to take them to task for the mundane present. Hagerman's agenda, in addition to physical training, included a psychological shape-up.

The members of her team would have to learn to act right and take care of themselves. Hagerman knew better than merely to suggest that the girls write thank-you notes after they housed with a family: she guaranteed that the notes would get written by collecting the notes and mailing them herself.

She took the same hardline approach to nutrition. When she saw Pat Foltz toting diet drinks to Shawn's morning match, she inquired whether Shawn always drank so many diet colas, and even when the players were out of her sight she had her ways of maintaining control. There was a budget for meal money for Junior Wightman Cup team members. Hagerman planned to dispense lunch money and then insist on receipts, so that she could see if the girls had spent it wisely. She kept a mental list of who suffered from what physical ailment, and when a player with a sore shoulder walked by, Hagerman stopped her to find out if she was taking good care of herself.

She noticed Melissa Gurney padding around the club in bare feet and called after her: "Watch out, or you'll get sunburned feet." Melissa said she would be careful, but she needed to get the tops of her feet a little tan so there wouldn't be that silly mark where her tennis socks stopped.

Robert Lansdorp, who had shed twenty-five pounds and evened off at 210, was sprawled shirtless on a lounge chair between the courts, having managed once again to find himself a motel room. He was here to begin to put his house in order: the trip overseas had been one disappointment after another, from the Junior Italian Open to the French Open to Junior Wimbledon. Shawn Foltz was the single exception, the one student who had played the way she should have, only to suffer anxieties for having done so well.

Lansdorp had to get everybody back on track in time for the big end-of-summer tournaments—the USTA Junior Clay

Court Championships, the USTA Junior National Championships, the U.S. Clay Court pro tournament, and the 1984 U.S. Open—so he made an appearance in Burlingame. He found that his presence had a strong impact on how the girls played. They felt special when he watched one of their matches, and they felt robbed when he didn't, which was why he paid careful attention to the schedule and made sure he gave all of his students some time. The girls seemed to care, even more than the boys did, about whether he took them seriously enough to come to their matches. Tomorrow he planned to drive up to San Rafael to catch Cinda Gurney's match.

The quarterfinal matches in the 18s began on Friday, and that morning a hand-lettered sign was posted at the entrance to the Peninsula Tennis Club announcing a three-dollar admission charge for adults and informing players that proper tennis attire, collared shirts and no gym shorts, was required. Now that the anonymous players had been weeded out and tomorrow's celebrities remained, this tournament was suddenly a marketable event with an image to uphold.

Robert Lansdorp had two students playing the 18-and-under quarterfinals—Melissa Gurney and Shawn Foltz. Melissa appeared in the clubhouse wearing a new tennis outfit she bought in Paris during the French Open. She had saved her own money to make the purchase, since there was no practical reason to buy the ensemble; Melissa had gotten clothing from Adidas for about four years. It was an irresistible souvenir of her trip—a trim vanilla skirt and shirt with pencil-thin colored stripes, which elicited envious gazes from the other girls in the clubhouse. Shawn sat in the back of the room alone, listened to her Walkman, and read the newspaper.

Since Ram and Carolyn Gurney had lived in northern California, this was a chance for an informal reunion. Carolyn's taste usually ran to wraparound skirts and sensible tailored blouses, but this morning she was a bit more dressed up, in a beige dress piped in brown and a short matching vest with the color scheme reversed. Soon other women of a similar age and style came up to her, some dragging young children, and they traded kisses and comments about how all the youngsters had grown. She led the group to the bleachers behind the far court to watch Melissa play, and the other women took seats on either side of Carolyn, in front of her, and behind her, as if to insulate her from any disappointment. She, being the hostess at this particular party, handed out Lifesavers to her guests.

It was the most satisfying kind of match for partisan spectators to watch. Melissa's opponent was good enough to give the games an edge of excitement, but not really good enough to pose a serious threat. Carolyn and her friends got to see Melissa play with all the enthusiasm and eagerness that came with self-confidence. When Robert Lansdorp dropped by to watch, he pronounced happy judgment: Melissa was playing "tougher and tougher."

Carolyn's friends took a purer, if more naïve, pleasure in watching Melissa play. They knew little, if anything, about the commercial ramifications of Melissa's talent. All they knew was that a child many of them had not seen in years had grown into a self-possessed young girl with an exceptional ability. They sat contentedly in the shade of a tree and reminisced, and laughed, and applauded Melissa's efforts simply because she was the daughter of an old friend, and it pleased them to see her doing so well.

Melissa won her match in straight sets to advance to the semifinals, but Shawn's match against Eleni Rossides dragged on. Shawn took the first set 6–1. In the second set she let herself think about the fact that it was the second set, and how desperately she did not want the match to go to three sets. She fell behind 4–1, and her composure slipped. When Shawn missed what she thought was an easy shot she yelled "Shoot," loudly.

The umpire for Shawn's match immediately called a code violation against her for obscenity, thinking that Shawn had said "shit." Shawn began to argue, explaining that she knew better than to swear during a match, while Pat fretted helplessly. Shawn was in a middle court, too far away to hear anything Pat shouted, or see her mother's gestures. "He's going to upset her," she whispered, her shoulders hunched.

Shawn took the game but lost the set, 6–3. Pat rushed to the gate at the edge of the court, and Lansdorp suddenly appeared as well, to give Shawn a pep talk. They ushered her away from the court and tried to calm her down. Ten minutes later, she reappeared, armed with two more diet colas, to resume the match.

Lansdorp sat in the bleachers behind Pat. He had never heard Shawn talk to herself so much during a match, and he took it as an indication that she felt uncertain of her game. She was playing "tentative," a tougher problem for a coach to solve than any technical mistake. "She ought to come to the net more, be more aggressive," he complained.

Shawn was temporarily wrapped up in her troubles. The desire to excel was a strong motivation for a young player, until it was bent by the pressure of being close to the top. At the beginning of the season, a new girl in the 18s could take chances and play an expansive game against a better player, in the same way that a new pro could wail away at a veteran; the underdog had nothing to lose and an upset to win. Once a player got within reach of a good ranking—once she had begun to prove herself, as Shawn had—she had less space in which to maneuver. It was no longer just a matter of moving forward. She also had to protect what she had already accomplished.

It could be an invigorating or exhausting challenge, depending on a girl's state of mind. Right now, Shawn was intimidated by the notion of her own excellence and the pressure to maintain it. When she hit a ball into the net, she stopped and, her voice wavering, said, "I guess I just don't *want* it bad enough, you know? That must be it."

Pat did the only thing she could do, which was to think positive thoughts to compete with the negative things Shawn was saying to herself. All through the third set Pat did a running commentary:

"Great shot, Shawn."

"Great, honey."

"C'mon, baby doll."

"Atta girl."

Her words ran in counterpoint to her daughter's, who announced, after a frustrating lost point, "That's enough to make someone throw up. Right here."

Shawn still won the match, 6–1, 3–6, 6–3, which bought her the opportunity to be defeated by Melissa Gurney the next day, 6–2, 6–2. Melissa was going on to the USTA National Junior Championships in Memphis, Tennessee, during the first week in August. Shawn chose instead to be the hometown favorite at the U.S. Open Clay Court Championships, held in Indianapolis at the same time.

14

Decisions

July and August were interminable for Debbie. The draw for the 1984 U.S. Open, which would begin on August 27, was 128 players, but the USTA held back eight of those slots for wild cards. Debbie could not get directly into the main draw with her 128 ranking. Her name was put on a list of players who were eligible to play the qualifying rounds, which was essentially a waiting list. If any girl with a better ranking became injured, or ill, or decided not to play the U.S. Open, the first girl on the qualifying-round list would move up into the main draw.

The waiting list would be revised on August 20, four days before the qualifying rounds began, according to the most recent WTA computer listing. There was only one pro tournament, the U.S. Open Clay Court Championships in Indianapolis in early August, where Debbie could attempt to raise her ranking. She could, and did, apply for one of the wild cards for the Open, but, given the Spences' history of run-ins with the USTA, neither she nor her father had much hope that she would receive one.

In the meantime, she, Tom, and Francine debated her status. Debbie wanted to turn pro for the U.S. Open, but Tom was uncertain. What if she didn't get off the qualifying-round waiting list into the main draw, and didn't get a wild card? Could she stand the pressure of turning pro and then having to thrash her way through qualifying matches—or, more to the point, could she turn pro, lose in a qualifying round, and not lose her nerve?

As the weeks wore on, and highly ranked players dropped out of the tournament, Debbie slowly moved up on the waiting list. She went to Indianapolis and played well—she liked playing on clay, which allowed her time to plot strategy, and set up her shots with care—surviving two rounds before she lost to Bulgaria's Manuela Maleeva. Then she came home to wait.

By Tom's informal calculations, Debbie's performance at the clay courts should have moved her ranking up high enough to get her into the main draw. Still, he had to plan for every possibility. He made two sets of travel arrangements. First he got Debbie and Francine plane tickets for Wednesday, August 22, in case Debbie had to play the qualifying rounds. He couldn't get a room at either of the two hotels that offered reduced rates to U.S. Open players because he had waited too long—so he booked another hotel for the qualifying rounds and two nights of the main draw. He assumed that Debbie would have lost by then.

Then he booked a second flight from Los Angeles to New York on Friday, August 24, in case Debbie got right into the main draw. He didn't change the return flight or the hotel; he wasn't even optimistic enough to extend a room reservation that wouldn't cost anything to cancel. The events of the last few months had made him doubtful that anything was going to work out the way it should. Tom had begun to anticipate disappointment.

He still wasn't certain that this was a good time for Debbie to turn pro, so Tom called Parkes Brittain at Advantage International for advice. If an agent said that Debbie ought to turn pro—and if, perhaps, he offered to represent her, irrefutable evidence of his belief in her potential—then Tom might be less reluctant. As it stood now, he was involved in an emotional conflict with Debbie. He wanted an outsider's objective opinion.

Brittain responded pragmatically. His position boiled down to: Why not? Debbie had just turned seventeen and was about to begin her senior year, but she resented even the minimal requirements of independent study and had no interest in college. College tennis was out. She was tired of the juniors, and had always responded well to a new set of goals. Turning pro now was the only move that made any real sense. If Debbie did well and moved up the computer, the agents and sporting-goods companies would seek her out.

If she didn't fulfill her potential—that dark, unspoken alternative—at least she would be earning prize money against her expenses.

Basically, he echoed what Tom already knew. He did not offer to represent Debbie, but Tom managed deftly to interpret that as an advantage. "What we've got here is an unproven commodity," he said. "If I went to an agent now, what could he do for me? She hasn't broken through. I mean, she hasn't been a Tracy Austin. She's only ranked around a hundred, a hundred and thirty. We can't do anything with that.

"So an agent couldn't get endorsements. And they take twenty to twenty-five percent! So if Debbie's only making twenty-five hundred to three thousand dollars a tournament and we have to give an agent twenty percent, she doesn't come back with much after expenses."

In fact, an agent usually took twenty to twenty-five percent of endorsement money, and only ten percent of prize money, but the exact figure didn't matter to Tom, who was primarily concerned with rationalizing a disappointment until it sounded like good news.

As August 20 approached, Debbie stepped up her workout schedule with Shawn Foltz, who had returned to California after the Clay Courts. Tom continued to hit the financial figures back and forth. The U.S. Open was the most lucrative tournament of the season. A player made $1,800 for playing the first round of singles competition. Maybe he owed Debbie the chance to bring home some serious money her first time out. After the Open, she'd be down to playing $50,000 Ginny tournaments for months on end, earning less than the Open's first-round prize for three rounds of competition. Unless he intended to hold her back for months, he had to answer Brittain's question: Why not?

Tom had hoped for a surer sign—a clear indication that turning pro was absolutely the right thing for Debbie to do—but there was no aggressive agent, no talk of a big press conference, no breakthrough Virginia Slims tournament where Debbie hit the semifinals and got her picture in the paper. There was only the simple truth that the Spences had lived with for years: Debbie was an exceptional tennis player who might make it to the top someday, and a still-questionable commercial commodity. It was almost time to place a bet on her future, and the odds refused to budge.

Both IMG and Advantage International went to work for Melissa Gurney again, to try to get her a wild card into the main draw of the U.S. Open, but she soon proved that she could take care of herself. Melissa won the 18s USTA National Junior Championships in Memphis, in mid-August, which meant that she could expect to receive a wild card directly from the USTA. She played an international grass courts tournament in Philadelphia and then met the rest of her family in Buffalo, New York, site of the annual Gurney family reunion, to wait for word on the U.S. Open.

If she got into the main draw, the entire Gurney clan, including Ram's parents, would come to Flushing Meadow to watch her play—partly out of pride, and partly because the Open marked a new phase of Melissa's career. Unlike Tom Spence, who often seemed intimidated by the choice that faced his daughter, Ram Gurney accepted the notion that the logical resolution of a great year in the 18s was a pro career. It had nothing to do with the starlet fantasy the agents continued to weave around his daughter. Ram stuck to his narrow focus on the relationship between achievement and forward motion; as long as Melissa played well, he was not going to stop her. When he evaluated her performance in the 18s, he came to a clean conclusion. "This will be the last year for Melissa in the juniors," he said.

During the second week of August, Melissa Brown of Scarsdale, New York—ranked tenth in the 18-and-under junior age group and forty-ninth on the WTA computer—turned pro. The local newspaper, which happened to be the *New York Times,* ran an article about Melissa and her family, with a photograph of the young player, on August 16. She had made the move without benefit of an agent, and without any endorsement offers, because her family felt that the time was right. The 1984 U.S. Open would be her first pro tournament.

When Tom Spence heard the news, he responded with almost jaunty enthusiasm, invigorated by a new challenge. This was like a dare, a call to competition.

"Y'know," he said slowly, with a surprising lilt to his voice, "we've sort of been thinking about that ourselves." He tried out the idea aloud, as if checking the fit of a new suit. "We'll just sign," he said, "and if she makes money, we'll take it. We'll give it a year and see what happens. If she does well, we'll have something to promote."

Suddenly, only days before the U.S. Open, the chances of turning pro were "seventy-thirty that we are," Tom said, holding back just a bit until he found out if Debbie would be in the main draw. Like so many tennis parents, he used "we," not "she," when discussing his daughter's future. Debbie might be the one to become the professional athlete, but this was the culmination of ten years of family effort. The distinctions between father, mother, and daughter were rather blurred by now. Everyone had something at stake here.

Finally, on Tuesday, August 21, Tom called the WTA for the last time, "to see where the clay courts put her." He was informed that Debbie Spence's computer ranking had jumped up to number eighty-eight. She was in the main draw of the 1984 U.S. Open. Matches began the following Tuesday. She would have to register before she played.

The last obstacle to her turning pro was gone. Tom called Francine, who had gone to Tulsa, Oklahoma, to help Terri and her husband get settled in their new apartment, and told her to get home in time to leave Friday morning. In typical last-minute confusion, she got home too late Thursday night to repack and leave early the next day. Tom switched his wife and daughter to a Sunday morning flight—and Francine prayed that no one would notice the change when they checked in, since their discount fare required advance reservations.

Francine and Debbie got on the phone long-distance and begged the Loew's Summit Hotel in Manhattan to find one more room at the special tennis discount rate. A sympathetic reservations clerk got them the reduced rate, they packed their bags, and were gone.

Francine had wanted Tom to come to New York as well, to watch his daughter turn pro, but he chose not to go. Earlier in the summer, he had considered the notion and dismissed it as a financial and emotional extravagance.

"Sentimental," he had said, shaking his head. He hadn't changed his mind.

15
U.S. Open—August 1984

I

On Monday morning Francine and Debbie overslept. They finally stumbled into the coffee shop off the lobby of the Summit Hotel at 10:00 A.M. Francine tried to fight off her jet lag with a cup of black coffee while Debbie diligently worked her way through a single scrambled egg and toast with the resigned air of someone who knew she was eating right and probably would have preferred a Danish.

She wore a souvenir T-shirt, given each year to the winners of the Continental Cup, its ribbed neckline and sleeves torn off to make it more stylish. In this business, a player wore her résumé on her back—during competition, a firm's free clothing, and during practice, a garment that defined her position in the hierarchy. There were 128 women in the main draw, 32 girls in the Junior Open, and various stragglers who had lost in the qualifying round but were hanging around to play doubles or mixed doubles, so anonymity was a real threat. The T-shirt identified Debbie as someone special.

The draw for the Open was posted on an easel at the back of the hotel lobby. When Debbie and Francine had arrived Sunday night, they were confronted with the troublesome news that Debbie's first match would be against Alycia Moulton, ranked twenty-ninth in the world, who, just this weekend, had taken Chris Evert Lloyd to three sets in the Canadian Open before Lloyd finally beat her. Francine joked that it was actually good news: Moulton would be so exhausted from the effort that Debbie would be able to beat her. Debbie reflexively pressed her fingers under her jaw line, as if to reassure herself that she was in good health. No swollen glands. Maybe she could beat Moulton.

Debbie had a practice court reserved for noon, so at 10:35 she and Francine wandered outside to catch the eleven o'clock bus to Flushing Meadow, only to learn that there was no eleven o'clock bus. The buses ran every hour on the half-hour. They had missed one by five minutes and now had fifty-five minutes to kill. Debbie headed across the street to Cosmetics Plus, a discount store whose mirrored walls reflected rack upon rack of shampoos, conditioners, tan enhancers, and sunscreens, around a huge central counter stacked with well-used testers of every conceivable cosmetic.

She stopped first at the nail-polish display in the front of the store. Her dark red polish had cracked and peeled a good quarter-inch up her nails. She considered several colors, checked the prices and found them reasonable, and announced that she was definitely coming back later to make a purchase. Then she toured the rest of the store, wandering up and down the aisles for a half-hour while Francine waited near the entrance, pleasantly paralyzed by the thrill of being in Manhattan, and at the U.S. Open, for the first time in her life.

Debbie came back excited. The store had "products from all over. From France," she reported. French cosmetics reminded her of playing in the finals of the 1983 Junior French Open, a happy memory, an omen that things would go well here. She walked right past her mother, out the door and down the block, got onto the bus, stuck little orange foam headphones into her ears, and turned her Walkman on. They had not said a word to each other about when Debbie would register, and how it would feel to turn pro, nor had they said anything to anyone else. Francine had given in to Tom's insistence that they not draw attention to the move, but she was chafing at the restraint. Her daughter was about to become a professional tennis player. Why shouldn't people make a big deal of it?

"I'm all for publicity," she confessed. "Parkes said she should just quietly sign her name, but I think it'd be *fine* if someone noticed. Pressure? Being number one in the juniors was the worst. This isn't that kind of pressure. These kids love the attention."

Francine had a Walkman, too, for her country music and religious tapes, but she was too worked up to listen. She preferred to stare out the bus window at the city and listen to New York.

"I had a dream last night," she said. "I was in New York and I was running, running so fast. And I thought: What could make me run so fast? Maybe it's the air here, instead of the smog in Los Angeles. It's so fresh." Or maybe it was the sense of opportunity. Her daughter was about to begin her career, and Francine, always immune to the flat, finite reality of statistics, rankings, and contracts, felt only hope. She and Tom had succeeded in giving Debbie something they had never had—endless possibilities.

By the time the bus arrived at Flushing Meadow, just after noon, Debbie's practice partner had begun working with another girl. Debbie scouted around until she found Melissa Gurney, who had gotten a wild card into the main draw, Robert Lansdorp, and another of Robert's students. She started hitting with Melissa while Carolyn Gurney and Francine found a couple of plastic chairs, plunked them down on the cement walkway next to the court, and commiserated on their first-time nerves.

Carolyn had just been up on the second floor of the U.S. Open Club Building, where Tuesday's draw was posted outside the players' locker rooms. Neither Melissa nor Debbie was on it. They would have to wait until Wednesday for their first match—and on Tuesday practice courts would be at an absurd premium, because most of the courts would be taken up with match play. Robert Lansdorp, who was being paid by the Gurneys to be at the tournament and work with Melissa, was already trying to arrange a practice court for her at nearby Queens College. Francine made a mental note to ask him if Debbie could go along.

Melissa's first match was against Terry Phelps. "She's six foot and a hometown girl," said Carolyn, who, in her anxiety, made Phelps four inches taller than she actually was, "and she's probably really up for this. But at least it won't be a traumatic match, a 'go back where you came from, kid' match. It's not a Pam Shriver. But she is ranked way up there, around thirty-seven." Phelps, in fact, was ranked fifty-seventh.

Francine thought about Alycia Moulton, ranked even higher than Carolyn's erroneous estimate, and glanced over at the girls.

"But it will be good experience for them," she said.

"That's one way of looking at it," said Carolyn.

She excused herself and headed for a pay phone to call Buffalo, New York. The family had assumed that Melissa would play on Tuesday, not realizing that the size of the draw required two days of first-round matches. Ram's father had canceled all of his Tuesday appointments, and he, his wife, Ram, and Ram's sister had made plane reservations for Tuesday. Now Carolyn was in the midst of a frantic long-distance reorganization, as she and Ram juggled plane tickets and hotel rooms while her father-in-law attempted to cancel his cancellations and clear the day on Wednesday.

As Carolyn headed away from the court, Francine thought about Tom. Before she left she had encouraged him to fly to New York if Debbie won her first match, but she had not told Debbie of that possibility, and did not really expect Tom to come.

"I do wish Tom could be here," she said. "But that's just the extra pressure she doesn't need."

Debbie hopped from practice court to practice court for three hours, stopping only to pick up another cold drink and quarrel with Francine about whether, and when, to talk to Lansdorp about a practice court for Tuesday and a mixed doubles partner. Debbie was playing doubles with Shawn Foltz, who had lost in the singles qualifying rounds and was hanging around, waiting for the Junior Open to start. Debbie wanted to play mixed doubles, too, but she had no partner, and Lansdorp had mentioned that he might be able to find someone for her. Francine thought that Debbie should take a break, find her coach, and get everything settled, but Debbie just wanted to keep hitting.

Finally, at 3:30, they headed for the second floor of the U.S. Open Club Building. Debbie wanted to check the draw sheet one last time before they boarded the bus for the ride back to the Summit. The only other stop she had to make was in the white trailer parked outside the players' entrance to the tennis center, where every player had to register formally for the tournament.

Debbie stopped in the locker room to wash up and put on fresh makeup, and then she and Francine went downstairs. As they walked down the hallway, past the hospitality areas for IMG and ProServ/Volvo, and the players' lounge, an older girl walked by, smiled, and said hello.

Debbie smiled back and then turned to Francine. "That's Elise Burgin," she said. "I beat her." Burgin, a student at Stanford University, had been Debbie's second-round victim at the U.S. Open Clay Courts in Indianapolis.

They made their way around the courts in silence. Fifty feet from the players' entrance and the trailer, without looking up, Debbie suddenly said, "So. Should I sign pro?"

"Yes," said Francine, emphatically. "Tell them you want to change your status. Say you want to register pro."

"Yeah?"

"Yes. Ask them what to do. Tell them you signed a letter saying you wouldn't be, that you'd be playing as an amateur, but you want to change your status."

Debbie took her Walkman out of her bag, plugged her headphones into her ears, and walked up the wooden steps into the trailer without saying another word. Francine hesitated for a split second before she followed her daughter inside, where three women sat behind a metal folding table. One of them handed Debbie a form to fill out. At the top there was a place to check off either "amateur" or "pro." A pro got to choose between picking up her prize-money check or having it mailed to her home.

Debbie filled in all the information, stared at the blanks next to "amateur" and "pro," checked off "pro," and stared a moment longer. Then she held it up for the woman behind the desk to see.

"Um," Debbie said, clearing her throat. "When I signed a form before I checked 'amateur.'"

The woman took the form without looking up.

"But now you're a pro?" she said, in a disinterested monotone.

"Yeah," said Debbie.

"OK," said the woman. "You have to get a photo I.D. and you get a sweatshirt. Small, medium, or large?"

"Small."

The woman put Debbie's form down on the table and rummaged through a box for a small sweatshirt, which she pushed across the table.

"And here's your packet," said the woman, handing Debbie a manila envelope. "You get free tickets for the first two days."

Francine took a step forward. After a year of waiting and hoping, the proceedings were a bit too cut-and-dried for her. No one seemed to be the least bit impressed that Debbie Spence was now a professional tennis player; the moment lacked ceremony. Debbie deserved better treatment. This business about two days' tickets—which implied, as Tom had when he made the hotel reservations, that Debbie couldn't possibly last any longer—was hardly an auspicious greeting for a new pro. It didn't matter that this was policy for all pros. Francine was insulted.

"What if she keeps winning?" she asked.

"Then we hand the tickets out on a day-by-day basis," the woman said.

Debbie held up the sweatshirt, which was white and had the words *U.S. Open 1984* printed in a small triangle over the breast.

"It's a nice sweatshirt," she said, to no one in particular. "A pretty big small though."

She adjusted her headphones and turned to leave.

Francine picked up the form, which was still sitting on the table. "I just want to make sure," she said, "that this form overrides the other."

"Yep," the woman said.

"She was an amateur," said Francine, "but now she's a pro. She had signed the other form. But now this is official. Right?"

"Right."

"So that's all we have to do."

"Mom," said Debbie, rolling her eyes and heading for the door. "Are you sure you don't want to ask *again?*"

"Well, you have to make sure."

"God, can you believe this?"

"Oh, Debbie. Did I embarrass you again?"

"You sure did."

Debbie Spence, just-turned seventeen-year-old tennis professional, went next door to another trailer to pick up her photo identification card. When she came out, she saw Melissa Gurney, who was about to register, but Debbie said nothing about what she had just done. Instead, she started joking with Melissa about how awful the picture on her I.D. card was—a picture taken last year, when she had lost in the first round of the qualifying and lost too soon in the juniors. She didn't want to have anything to do with the girl in the photograph, who had a fatter face, and plain straight bangs and plain long straight hair, and who lost. Debbie wanted a new picture to go with her new life, a picture of a girl who had a chic haircut, whose facial bones were beginning to peek through. A girl who was already starting to compute how much money she might earn this year, and deciding where she intended to spend it.

"Mine is the worst," said Debbie.

"Mine is *so* ugly," said Melissa.

"Lemme see it."

"I don't have it on me."

"Yeah, sure," said Debbie. "I look so fat. My hair wasn't even curled. Next year when they say, 'Were you here last year?' I'll just lie and say no."

Francine insisted on taking photographs, without mentioning exactly what moment in history she wanted to immortalize, but Debbie, feeling a little bit wild, refused to hold still for a normal pose. She borrowed a pair of reflector sunglasses, and then loaned her sunglasses to Melissa and posed while she put on lip gloss. Then she turned abruptly and headed for the bus, leaving Francine to pick up her racquet bags. Francine grabbed one upside down, and three racquets fell to the ground.

"Debbie," she called.

"Yeah, Mom?" Debbie turned and looked. "Great."

"Could you pick them up?"

"You pick it up. You dropped it."

Francine's voice got shrill. "I am not a maid. I do not want to feel like a maid."

"Sure, you are," said Debbie, walking over to pick up the racquets. "You're a mother."

As Debbie walked on ahead, Francine vowed to get hold of Lansdorp as soon as they got back to the hotel. "We have to talk to him," she said. "He's supposed to find Debbie a mixed doubles partner. It's more money." Surprised, she burst out laughing. "It *is* more money. I forgot."

Francine and Debbie were in room 834 at the Summit, which was the sort of disaster that resulted from two people packing at the last minute for a trip that could last from four days to two weeks and required four people's worth of clothing. There were mountains of cotton practice clothes and tennis ensembles for Debbie, shorts and tops for Francine, and two more sets of clothes for their forays into Manhattan. A row of squishy fabric bags spilled their contents along the dresser top. Francine's hard shell suitcase sat on a chair. There was an open bag filled with cosmetics on top of the TV, alongside Debbie's battery-powered combination radio and cassette tape player.

As soon as they got back to the room Monday afternoon, Debbie shut herself in the bathroom and turned on the shower. Francine, a bit giddy from the day's events, rummaged through her purse looking for the phone number of the Essex House, the other official tournament hotel, where Robert Lansdorp was staying. She tossed the contents of the purse onto the bed: cassette tapes of Linda Ronstadt, country music, and Christian teachings; two granola bars in case Debbie needed some quick energy; and two oversized greeting cards without envelopes. They were inspirational cards, one entitled "What I Need" and the other "Gentle Words of Encouragement," which Debbie had bought for herself in the gift shop at the El-Con during the Easter Bowl last spring. Francine, pleased that her daughter found comfort in religious cards and concerned about keeping Debbie "psyched up," had brought the cards with her to New York.

She sat down on Debbie's bed and called Lansdorp. "I was wondering," she said to him, in a deferential tone of voice, "if you might have found a doubles partner for Debbie, and if you might have an idea about where she could practice tomorrow, or if you might have time to hit with her or let her come with you."

Lansdorp told Francine that mixed doubles were out of the question, since the draw was too small for Debbie to qualify. Then he suggested that Debbie join him and Melissa Gurney for tomorrow's practice session, which had been Francine's primary concern. She did not want Debbie to have a whole day with nothing to do before an important match. It would be too easy for her daughter to get worked up if she wasn't occupied.

"Now, I'm prepared to pay you for any time you spend with Debbie," said Francine happily. "I'm filthy rich."

Lansdorp told her not to worry about the money. She thanked him profusely and then began to laugh.

"No, you keep your pockets open for all my money," she said. "Remember, I'm filthy rich."

Debbie emerged from the bathroom, put on her makeup, her official U.S. Open sweatshirt, blue sweatpants, and white pointy-toed shoes with slim heels. She and Francine intended to walk from the East Side to the Essex House, on Central Park South, to see Pat and Shawn Foltz. Debbie and Shawn had made vague plans for dinner, and Debbie would have gone alone, but Francine was determined to see Central Park.

Mother and daughter headed out together. Before they got a block away, Francine pulled out a movie camera and began filming inanimate and obstinate objects—the Helmsley Building at Park Avenue and 46th Street, the horses that drew carriages through Central Park and were, by 5:30 at night, too bored or tired to move, and her daughter, who kept trying to dart twenty feet ahead of her mother and refused to mug for the camera.

"I don't *know* her," howled Debbie, mortified at having to be seen with such an unworldly woman as Francine.

By the time they arrived at the Essex House, Shawn and her mother had made other plans for dinner, but they agreed to meet back at the hotel in a few hours for a visit. Debbie and Francine walked around the corner for a five-dollar hamburger, which was the least expensive offering on the menu, and then went back to the Foltzes' room, where Francine and Pat shared stories about the dangers of life in Manhattan.

Debbie and Shawn announced that they were just going down to the lobby to see if any of their friends were around and then proceeded to take an illicit stroll around the block. Even though Shawn had lost in the qualifying for the main draw, she was having a wonderful time. Singer Kenny Rogers, an avid tennis fan, had been out at Flushing Meadow during the qualifying matches and recognized Shawn from her role in *Spring Fever.* He introduced himself, complimented her on her game—and said he might show up to watch her and Debbie play doubles.

The next morning, Debbie confided to Francine that she had come up with a great plan. Tom had once said he was willing to support Debbie for two more years. She wanted him to do that—to pay all of her expenses on the pro circuit while she saved all the prize money she won. "It won't be that much," she told Francine. "Maybe forty thousand dollars a year. This way it'll give me a good start."

Francine was amused by the idea. What Tom had meant, of course, was that he would support Debbie for two more years if she decided not to turn pro. He was not going to be enthusiastic about subsidizing Debbie's tennis while she socked away $80,000. Francine wondered if Debbie remembered her promise to pay her father back for her $14,000 sports car, but she decided not to mention it today.

Debbie left the hotel early to meet Robert Lansdorp at Flushing Meadow, so Francine blithely announced her intention to spend Tuesday seeing the sights—the Empire State Building, Grand Central Station, Rockefeller Center. But not an hour passed without reference to Debbie. Francine would look at her watch and wonder if Debbie had gotten enough practice time, if Lansdorp was giving her enough attention, if she was truly back to her physical peak. By four o'clock, when Francine collapsed at a table at an outdoor café in Rockefeller Center, all she could think about was Debbie's match tomorrow, the first of her pro career.

II

If looking tough was the key to victory, Debbie strode out of the elevator Wednesday morning a winner. She was invulnerable. Her eyes were hidden behind big plastic sunglasses, her ears plugged with headphones, her body swathed in a fancy red-white-and-blue satin bomber jacket with the insignia FILA SQUADRA 84 on the front and SPENCE embroidered across the back.

Her no-nonsense image lasted about fifteen seconds. Then she stopped at the edge of the hotel lobby, took off her sunglasses, and inquired: Was there something funny about one of her eyes? Francine assured her that the swelling in her right eyelid was minimal, hardly noticeable at all, probably just a reaction to her makeup. Reassured, Debbie walked out front, where the bus and two official U.S. Open cars were waiting.

Although Debbie was supposed to take the bus, Francine marched right over to one of the cars and asked the driver if he would take them to Flushing Meadow. She wanted to remind her daughter that this was a special, exciting day, even though it had not had an auspicious beginning. Debbie had woken up this morning with a swollen eyelid and blood on her nightshirt from a cold sore on her lip, which had opened during the night. It was hard to feel that you could conquer the world, or at least Alycia Moulton, when you looked like a mess.

Now Francine regarded her daughter critically. "This morning I thought, 'Uh, oh, now she's got excuses.' But she's in pretty good spirits."

She got into the car with her daughter and another tennis player. The driver was a member of the U.S. Olympic fencing team, an amateur athlete who was delighted at the chance to make $100 a day, plus the use of the car at night, plus meals, for a two-week job.

The other tennis player congratulated the driver on the cushy job, and asked whether the money would have to be reported on his income tax. The tennis player had heard that the money was tax-exempt, which made the job an even better deal. The driver, a student at Columbia University, laughed.

"What difference does it make?" he said. "I'm right there at the poverty level anyhow."

Debbie, who would make $1,800 today if she lost and over $3,700, and the opportunity to earn more, if she won, laughed politely.

The players' lounge in the U.S. Open Club Building, like the IMG and ProServ/Volvo digs down the hall, was defined by green partitions and festooned with green and white banners hung from a wire stretched across the ceiling. There was a long food counter at the back of the room, where players and coaches could get salads, sandwiches, hot meals, drinks, and a hefty array of cakes and pies for free—and their guests could buy a meal for substantially less than the going rate for civilians. The back half of the room was full of round tables, for diners. The front half was crammed with chairs and couches and small tables, and a board upon which the schedule of matches was posted. After a day, since no one recognized the demarcation between dining room and living room, it was also littered with the remnants of hastily eaten meals.

Over in the corner of the lounge two women sat behind a table draped in gold fabric, which was the temporary office of Thomas Cook Travel, the official travel agency of the WTA. It was a sobering, if unobtrusive, reminder that most of the people who were crowded into this room were going to lose, and might need to change an airline reservation. A few couches away a nervous potential victim lay with his head buried in the cushions. When a concerned coach or friend stopped by to offer encouragement, he would thrash about as if he had a fever and could not find a comfortable place to rest.

When Debbie and Francine arrived they made the rounds of the tables while Debbie waited for her eleven o'clock practice court. They stopped to say hello to Michelle Torres, an amateur who hardly played the juniors anymore, had a computer ranking in the top thirty, but had yet to turn pro. Francine asked Muriel Torres, Michelle's mother, when her daughter might make the move. Muriel hesitated. Michelle was recovering from foot surgery, and all the recent negative publicity about young girls facing physical and mental burnout made them think that later might be better than sooner. Mrs. Torres did not inquire about Debbie's plans, so Francine said nothing.

The truth was that Michelle, like Debbie, had just registered as a pro, but Mrs. Torres, like Tom Spence, wanted to spare her daughter any additional pressures before the tournament began. Francine, less disciplined on the issue of secrecy, wandered over to the food counter a bit disappointed. If Mrs. Torres had only asked, Francine would have felt compelled to tell the truth.

"I would have said, 'Well, as a matter of fact, *we've* just done it,'" she said, with an eager giggle.

A table away, Robert Lansdorp ate his lunch alone. He said hello to Francine and Debbie, and made sure Debbie was on her way to practice, but he chose not to join them. Small talk was a waste of time. Lansdorp was busily playing matches in his head, thinking about his students' chances.

At the USTA Junior Hardcourt Championships last month, he could afford to sit in a lounge chair and take the sun, confident that his girls were among the best players in the tournament. Here they were the novices, the ones who might cave in to stage fright and lose matches they perhaps shouldn't have lost. The summer had been a somber reminder that playing in the pros required psychological, as well as physical, stamina. Lansdorp could only hope that Debbie, Melissa Gurney, and Stephanie Rehe were in good mental shape. It was too late for anything but fine-tuning; a suggestion about a stroke here, the perfectly pertinent word of encouragement there.

There was a lot at stake for the director of the nearly one-year-old Robert Lansdorp Tennis Academy. People here still remembered how his last protégée, Tracy Austin, had made it to the quarterfinals of the U.S. Open when she was fifteen.

If one of his girls broke through this year, he would get a lot of attention, which IMG might be able to translate into an endorsement contract, or a sponsorship for a real academy sometime in the future. He had three prodigies in the main draw. He rolled their chances over in his mind.

Debbie's first match was going to be a severe test of her mental game. Moulton would have presented a problem for Debbie even under the best of circumstances. She was an aggressive player who played a power game at the net, while Debbie preferred a slower baseline game that depended on accuracy and strategy. If Moulton started cramming the ball down Debbie's throat, Debbie might collapse. Besides, everyone had heard about Moulton's match against Chris Evert Lloyd. The crowd would expect her to make short work of a kid like Debbie. And, even though Debbie hadn't publicized her new status as a pro, she was under a lot of self-inflicted pressure. She could choke if she began to play badly.

Melissa Gurney had what looked like an easier match against Terry Phelps, but Lansdorp knew how delicate an instrument a young player was, especially one who was at the U.S. Open for the first time. Melissa had the ability to win, Lansdorp decided, unless she became overwhelmed by her surroundings. She was better off than Stephanie Rehe, who had survived the qualifying rounds only to face Barbara Potter, ranked twenty-fifth this year but no stranger to the top ten.

An objective observer might have concluded that Spence and Rehe were in trouble, while Gurney had a chance. But no one involved in the competition, on any level, could afford to be objective at this point. The coaches, agents, parents, and even the players were all speculative investors in a volatile, unpredictable business. They banked a professional reputation, or some portion of an adolescence, on victory, knowing all the while that, each time out, every girl but one would lose. They were all too aware of the myriad things that could trip up even the best player, from the incessant roar of jets from LaGuardia Airport overhead to the mercurial loyalties of the crowd. Still, they had made their bets—

the wagers were years old—and needed to believe that they had gambled wisely. They were all involved in ongoing, internalized pep talks.

"Debbie can win if she's tough. But she won't be happy playing Alycia because she doesn't like girls who come to the net," Lansdorp declared. "Gurney can win if she doesn't get nervous, because Phelps is just a consistent hitter, no excitement. Rehe can win if she breaks Potter's serve and Potter collapses."

Somewhere on the grounds of the USTA National Tennis Center, the players who would face Spence, Gurney, and Rehe—and the members of their entourages—told themselves just the reverse. They needed to believe, as fervently as Robert Lansdorp did, in the opposite set of conclusions.

Francine lingered in the players' lounge while Debbie practiced, and then wandered outside to watch some of the matches. But her eyes kept darting over to court 21, where Debbie's match was up next. When she figured it was time for Debbie to be done with her workout, she went back to the lounge to intercept her. She trailed along as Debbie headed to the locker room to change.

"Don't take too long," Francine said. "Somebody could sprain an ankle."

Debbie grunted. She preferred not to be reminded of her default at Junior Wimbledon.

"I have to know where you are *every minute,*" Francine called after her.

By 12:30 Debbie was sitting on one of the couches at the edge of the players' lounge, dressed in a fresh Fila outfit. She drank a Tab, listened to her Walkman, and riffled through a paperback book, to blot out distractions as much as anything else. Every few minutes Francine walked upstairs to the locker room to make sure the match had not been called.

On one of her trips she heard someone say that the match between Catherine Tanvier and Leigh Thompson had just ended, and she ran back to the lounge, grabbed Debbie, and rushed to the court, past a group of little girls who were camped outside the lounge, hugging their autograph books to their chests and watching for famous players. But Francine had misunderstood. The match was tied at 4–all in the second set. The girls had at least two more games, and possibly a whole third set, yet to play.

Instead of returning to the lounge, Francine and Debbie just leaned against the chain link fence that surrounded the court, and watched the match. Their adrenaline had started pumping at the thought that Debbie was about to play, and now they were too wired up to go back and sit down.

Mercifully, Tanvier took the match in straight sets, so Debbie did not have to wait too long. As soon as the other players cleared the court, she gathered her racquets and, without a word to Francine, walked onto the court and began her pre-match ritual. She introduced herself to the umpire, sat down in one of the two folding chairs set out for the players, unzipped her racquet bags and checked her racquets, got herself a cold drink, and straightened her outfit and her hair. She did not look over her shoulder at her mother. When she was ready, she simply sat quietly, her back to Francine, and stared at the court.

A few minutes later, Alycia Moulton appeared. At five-foot ten-and-a-half, she was an imposing physical presence. She strode onto the court, wearing the high-top tennis shoes that were the latest in tennis footwear, a graceful woman with a big rolling stride and an impenetrable slight smile. With her long, braided dark-blond ponytail and court tan, she was a handsome, twenty-three-year-old pro who had been ranked in the top forty consistently since she turned pro in 1982.

Since this was not a match between two well-known players, it was consigned to a court without any bleacher seats. Francine immediately took up a position against the low fence, checked to make sure that the umpire's elevated chair did not obstruct her view of either side of the court, and gripped the top of the fence with both hands. She had vowed to remain in control of her nerves, no matter what—no matter how many times she had made that vow, and broken it, in the past. It was the least she could do for Debbie.

"I'm going to control myself real well here," she said. "At least outwardly. Inwardly I'm a wreck."

Alycia Moulton won the coin toss and decided to serve. Although she allowed Debbie to tie up the first game by double-faulting, she managed to hold her serve. But then Debbie quickly took the second game without allowing Moulton a single point, and broke Moulton's service with well-placed passing shots to take the third game as well.

Francine began a quiet conversation with herself as the fourth game got under way. "Debbie looks like she's ready to attack," she muttered. "Be tough, Debbie."

Debbie stayed ahead through seven games by doing what a new pro was supposed to do: she played go-for-broke tennis, scrambling around the court in a blur of speed. If Moulton tried drop shots to lure Debbie to the net, Debbie zoomed up and returned them for winners. Moulton broke her serve to tie the set at 4–all, but Debbie retaliated by breaking Moulton's serve again to pull ahead, 5–4.

As Debbie stepped up to serve for the first set, Francine closed her eyes. She bounced up and down and bent her knees, as if she could achieve the transmigration of flexibility from her body to her daughter's. Andy Davidson, the teaching pro who sometimes worked with Marianne Werdel and Camille Benjamin at the Bakersfield Tennis and Racquet Club, suddenly appeared to give another southern California girl a boost. His players were not in the running. Marianne had not been able to get back onto the computer in time to qualify for the main draw and had no interest in playing the juniors. Camille was here, but had already lost her first-round match. Andy leaned on the fence next to Francine and applauded loudly whenever Debbie made a good shot.

She took the last game, and the first set, with an ace. Francine, who had spent most of that game staring at the ground and shifting from one foot to the other, clapped wildly and grinned at her daughter, who seemed determined not to look over at the crowd.

"OK," said Francine, with a nervous sigh. "Now they can stop the whole thing."

A spectator standing nearby inquired if Francine and Debbie were sisters.

Debbie Spence and Alycia Moulton traded games through the second set until the eighth game, when Moulton broke Debbie's serve without allowing Debbie a single point, to lead five games to three. It was too quick and decisive a loss, and for the first time in the match Debbie glanced over to her mother for reassurance. Francine nodded at her daughter, but she was having her own problems maintaining her composure. Her repertoire of nervous gestures had expanded to include wiggling her knees back and forth, crossing and uncrossing her legs, and clutching the fingers of one hand in the other.

At one point she lurched sideways and bumped against a stranger. "I'm sorry," she apologized. "I was going for that ball." She muttered to herself that being a spectator was the worst part of tennis, and joked that it would have been nice to make this a one-set match.

She talked straight through the next game, which Moulton took, to win the second set 6–3. "I have to," she said, "to blow off steam."

In the third set Debbie started to come unraveled. Stray hairs worked their way out of her barrettes and flew in all directions, and her eye makeup was smudged under her eyes. Her face was splotchy and drenched in sweat. She began to talk to herself, out loud, as she and Moulton continued to trade games.

The lead seesawed back and forth until Moulton, ahead 5–4, prepared to serve for game, set, and match. Francine grimaced. "This," she said, "is no longer fun." It was nerve-racking: Debbie quickly pulled ahead to lead 0–40, only to lose her concentration and give away two points. She recovered and broke Moulton's serve and then, delighted at having temporarily saved the match, she took the next game as well. Now she was ahead 6–5. Francine's grim mood instantly swung over to ecstasy.

"Now I'm OK," she announced. "It's when it's the other way around that I'm not. The only problem now is that Wonder Woman"—she smiled at the nickname she had just slapped on

Moulton—"is serving. But that's OK. She'll double-fault it away."

Her loopy optimism was as excessive as the despair she had felt moments before, but there were no middle emotions, no luxurious subtleties, for tennis parents. This was a life of garish extreme—the kids won or lost, they and their parents were happy or sad, and the gradations of feeling they tried to create were, for the most part, forced and unconvincing. Now that Debbie was a pro, any attempt to look at the bright side of a loss would sound absolutely silly because of the economic repercussions. It was small consolation to have made a respectable showing against a seasoned pro if the other girl walked off the court with twice the prize money and the chance to earn more.

The thrill was short-lived. Alycia Moulton did *not* double-fault the match away. She won the game and forced the match into a thirteen-point tie breaker, an agonizing test of a player's ability to remain cool. It was as if nothing that had happened in the past two hours mattered. Whoever got seven points first won the match.

Debbie had been up 0–40 again in the last game, one point away from winning the match, but now she was only seven points away from a loss, and at a distinct psychological disadvantage. She had blown her lead in the third set—truly the mark of a wobbly novice.

She glanced at Francine between every point now, her mother's face a frozen mask of what she hoped would pass for encouragement. But Debbie did not collapse, as she had in so many matches during the past year. This was her first match as a professional tennis player—as an adult—and she had to prove to herself, and her parents, that she was ready. No more childish surrender to self-doubt.

To the crowd's loud delight, Debbie Spence took the first four points of the tie breaker, gave up one point to Moulton, and then finished her off, 7–1. Debbie Spence had just scored an upset in the first match of her pro career. She scooped up her racquets and stumbled off the court a disheveled, jabbering wreck.

Francine was right outside the gate, bouncing up and down, but to congratulate Debbie she had to stand in line behind two little girls—wearing T-shirts from the Wimbledon Racquet Club and the Sri Chinmoy Tennis Classic, respectively—who accosted Debbie and demanded autographs. She scrawled her name and then stared at her hand, which trembled noticeably.

"I was *so* nervous," she said. "Look at me. I'm shaking."

Then the true significance of the event hit her.

"Mom," she shrieked. "I won so much money. I'm so happy. Thousands of dollars. Right in my bank!"

Francine hugged her as a knot of people formed around them. Spectators, including two sets of parents of much younger players who had just had their fantasies confirmed, came over to congratulate them both. Passersby, always interested in discovering a new talent, asked who Debbie was, who she'd beaten, and how old she was, and then consulted their draw sheets to figure out when they could catch the next Spence match.

A moment later Robert Lansdorp strolled over to congratulate Debbie. He had been watching Stephanie Rehe, who lost to Barbara Potter in three sets, but now he was full of praise and questions for Debbie.

"Whaddaya gonna be now?" he joked loudly. "Number thirty in the world?"

Euphoria was a brave state: Debbie retorted that it was about time he showed up to watch her, and headed toward the locker room with Francine. She chattered nonstop. With this victory to back her up, she could tell people that she had turned pro—there had been rumors going around, which she had sidestepped, but now she had something to brag about. She deserved to be a pro; she didn't have to be evasive anymore. And this was only the beginning. Debbie confessed her belief that a three-set win was a good omen.

"This other time at a tournament I won a match in three sets and it went well," she said, "so I thought, OK. If I win this one in three the *whole tournament* will go well, and if I don't it won't."

As Debbie and Francine came around the side of the U.S.

Open Club Building, they saw a crowd of youngsters milling in front of the entrance, watching for a favorite player to pass by. Suddenly one of the girls pointed at Debbie and a dozen young fans ran up to her and held out pens and paper. A conscientious new pro, aware of her responsibilities to the crowd and to women's tennis, Debbie dutifully signed each autograph before she headed upstairs for a shower.

Then, cognizant of her dual potential, as a player and as a public figure, she put herself together. If an agent, a tournament official, or a sporting-goods rep stopped her to say congratulations, she wanted to make a good impression. She applied fresh pink eyeshadow, mascara and lipstick, grabbed a Tab and some popcorn, and headed over to watch Melissa Gurney's match. Francine followed a few steps behind her daughter; she sensed that Debbie's new image did not include a hovering parent.

Debbie envied Melissa what seemed like an easier draw, a draw that could get her a lot of media attention. If Melissa beat Terry Phelps she would face Rosie Casals, a legendary figure in women's tennis, but an eminently breakable icon. Casals was weeks away from her thirty-sixth birthday, and in the last four years her ranking had slipped from a high of sixth in the world to as low as ninety-eight. She had been ranked in the top five in the country as a sixteen-year-old, but that was back in 1964, before Melissa, Debbie, or the Virginia Slims Circuit was born. Melissa had a chance to get herself noticed. People would love a story about how a fifteen-year-old junior player had beaten one of the grand old ladies of tennis.

Still, Debbie was excited enough by her win to think she might have a chance against Lisa Bonder, her next opponent. Lisa was seeded ninth in the tournament, and as Debbie walked toward a back court she tried to calculate how a victory would improve her computer ranking. The way she figured it, beating Bonder would bump her up to a ranking in the sixties, high enough to get into the main draw of a lucrative Virginia Slims tournament without having to suffer through the qualifying rounds.

Wouldn't that be something to tell her father on the phone

the day after tomorrow! She and Francine had just called Tom from the locker room to tell him that Debbie had beaten Alycia Moulton, and Debbie had pridefully challenged him to guess her score.

"Oh-and-oh?" he guessed.

As if 6–4, 3–6, 7–6 weren't good enough. If she beat Lisa Bonder he wouldn't have much to complain about.

By Thursday Melissa Gurney's informal entourage had ex-panded to include not just her parents, sister Robyn, uncle, cousins, and grandparents, but Robert Lansdorp, Jim Curley of IMG, and Parkes Brittain of Advantage International. Despite a little initial nervousness, Melissa had beaten Terry Phelps handily. The bleachers were packed for her next match against Rosie Casals. It was essential that the people who stood to profit from her performance be here, lest they be accused, as Robert had been by Debbie the day before, of insufficient interest.

They were hot on the trail of the next Tracy Austin. It made no difference that the original Tracy Austin had not yet returned to the circuit full-time, almost a year after she went to Australia to get back into shape. No one was bothered by the news that Gunze, the Japanese sportswear firm, had recently renegotiated her contract when it became clear that Tracy's long absence from competition would not soon be over. The individual might be in trouble, but her image was untarnished, larger than life.

They continued to believe in her—and they were ready to believe in Melissa Gurney. Jim Curley, sweating in a suit and tie in the hot, humid afternoon, waved and smiled at the Gurneys and climbed to a seat in the top row of the bleachers. An agent had to dance a delicate two-step; he had to be attentive without being overbearing. Curley wanted the Gurneys to know that he was around, but he didn't want to be pushy.

He felt that Melissa Gurney had the combination of talent and charm that it took to be a successful—commercially viable —pro. He had never actually seen her play before today, but other people at IMG had. "They said, 'This is someone you should keep an eye on and get close to,' " he recalled. "So I spoke with Robert and said, 'If they're interested in sitting down I'd like to introduce myself.' "

So far he had been cautious in his approach. "The time to turn pro is when the family, the coach, and, most important, the player is ready" was his philosophy. "There comes a time when everybody thinks it's right. It could be six months, could be a year, maybe a little longer. We're talking about very impressionable young girls, and we have to be there to help them, not to press them."

As soon as the Gurneys were ready to make the move, though, Curley had strategies. He felt that the best way to protect Melissa from the shock of suddenly being a pro would be to carefully choose a tournament schedule that would help her build her self-esteem. Since IMG promoted tournaments and provided players for exhibition matches, the agency could place Melissa in situations where she would get experience without risking a morale-bending match against a top-ranked player.

"You don't want to throw her to the lions too soon," he said, laughing. "You don't want to put Melissa in an event where she's playing Chris or Martina or Hana Mandlikova. At the beginning you have to work on confidence." Advantage International did not have its own tournaments, so Parkes Brittain could not offer similar protection, which compensated somewhat for his having approached the Gurneys so much sooner. Curley did not seem worried about the competition.

In fact, he was already doing what he could to "position" Melissa Gurney, to make the pro tennis world aware of her both as a player and as an attractive young woman who might soon be available to endorse products. He knew that companies sent scouts to tournaments like the U.S. Open to look for marketable players—not just sporting-goods companies, but anyone who thought that a healthy talented youngster could lure customers. He talked up the players IMG represented, or wanted to represent, in the hope that a scout would drop by a player's match.

Melissa won handily, 6–0, 6–3, in front of a large, noisy crowd. It didn't matter that Rosie Casals was past her peak as a singles player, that Melissa might have encountered a tougher match from a more anonymous foe at the top of her form. What was important was that a child had trounced one of the pioneers of women's tennis, and had imprinted her name in the spectators' collective memory by virtue of that victory. Insiders already knew who Melissa Gurney was, knew to watch her every move with hungry anticipation. Now the mass audience knew her, too; she had taken another step toward celebrity.

As soon as the match ended, Jim Curley was on his feet, as was Parkes Brittain, both heading toward the Gurneys to talk about the bright future. Brittain felt that Melissa's performance here was a mandate—she could turn pro at any time. The only thing she might want to do was remain a junior until the Orange Bowl in December, the prestigious international junior tournament that Debbie Spence had won in 1983. Melissa might want to add that victory to her collection.

"But then, why bother?" he said, with a huge smile. "I think she's certainly proved herself right here." He trailed after Melissa and her mother, who were looking for Ram. Ram's nerves had gotten the better of him, and he had paced back and forth, out of eyeshot, for most of the match.

Suddenly, Robert Lansdorp strode into view. In a loud, brash voice, he announced that the match "stank." Melissa hadn't moved around the court quickly enough to suit him, and he was thinking of having her do some running this afternoon. Whether he was right or not, he upset Carolyn and Melissa, and took the edge off of what had been a happy moment. Carolyn quickly moved next to her daughter, put a protective, guiding arm around her, and led her away toward the locker room, the two agents in hot pursuit. Melissa had defeated a famous opponent and was one match away from the quarterfinal round. This was no time to think about real or imagined shortcomings.

Later, Lansdorp would insist that he only came on strong because he believed that Melissa could break through and create a sensation—but only if she worked hard. He felt she had won against Casals "too easy," that she had let her level of play slip once victory seemed certain. Since his professional future rode with hers, he could not afford to sit by and let her take that kind of chance.

"She got bored," he said, "but you can't *do* that. You've got to play tough. What if the other person gets a second-set win and all of a sudden you're out there for three sets? If she couldn't do any better it would be a different story. But she can. She can get into the quarterfinals."

Melissa did not get into the quarterfinals; she was beaten in the third round by Petra Delhees Jauch of Switzerland, 7–5, 6–1. It didn't really matter. The powers that be in women's tennis, the coaches, agents, and promoters, had determined that Melissa Gurney—prettier than Debbie Spence, younger, coming off a more consistent year—had a bright future. She had an almost magical credibility that made a loss a fleeting disappointment, and nothing more.

Thursday night Debbie and Francine sat in their hotel room with Warren Rice, who had accompanied Debbie to the 1983 Junior U.S. Open and had arrived this afternoon, again at his own expense, to serve as an unofficial traveling coach. To Debbie, he represented Tom Spence's expertise without the parental pressure—and to Warren, Debbie represented yet another opportunity to make a place for himself in pro tennis. Perhaps, he thought, he could create a job for himself as a combination coach and business manager.

Right now, though, profits were only pleasant fantasies. The economic reality was as tight as it had ever been. Since there were no rooms left at the Summit at the discount rate, Warren would sleep on the floor of the Spences' room. Before everyone went to sleep, they talked about tomorrow's match.

They decided that nerves, not Lisa Bonder, were Debbie's true foe. So they came up with two slogans for Debbie to say to herself, words that would bolster her confidence and keep her from losing her concentration: "Play to win" and "I can do it."

On Friday, Robert Lansdorp personally conducted Debbie's warm-up session and promised to stay in the bleachers for the whole match. "The *other* girl has to be nervous," Lansdorp announced, when Debbie went upstairs to the locker room to change. "She knows how tough Debbie is. But Debbie has to start out well. She can definitely win this. I've talked enough to her. If she doesn't believe it by now, there's not much hope."

Debbie appeared in the players' lounge about a half-hour before her match, and Warren tried to distract her by chatting with her and some of the other girls. Francine did her best to appear calm. When the match was finally called, she hung back with her daughter for a moment. She wanted to make sure that Debbie remembered what to say.

" 'Play to win,' " she whispered to Debbie, "and 'I can do it.' "

Francine put up a brave front, but as Debbie walked on ahead with Warren, her mother fretted about something that had been preying on her mind since Debbie's match against Alycia Moulton two days earlier. Francine kept thinking about how Debbie had glanced at her when the second set started going badly. It was not a good sign.

"I'm a nervous wreck," she said. "But I'm going to be calm on the outside. But she *did* look over at me last time. Gosh, when she was little she'd do it all the time—hit the ball, look at me, hit the ball, look at me. And she'd say, 'How come you weren't smiling?' She's better than that now. . . ."

For Debbie's sake, Francine did a good imitation of an optimistic parent. When they got to the court she was smiling and laughing as if she didn't have a care in the world. She patted Debbie on the back, watched her walk onto the court, and then said, in a loud voice, "We want to sit where we can influence the applauding." After some discussion, she and Warren chose seats a few rows up, right in the middle, while Lansdorp perched at the edge of a row on the opposite side of the court.

This was a match with entertainment value, which accounted for two sets of bleachers, three sports photographers, and a CBS Sports television crew. Lisa Bonder—an attractive eighteen-year-old, and the ninth seed—faced the girl who had beaten the girl who had taken Chris Evert Lloyd to three sets.

Debbie found herself playing in front of a new kind of spectator, people who had paid money for a good show and wanted a return on their investment. Lisa Bonder and Debbie Spence were both baseliners, a traditional style for American women, but not as thrilling, some thought, as the net game that Martina Navratilova had made popular. People in the bleachers complained loudly that they were not getting their money's worth.

"Two baseliners!" yelled a man who sat behind Francine and Warren. "You could leave and not have to come back until next Tuesday."

Francine managed to ignore a string of comments like that. She seemed to have successfully shut out everything but the first set, which was staying even. Lisa Bonder broke Debbie's serve in the second game, Debbie retaliated by breaking Bonder's serve in the fifth game, and as Debbie served to begin the sixth game the television camera swung to look at her.

Francine saw the camera swivel. She looked behind her. The stands were filling up. Debbie was hanging on three games to two against a top pro and people were starting to notice her. The girls traded service breaks again, and then Debbie took the next two games to lead 5–4. If she held serve, she would win the set—but she faltered and let Bonder take a crucial game.

Debbie still won the first set 7–5, but Francine was less than ecstatic. Debbie had not won because she did something exceedingly right; she won because Bonder made mistakes. Three unforced errors by Bonder were no testament to Debbie's skill. They were "a gift from heaven," for which Francine was grateful, but Debbie could not take a whole match on lucky breaks. Francine leaned forward to study her daughter's face as she walked off the court, and she did not see the confidence she hoped to find there.

"I don't care about anything," she said devoutly, "as long as she wins."

Lisa Bonder took the first game of the second set. As Debbie stepped up to serve, she rubbed her eye, the one she'd worried about before her match against Alycia Moulton. Now there seemed to be real cause for concern. "Her eye is swollen," said Francine, without taking her eyes of her daughter, "and when she gets sweaty it hurts, and then she rubs it. She said she couldn't *see* for ten minutes in that other match."

She nudged Warren, who took one look at Debbie's face, and made the sign for "time-out for injury" with his hands. He held his hands up until Debbie noticed him, but she shook her head and prepared to serve. Lisa Bonder broke her serve and then held her own.

Debbie did not give up. She ran down every ball, no matter how impossible a return might seem, and the crowd responded. People who had no idea who Debbie Spence was began to root for her, because she was the underdog and because she was giving the 110 percent her father had taught her to give. She came to the net a couple of times, to great cheers. She tolerated two questionable line calls that went against her and proceeded to break Bonder's serve anyhow. She came from behind to tie the second set at 5–5.

A few rows down, three little girls screamed at the top of their lungs, first for Lisa Bonder, then for Debbie Spence. They had no allegiance; they'd simply caught the crowd's fervor without understanding its partisan nature. They changed sides, and yelled louder, with each volley. Francine studied them for a moment. "Pay those little kids," she said. "Hand them a buck."

It wouldn't have mattered. Bonder took the last two games quickly to win the second set 7–5.

The bleachers were now so packed that people who were sitting down could not get out, and people who wanted to sit down clogged the walkways at either end of the bleachers and had to settle for reports filtering from above. Lisa Bonder was tired, groaning when she failed to make a shot. Debbie Spence was rattled. When she lost the first game of the final set without scoring a single point, she turned toward Francine and mouthed the words "Four points in a row."

"She *can't* concentrate on that," said Francine.

It was too late. Debbie's confidence had deserted her. She made a last rally, and tied the set at 3–all, only to see Bonder come back to take the next three games, and the set, and the match. The crowd applauded and cheered wildly for both girls —from a fan's perspective it had turned out to be a great match, full of suspense and drama—but Francine knew that their appreciation didn't make much difference right now.

"Debbie's going, 'Who *cares?*' " she said, as she pushed through the crowd to get to her daughter. "It's no consolation. She's going to be so mad at herself."

Parkes Brittain had positioned himself at the exit to tell Debbie how well she'd played, and Robert Lansdorp, who was outside talking to the Gurneys, broke away to talk to her. Nick Bollettieri, Lansdorp's East Coast competitor, had a comforting arm and a few words of advice for Debbie, who had visited his academy briefly in August for a workout before the U.S. Open Clay Court Championships.

The adults saw the match differently than Debbie did. They saw how close Debbie had come to beating Bonder; although she had lost, she had redeemed herself in their eyes by playing a tough, crafty match. But Debbie saw everything in extremes —black or white, win or lose—and all she wanted was to slip away with Francine and Warren.

In a plaintive voice, just this side of tears, she confided her sorrow to her mother as they walked back toward the locker room. "I could have won *thousands* of dollars," she said. "If I won this and another one I could have gotten seven thousand, maybe fifteen thousand. Instead I go home with thirty-six hundred."

Francine reminded her that $3,600—actually, $3,733—was twice what Alycia Moulton had received. And she reminded Debbie of what she had said after beating Moulton, how she had crowed about being half Francine's age and making so much more money than her mother did as a teacher.

They didn't make it upstairs to the locker room. Debbie collapsed in a heap in the hallway outside the players' lounge and agents' hospitality suites, a white towel over her sodden head, her eye makeup running down her face in watery tracks that were half sweat, half tears. Francine and Warren and a writer stood there uncertainly for a moment and then sat down on the artificial-turf carpeting. Debbie could only stare at them imploringly and say, over and over, that she needed help.

Francine's response was to be practical. She immediately pulled Debbie's schedule out of her bag and asked Warren whether he thought Debbie should play an upcoming Ginny tournament in Salt Lake City, Utah. Perhaps Debbie shouldn't bother with a tournament that offered fewer computer points and less prize money than a Virginia Slims tournament.

It may have seemed coldhearted, but under the circumstances it was the pragmatic thing to do. This was the way life would be from now on. The competition was rougher, the losses had financial, as well as emotional, consequences, and that was that. Debbie could not afford an emotional outburst every time she lost. Perhaps her distress would subside if no one addressed it directly. In an almost hypnotically soothing voice, Francine continued to discuss the future.

Warren Rice measured Debbie's mood and saw an opportunity for himself. He pulled Francine aside for a moment and made his suggestion: he could move into the Spences' house for a week to start a complete conditioning, nutrition, and practice program for Debbie, for which they could pay him a fee. Debbie needed someone to take her in hand and get her ready for the circuit.

Debbie overheard the conversation, and when Warren walked away to get the official form to pull her out of the Salt Lake City tournament, she complained bitterly to her mother that what she needed was a good friend, not somebody who wanted to be paid. She needed help, she insisted again, which seemed a synonym for love and concern. Those were not things you could pay people to provide.

She pulled the towel further over her face, and in a

strangely disembodied voice began a monologue of despair. Right now she hated herself, and everyone else who had not been able to save her from defeat, and she took perverse delight in enumerating all the elements that had conspired to rob her of victory.

"I've got a slipped ligament in my back," she began. "Not really slipped, but when I was practicing at home I couldn't really get my serve right because it would hurt.

"And I need to work harder. I mean, the last couple of weeks Shawn and I were *really* going to work. Get up in the morning and run and eat right and go to sleep early. And all we ended up doing was practicing a couple of hours a day.

"But if I work longer I get tired, I mean, with the mono. I used to be able to go a three-set match. But today I was just so weak. *What if it's coming back?*

"I don't eat right, I know, but it's so hard. My mom won't cook vegetables!" she said, with an accusing glance in Francine's direction. "I used to eat an apple and an orange. When I was in ninth and tenth grade I'd get an apple instead of cookies, y'know, and I'd eat it and get all filled up and that was good. But now I'll grab a Twinkie or I eat junk food. And I know I shouldn't. I ought to lose about fifty thousand pounds.

"About six months ago I had a problem with my stomach because I was eating too much greasy fried food, y'know, like pizza, and I eat it all the time again. I guess it's a miracle I don't have a stomach problem now."

She took off her tennis shoes and socks and held a swollen, red foot in both hands.

"Look at these blisters. I won't be able to walk. And my father's no help at all. I need people who support me. He just tears my game down. I don't even hit good when I hit with him anymore. The two days before I left, I hit awful."

She considered it all for a moment. In her mind's eye she was a fat, untalented, unloved, undisciplined fool, abandoned by family and friends, who were probably right to give up on such a worthless human being. Her voice slid up into a wail.

"I feel," she said tremulously, "like such a loser."

"Debbie," said her mother, aghast. "You're talking to a writer!"

Debbie sniffled and fell silent.

When Robert Lansdorp walked into the U.S. Open Club Building and saw Debbie Spence crumpled at the end of the hallway, he knew what he had to do. Part of his job was psychological maintenance. He rescued kids from self-pity and helped them concentrate on the future.

He sauntered over, in an approximation of carefree optimism, and made his pronouncement: The second round of the 1984 U.S. Open was now ancient history. For the record, he thought Debbie had the match wrapped up in the second set. Only inexperience had kept her from an upset victory. If she continued to play as she had in the first two sets, she could be ranked in the top ten within a year. That should be her focus, he advised. There was nothing to be gained from berating herself over a single loss.

Francine was visibly relieved, but Debbie still stared at the floor and played with her shoelaces. When an acquaintance passed by and offered condolences, she turned away.

She only perked up when Shawn Foltz arrived, sat down on the floor, and gave Debbie a hug and a kiss. Shawn understood that Debbie needed to be upset—that sometimes the best way to get past this kind of disappointment was to act as though the world had ended, plummet all the way to the bottom of despair, and then crawl back up. If a girl clung to her cool image instead, the distress would just eat away at her from inside.

Shawn cuddled her doubles partner in a sweet, almost motherly fashion, made sympathetic noises about Debbie's feet, weight, and swollen eyelid, and gently complimented her on a match well played.

She had practical, as well as personal reasons. In less than an hour Debbie and Shawn were scheduled to face the fifth-seeded doubles team, Wendy Turnbull and Anne Hobbs, in a first-round doubles match. Kenny Rogers might show up to watch. Shawn didn't want a doubles partner who was moping around the court, for her sake and for Debbie's. The best thing

Debbie could do would be to show up at the doubles match looking good. Sitting here in the hallway, advertising terminal despair, was not very smart. Debbie could have a little more time to be cranky, but then she would have to snap out of it and get ready for the match.

Lansdorp asked the girls what kind of doubles they would play, hoping to evoke a positive response.

"Tanking," said Debbie. She was not in a victorious frame of mind.

At that Shawn stood up and tried to pull Debbie to her feet.

"You will *not* tank this match," she said, in an exasperated voice. "You've got to make your living, girl."

"If I don't do well in San Diego I'm going to quit," said Debbie, defiantly, referring to another upcoming Ginny tournament she had been thinking of playing. The look on her face was a pleading dare that said, Go ahead. Tell me I'm crazy to talk about quitting.

"What do you mean?" laughed Shawn, with a teasing grin. "Do you want to be number one right away?"

"Yeah," said Debbie.

"Well, you can't be," said Shawn. Then she repeated what her mother told her when she got depressed—what Pat had told her this very week, after the double disappointment of not getting a wild card and then losing in the first round of the qualifying matches. None of the people who made money off of tennis could quite afford to believe it—and even the most compassionate parent had to doubt it, sometimes—but it was the best consolation a mother could offer her daughter.

"You take it slow," was the lesson Shawn now shared with her friend, "and you'll be surer when you get there."

"But how many shots am I going to blow?" said Debbie, getting to her feet. "Two three-set matches." She was referring to today's match with Bonder and her third-round loss at the U.S. Open Clay Court Championships a month before. In her devotion to misery, she'd conveniently forgotten her two-day-old victory against Alycia Moulton.

Shawn refused to play along. She just stood there and waited.

Debbie looked at her watch. She had about thirty minutes to shower, change into a fresh outfit, fix her hair, apply her makeup, get psyched, and get down to the court. She was starting to feel better; it helped to spew out every awful thing she could think of after a loss.

She did have a responsibility, as a pro, to take her matches seriously. She and Shawn had little chance of winning this match, but it would be childish—amateurish—to give up without a fight. Besides, the first-round doubles paid $935 to the losers and guaranteed $1,600 to the winners. Even if she lost this afternoon, she'd make some nice money.

Debbie thought about how much fun it would be to stick around Manhattan for two extra days for a serious shopping expedition. After all, she was earning a living now. As long as she had a hotel room and an income, why not stay to watch a few matches and spend her hard-earned cash?

She smiled at Francine.

"I'm going to take four days off," she announced. "I guess that's okay. When are you going home, Mom?"

She did not wait for Francine's response. There wasn't any time. Debbie Spence grabbed her racquets and headed upstairs to get ready to go to work.

Epilogue: U.S. Open—August 1985

The top junior girl in the country is in a safer, more insulated place than she knows. Maybe Debbie Spence didn't receive all the special favors she felt she deserved during her reign in 1983, but she had concrete, reassuring proof of how special she was—in the form of her official USTA ranking. She could take refuge in statistics, complain about unjust treatment, and still consider herself a star in the making. She was, after all, the best.

Melissa Gurney followed Debbie into the number one slot in 1984, co-ranked with Stephanie Rehe, and, along with her sister Cinda, was named Junior Player of the Year by *Tennis* magazine. She got the kind of reception girls like Debbie dreamed of: IMG and Advantage International fought for her favors with wild cards, exhibition matches that got her media coverage, and talk of endorsements. In January 1985, when she was in Washington, D.C., for a tournament, Melissa played mixed doubles with Vice-President George Bush. The match was arranged by Advantage International's Jeff Austin, Tracy's older brother, who knew the vice-president's son.

But a pro has to know how good she is, and will be, without constant reinforcement and attention. She has to believe in herself even though she has gone from being number one to being one of dozens of very good players on the tour—her outstanding junior record reduced to a statistical footnote in the annual Virginia Slims media guide. She has to learn to lose, frequently, and sometimes badly, and not give up.

She has to have faith in her ability without necessarily having proof of it in tournament results. She needs a personal, internal sureness that can elude girls who have always depended on external evidence, whether it be a ranking or an agent's interest, to help them judge how they are doing. And she has to find that faith quickly, so that she can start to win again. The pro circuit, even more than the juniors, works at a breakneck pace, and anyone who falters will be left behind.

In Hollywood the rule is: You're only as good as your last movie. In women's tennis, a new pro is as good as her last tournament. She will be given a little time to adjust—as long as she remains personable and optimistic for the duration— but then she must meet everyone's expectations. The public, the media, the agents and their corporate clients can be terribly fickle.

The Women's Tennis Association, concerned that girls were rushing into a pro career before they could handle the physical and emotional rigors of the tour, would issue restrictions during the 1985 U.S. Open limiting the number of pro tournaments a player could enter before she was sixteen. But the WTA had conflicting loyalties, and could not ignore the proven commercial value of young players. The guidelines were not as stringent as they might have been because teenage pros enhanced the sport's image. Still, most of the families affected by the guidelines regarded the move as an irritating intrusion.

In August 1985, 128 women prepared to compete in the main draw of the U.S. Open, including eighteen-year-old Debbie Spence, who would mark the end of her first year as a pro, and sixteen-year-old Melissa Gurney, who had turned pro in May 1985, in time for Wimbledon.

Debbie had settled comfortably into a berth in the high thirties on the WTA computer, up fifty points in a year. She played twenty-two tournaments, "an exhausting year," she admitted, but there had been rewards: Debbie was a semifinalist in the Ginny circuit championships, won the Ginny of San Diego, and reached the quarterfinals of several major tournaments. She had played some of the best players without folding, and was proud of close losses to Helena Sukova and Hana Mandlikova. In one tournament, she took four games off Martina Navratilova, and tentatively advanced the notion that she could have won a set had a few crucial points gone in her favor.

For the year's effort she earned $60,000 and got to keep about half of it. The rest went for expenses—including travel expenses for Francine, since, in a generous moment, Debbie had decided to assert her independence by offering to pay her mother's way.

Melissa came onto the computer at eighty-eight in November of 1984. She had her big prestigious loss when she was still a junior, in October 1984, extending Chris Evert Lloyd to three sets in the Virginia Slims of Los Angeles, in a match that sparked extravagant media speculation about what she would be capable of when she was bigger, stronger, and more experienced. In May 1985, just before her sixteenth birthday, she ended the battle between the sports agencies by signing with Advantage International. After three pro tournaments, she arrived at the U.S. Open ranked fifty-fifth.

Her schedule in the coming year would be limited by her determination to continue attending high school. She joked that she felt "like I've earned about twenty cents." But her career was about more than prize money; it was about potential, and Melissa had plenty of that. After Wimbledon she had signed a five-year clothing and shoe contract with Reebok, which included rewards for attaining certain rankings or surviving into the late rounds of specific tournaments. Parkes Brittain's estimate was that Melissa would be "earning six figures by the end of the year."

In the meantime, the agency did what it could to keep her in the public eye. CBS-TV interviewed her on the eve of her appearance at Wimbledon, and the special U.S. Open supplement in *New York* magazine listed her as one of the young players to watch.

On the surface, everyone, in both families, was satisfied. Debbie felt cocky enough to turn down a racquet endorsement offer of $5,000 from Wilson because it wasn't enough money for a player of her stature, and replaced her Wilson with a Prince racquet. No longer willing to compete for what she interpreted as Coach Robert Lansdorp's dwindling attentions, she switched her allegiance to Chris Boyle, a thirty-five-year-old, second-generation tennis coach with whom Debbie had worked, off and on, since she was ten.

For Melissa, the combination of turning sixteen, turning pro, and getting her first endorsement contract was a heady thrill. She borrowed money from her father—against what she would eventually receive from Reebok—to buy a new grey Honda Prelude. And she, too, weaned herself from Lansdorp: despite his connection to IMG, she signed with Advantage International and, once signed, often worked out with Jeff Austin when he was in town, or with Ross Walker at the Kramer Club. In the Gurneys' newly expanded universe, Lansdorp no longer wielded the kind of power that had convinced them, two years before, to quit working with another coach rather than risk his wrath.

But just behind the girls' bravado was the restless need to feel special again. It turned out to be more difficult, and take more time, than anyone had anticipated. Francine Spence and Carolyn Gurney had both come to the conclusion that the key to their daughters' success would be patience, something that had always been in short supply on the junior circuit, and a level of self-confidence that could withstand a surely temporary anonymity on the pro circuit. The girls had to understand that not leaping directly to the top did not mean they were failures.

"First you have to get over your fear of losing," Francine said. "Then you have to know you can beat somebody good. Once you know that, you can commit all your energy to working up to the top. But you have to go one step at a time. You can't do it all at once."

Carolyn Gurney estimated that it would take her daughter "a year or two to get her footing, get established," and in the meantime she advised her daughter not to fret about her computer ranking and not to become demoralized. "The problem is, she's had too many close matches," said Carolyn. "She hasn't had the wins she wanted, and the losses have been so close. She gets discouraged. But it's all a matter of maintaining a perspective."

Debbie and Melissa had more trouble remaining philosophical: they were itching to break through and make headlines; they were just a bit wobbly, propped up by nothing more than memories of junior victories and supportive speculation about when they might hit their strides as pros.

"It's so frustrating to play the pros," Melissa would admit. "You have to remind yourself that you did *so* well in the juniors—you *can't* be a flop in the pros."

Shawn Foltz, now seventeen, had talked about turning pro in 1985. She was ranked number three in the 18s in 1984, behind Melissa Gurney and Stephanie Rehe, and ranked number seven in international juniors. Her computer ranking got as high as fifty-five, and then settled into the seventies.

But then, in the summer of 1985, she went through what she called "a slump," a period of several months when she wasn't winning any matches and was often ill, so she decided to hold back. If she were to turn pro while playing badly, she would be ignored. Shawn, too, was looking for the big win—the one that would call attention to her efforts and give her the confidence to turn pro. She had whittled her options down—she had not played enough junior tournaments to get a 1985 ranking, and she still attended high school via mailbox—but she didn't want to make the obvious next move until she felt ready.

She had changed coaches again, which gave her a psychological boost, and after the Open would move to Florida to train with Patricio Apey, whose most famous pupil was fifteen-year-old Gabriela Sabatini, a dark-haired Argentinian beauty and the sport's reigning teen phenomenon. But having a hot new coach, and proudly being able to claim the illustrious Gaby as a friend, were not enough: Shawn needed to prove herself on the tennis court.

"I want to feel totally sure of myself," she said. "Sure that I'm playing well—and sure I can earn enough money, because it's my career."

Of the girls who had come to prominence in southern California in the last two years, only Marianne Werdel had forestalled an identity crisis by deciding to remain an amateur—and she was under pressure from the other players for being the odd girl out. Marianne had accepted a tennis scholarship at Stanford University, her parents' alma mater, and would begin her freshman year in mid-September. But she had been playing well recently and had survived three days of qualifying rounds to get into the main draw of the U.S. Open. Some of the players told her she was crazy to go to college. If she was winning, she ought to stick with the circuit.

Corinne Werdel smiled politely at the notion. She did not see the young pros, the ones who had skipped college, doing all that well. She was quietly determined, as she and her husband Tom had been from the start, that Marianne have a life outside of tennis. Her daughter would register at Stanford no matter how well she played at the U.S. Open.

Both Shawn and Marianne did better than they had expected. Shawn scored an upset in the first round before losing in the second, and Marianne made it to the third round before she was defeated. But their advances went largely unnoticed: a player trying to regain her momentum and a girl on her way to college sat at the edge of the media circus. The spotlight was reserved for players like Gaby and fifteen-year-old Steffi Graf from West Germany—young girls who had already proven themselves on the pro circuit.

On the morning of the first day of competition at the Open, Debbie sat in an official car with her mother and Chris Boyle, listening to rock music on her headset while the driver, who had a different rock station on the car radio, inched toward the entrance of the USTA National Tennis Center, caught in a slow, snaking double row of spectators' cars.

When Bruce Springsteen's song "Glory Days" came on the radio, Chris Boyle leaned forward and turned it way up. In a previous incarnation he had been a publicist for the rock group The Doors, and now he played guitar and wrote his own songs. Like Debbie, he believed in the inspirational power of music.

"Let's get this girl *pumped*," he yelped. "It's her favorite song."

Debbie smiled and pulled a foam rubber pad away from her ear—and out of it came a tinnier version of the same song. It was one of those good luck moments. The Boss himself was speaking into Debbie Spence's ear.

Even Francine knew the words to her daughter's favorite song. As the car inched forward, Debbie, Francine, and Chris began to sing, roll their shoulders, and tap their feet. The car rocked rhythmically from side to side, like a big lumbering bug, and people in the other cars craned their necks to see if they recognized the blonde in the back seat.

She sang with the blithe abandon only a star, or a girl who believed she would be a star, could muster. What happened to the people in the song could never happen to her:

Time slips away
Leaves you with nothin', Mister, but
Boring stories of

Glory days, they'll pass you by
Glory days, in the wink of a young girl's eye
Glory days, glory days . . .

At that moment, buoyed by the music, and the company, and the day's promise, Debbie believed in herself. By the time her match was called, any semblance of invincibility was gone, worn away by hours of delay. The matches that preceded hers on court 6 ran terribly long. Although she had expected to start playing at four, her match was delayed until almost seven. She had warmed up, changed clothes, and eaten too early—and although her opponent, Austria's Petra Huber, was equally off-schedule, Debbie did not yet have the mental reserves she needed to survive such a frustrating day.

She marched defensively onto the court, took an early two-game lead, and then began to throw it away. She belligerently refused the fruit that Chris Boyle, at Francine's worried urging, passed to a ball boy. After Huber took the first set in a tiebreaker, Debbie seemed to lose control; instead of taking a deep breath and regaining her concentration, she rushed her shots and made hasty mistakes, almost as if she wanted the match to end.

Although Francine was still humming, "C'mon, c'mon, c'mon," with her daughter down 5–1 in the second set, Debbie had given up hope. Huber took the next game and the match, and Debbie stormed away, vowing never again to play "this *stupid* game."

While Francine chased after her, Chris Boyle hastily collected the equipment bags and went looking for the Spences. As sporadic cheers boomed across the darkened sky from the direction of the grandstand court, he hunted up one walkway and down the next, reflecting on how tough it was to lose.

He remembered losing a finals match when he was eleven, on what he still considered to have been a bad call. Enraged, he refused to accept his runner-up trophy. When it was pressed upon him, he took it and threw it on the ground. It didn't break, so he picked it up and threw it against a nearby wall.

"My father," he recalled, "kicked my ass up one block and down another. Then he made me pick up all the pieces and glue it back together."

The next day, Carolyn Gurney would find a phone message from Francine Spence, who had called to say good-bye and apologize for leaving so soon. Debbie's nerves, stretched tight by her need to be noticed, had snapped, and she gave in to despair. Despite the entreaties of her mother and coach, she insisted on flying home immediately, skipping the doubles competition which she had planned to enter with Shawn Foltz.

Melissa fared no better, losing 6–0, 6–1 to Sweden's Catarina Lindqvist, a tough, calculating player who ran Melissa ragged, placing ball after ball frustratingly out of her reach. But Melissa took the loss differently than Debbie had, possibly because her transition was cushioned by signed documents, from Advantage International and Reebok, that certified her worth. She remained in New York the week after her loss because she had business in town—including a meeting with Jeff Austin to plan the next month's activities, and a reception sponsored by Avis Rent A Car.

Although there was pressure involved in playing under a watchful corporate eye, Melissa could take some small solace in the notion that people had faith in her. They talked reassuringly about new players' slump, as if it were the most natural thing in the world. They might want—and need—her to win, but they gave her tacit permission to lose without feeling like a failure.

Debbie had no such buffer. Every time she lost, she gazed into a chasm alone: she faced the awful threat of being a nobody.

Maybe Debbie temporarily lost control of herself; maybe she fled New York and went home because she had to have a rest and knew of no other way to buy herself a few days' time. But she recovered quickly. She placed much of the blame for her loss on her new Prince racquet and decided to return to her old reliable Wilson. A week and a half later she left Cerritos for a Ginny tournament in Salt Lake City, Utah—and from there she would fly to Hawaii for a four-day vacation, courtesy of the tournament promoter, who offered Debbie the trip, and her expenses to Salt Lake City, as enticement to play a tournament she might otherwise have skipped. She hadn't broken through to the top ranks yet, but the 1984 Ginny championship semifinalist, now ranked in the thirties, had definite box office appeal on the Ginny circuit.

Before she left home, Debbie announced a new plan for the coming months: by Christmas she wanted to be in the top twenty. That was her goal.

"Then the agents will all try to do things for me," she predicted, "and I can see who comes up with the best stuff."

She had her father's doggedness—and, more important for the years to come, she had some secular version of her mother's fervent faith. At eighteen, she had passed through her adolescence with little time to figure out who she was, but, like so many other girls who turned pro, she knew exactly who she wanted to be. Turning pro was a rather severe test of a girl's belief, but the devout have always persisted in thinking that they would prevail.

These girls worshipped celebrity: an early drive to excel had been altered, along the way, by the desire to be a star. In their minds, talent was not enough; they needed to be singled out for their talent. For a girl who might not quite know herself, the next best thing was recognition. She could borrow from other people's perceptions. A girl like Debbie would see herself most clearly by studying her reflection in the public eye.